# DREAMERS AND SCHEMERS

The publisher and the University of California Press Foundation gratefully acknowledge the generous support of the Lisa See Endowment Fund in Southern California History and Culture.

# DREAMERS AND SCHEMERS

HOW AN IMPROBABLE BID FOR THE 1932 OLYMPICS
TRANSFORMED LOS ANGELES FROM DUSTY OUTPOST
TO GLOBAL METROPOLIS

## BARRY SIEGEL

UNIVERSITY OF CALIFORNIA PRESS

University of California Press, one of the most distinguished university presses in the United States, enriches lives around the world by advancing scholarship in the humanities, social sciences, and natural sciences. Its activities are supported by the UC Press Foundation and by philanthropic contributions from individuals and institutions. For more information, visit www.ucpress.edu.

University of California Press
Oakland, California

Library of Congress Cataloging-in-Publication Data

Names: Siegel, Barry, 1949– author.
Title: Dreamers and schemers : how an improbable bid for the 1932 Olympics transformed Los Angeles from dusty outpost to global metropolis / Barry Siegel.
Description: Oakland, California : University of California Press, [2019] | Includes bibliographical references and index. |
Identifiers: LCCN 2019009743 (print) | LCCN 2019015888 (ebook) | ISBN 9780520970649 (Ebook) | ISBN 9780520298583 (cloth : alk. paper)
Subjects: LCSH: Garland, William May, 1866–1948. | Olympic host city selection—1932. | Hosting of sporting events—California—Los Angeles. | City planning—California—Los Angeles. | Olympic Games (10th : 1932 : Los Angeles, Calif.)
Classification: LCC GV721.2.G37 (ebook) | LCC GV721.2.G37 S54 2019 (print) | DDC 796.48—dc23
LC record available at https://lccn.loc.gov/2019009743

Manufactured in the United States of America

27  26  25  24  23  22  21  20  19
10  9  8  7  6  5  4  3  2  1

*To Marti, as always*
*and to Ally, Mike and Lea, who are the future*

# CONTENTS

# ILLUSTRATIONS

# AUTHOR'S NOTE

It has been said that the story of William May Garland is the story of Los Angeles. He arrived in Southern California in 1890, just as the city's population reached fifty thousand, having surged from eleven thousand a decade before. He helped drive much of the expansion that followed in the first two decades of the twentieth century. Then, over the years 1920 to 1932, in an era when Los Angeles truly became Los Angeles, he led the city's quest to bid for and stage the 1932 Olympic Games. All that doesn't make him a knight in shining armor—there are complications—but it does make him interesting to me. I will call him Billy throughout this narrative, because that's what everyone—family, friends, colleagues—always called him.

That Los Angeles is not an old city, that Los Angeles rose over a matter of decades, is something I know firsthand. I grew up in LA, not in the frontier days, but at a time when there was no San Diego Freeway, no Santa Monica Freeway, no Century City, and no Dodger Stadium. From West Los Angeles, still thick with orange groves, my father and brother and I would drive miles east along Exposition Boulevard to watch the Dodgers play baseball in the Coliseum. We took for granted that Los Angeles had the Coliseum, but of course it didn't always exist. Billy Garland conjured the Coliseum, willing it into existence even after the public voted down a bond issue to fund its construction, because his quest for the Olympic Games—and LA's future—mandated a Coliseum.

Can individuals, in defiance of formative global realities, make history? Can imagination and even illusion play a role in shaping not just art but the future? The renowned California chronicler Kevin Starr posed this question in his book *Material Dreams,* being careful to say he wasn't denying "the shaping realities of all the other explanations historians are so willing to give these days," but rather was asserting "the parallel truth that individuals also make history." And so to his famous claim: "Los Angeles did not just happen. . . . Los Angeles envisioned itself, then materialized that vision through sheer force of will. Los Angeles sprung from a Platonic conception of itself, the Great Gatsby of American cities."

I expect some might object to this, not least for the seeming ode to a group of Los Angeles businessmen who—let's make this clear from the start—were part of that era's wealthy WASP hegemony. They exercised, partied and conducted their business in exclusive private clubs that barred Jews, Catholics, people of color and anyone with questionable social standing. They presided over a city segregated by class and race. They were virulently antilabor and resistant to immigrants from anywhere but western Europe.

So: Immoral scoundrels or bright-eyed visionaries? Dreamers or schemers? This is a familiar question, one that arises all the time in chronicles of early Los Angeles. The obvious answer: Weren't they all these things? I'm not inclined to grind human complexity, with all its moral contradictions, into a one-dimensional polemic. What interests me is the nuance and ambiguity, the shades of gray inherent in flawed but compelling characters. I like telling stories.

What was it like for a twenty-four-year-old to step off a train in a remote, wide-open frontier town such as Los Angeles, to hole up in a cut-rate boardinghouse, to look around, to see and hear and smell this new domain, to start imagining a world-class city out of whole cloth? And next to choose for a career the then dubious field of realty? Yes, that's what Billy Garland was, a real estate man—the premier realtor in an era when realtors drove the city's growth, when an emergent Los Angeles was hell-bent on hosting the 1932 Olympics. Billy's quest provides an unusually revealing window onto a particular time and place and way of life.

It was a momentous time and place—when LA came of age. This era has been well chronicled, but never through the lens of those who truly drove the transformation—the realtors led by Billy Garland. Their narrative, linked tightly to the bidding for and staging of the 1932 Olympic Games, represents nothing less than the birth of modern Los Angeles.

Back to Kevin Starr: "Thus the real-estate salesman . . . emerges as an archetypal Los Angeleno of the 1920s. A figure of folkloric significance, a Wizard of Oz, part preacher, part confidence man, the real estate salesman pitched the Southern California dream. . . . Despite the occasional frauds, the ever-present hoopla . . . a million Americans were in the course of a brief decade placed in homes and recycled into new lives. . . . From this perspective, the real-estate salesmen of the Southland, for all their brass bands [and] aviation stunts . . . were not hucksters at all but were rather shamans of a new, and it was hoped, better identity and circumstances. Like wizards of Oz behind green curtains, they spoke to that dream of a better life that was bringing a million and a half Americans into Southern California. . . . The roll call of modern Los Angeles realtors, or, more correctly its Burke's Peerage, commences with William May Garland, the Prince of Realtors as he was known."

This, curiously, was Starr's only reference to Billy in all his books. One sentence on one page in *Material Dreams*. I say, let's go further: Come with me as we watch the preachers and confidence men work their magic behind green curtains.

# PROLOGUE

Billy's Parade

In Southern California, the year 1932 began, fittingly enough, with an illusion: William May Garland, known across the region as the "Prince of Realtors," acting as the grand marshal at the Pasadena Tournament of Roses parade on New Year's Day. There he was at sixty-six, in a dark pin-striped suit and tie, with his trademark tortoise-rimmed glasses and snowy white hair parted down the middle, marching just behind a bugler, mounted police, and a drum corps. Seventy flower-covered floats followed, some propelled by motors, others by prancing horses. Not by chance, the Pasadena Tournament of Roses Association's own float featured the "Queen of the Olympic Games," a young woman enthroned amid a profusion of flowers on a dais above a base of huckleberry arranged to depict the various continents of the world.

Billy Garland could not have been happier. It had rained the day before, and the forecast had been for more rain this morning—"Rain, hail or snow will be just an added attraction," the tournament's president had declared. But instead the sun shone brightly. To the north and east, the rough, snow-covered peaks of Mount Lowe and Mount Wilson held back a dark shroud of clouds, leaving the parade imbued with a sparkling clarity. Those mountains must have looked like Olympian deities to Billy.

He had made it all happen: This Olympics-themed Rose Parade would merely be the prelude to the 1932 Olympic Games, to be held in Los Angeles that August. As president of the city's Tenth Olympiad

Committee, Billy had literally imagined the LA games into being. It had been an outlandish notion. The Olympics had always been held in one of the great European capitals. In 1918, when Billy first set out to bid for the games, Los Angeles was only the tenth-largest American city and not the least cosmopolitan. It more closely resembled a frontier town, with its leaders still kicking mud off their boots. What's more, it was a grueling six thousand miles from Europe—an expensive five-day ocean voyage followed by a five-day train journey across the American continent. Billy, nonetheless, thought bidding for the games was a splendid idea.

By the spring of 1923, through charm and force of personality, he'd somehow managed to convince the International Olympics Committee to agree with him. When the IOC members met in Rome on April 9, 1923, Billy prevailed almost entirely because of the connections he'd forged. As the meeting adjourned, after a vote in favor of Los Angeles' bid, one of the committee members from central Europe approached him and said, "Billy, I voted for Los Angeles because I like you personally, but where is Los Angeles? Is it anywhere near Hollywood?" Billy knew enough to play that card. "Yes, yes," he replied. "It's a suburb of Hollywood."

Billy couldn't help but recall that day in Rome as he led the Rose Parade past a throng of 750,000 citizens, everyone clapping and cheering on streets hung with more than four thousand banners. Billy took it all in: bands, bugles, beautiful girls, martial music, Scottish bagpipes and drums, the hum above of planes and a snub-nosed blimp, the riot of color on float after float. On one, a striking woman clad as a Greek goddess reclined against a graceful wreath, tossing roses to barefoot urchins. "Nations and Games in Flowers," they'd called this year's parade. Yes. Just as Billy had imagined.

Yet it was all a mirage: at this moment, neither a colorful pageant nor Billy's imagination could do more than temporarily distract the city, the country, or the world. As he bounded behind the buglers and drum corps, Billy faced daunting challenges he'd never imagined a decade before, when he sought and won the 1932 games. The Roaring Twenties, and Southern California's historic expansion during that decade, had come to a disastrous halt with the October 1929 stock market crash and the world's plunge into the Great Depression. On the day of the 1932 Rose Parade, unemployment in California stood at a stunning 28 percent. Evicted families pulled their tattered belongings down LA's clogged sidewalks. Soup kitchens rose in the shadow of the Coliseum. Suicide statistics kept climbing, with seventy-nine people so far jumping from the Colorado State Bridge in Pasadena, not far from the route of the Rose Parade. Desperate refugees from America's heartland arrived in Los Angeles every week, encamping in "Hooverville" shantytowns.

Europe and the rest of the world were staggering as well, slammed by devastating economic calamity. Country after country faced financial crisis, and three—Germany, Italy, and Japan—also faced the rise of fascist dictatorships. Everywhere bankruptcies mushroomed and unemployment soared. Everywhere despairing families surrendered their homes and life savings.

Against this backdrop, it did not seem possible that anyone could attend or participate in the Olympic Games, or that LA could accommodate them. With people hungry and homeless, it was difficult to defend the Olympics, difficult to justify sending athletes across the globe for a track meet. Even though Billy kept promising a "shot of optimism," doubters had started calling the 1932 LA Olympics "Garland's folly." The Tenth Olympiad promised to be an historic flop, one of the biggest failures of all time.

It didn't help that Billy no longer had all of his own corporate and political sponsors at his side. A good number had lost enthusiasm, and about half, despite the late date, wanted to withdraw their support. Even many stalwarts on the LA Olympic Organizing Committee were calling for a last minute cancellation of the games. The idea horrified Billy. It seemed unimaginable. A confrontation came, some weeks after the Rose Parade, at a meeting in a wood-paneled conference room at the venerable Los Angeles Athletic Club, where Billy was the long-time president. There was no charm or smooth talking now, no attempt at conciliatory persuasion. Billy condemned the "cold feeters." The men around the table bristled. Billy didn't care. We have given the International Olympic Committee our word, he insisted. Would you forget honor and walk away? He took in the brooding silence, the eyes cast down. He leaned forward, repeating: Would you forget honor and walk away? The next day, Billy ordered the printing of two million tickets for the 1932 Olympic Games in Los Angeles.

# BILLY'S MIGRATION

Of course he came from somewhere else, and headed west as a young man. Billy Garland was born in Maine on March 31, 1866, to the Reverend Jonathan May Garland and his wife, Becca, who had been deaf since a bout of scarlet fever at age three. Billy, a middle child, had an older brother, Rastie, and a younger sister, Rose. The family lived in Westport, an island then reachable only by ferry, where Becca's farming family had dwelt for one hundred years. Reverend Garland, a heavily bearded circuit-riding Methodist minister, often lodged with his parishioners.

When the children came of school age, the family relocated to Waterville, Maine, where they lived in first one, then another, rented home. Life was austere in their household, but Becca encouraged her children to attend college. She prevailed with Rastie, who graduated from Colby College and Albany Law School, and with Rose, who graduated from Smith College and New York Law College. Billy followed a different path.

After three years at Waterville High School, and a short period laboring on his uncle's farm, Billy, without graduating, moved to Boston, finding work there as a clerk in a crockery firm. Restless after one year, and troubled by a bad cough, he joined his parents in Daytona Beach, Florida, where they'd moved in 1884 to launch a stagecoach line and tend a five-acre orange grove. Billy lasted only a few months driving stagecoaches for his father's company.

Still restless, still bothered by a bad cough, he next tried his luck in Chicago under the sponsorship of his mother's relatives, who held

FIGURE 1. Looking west on Sixth Street from Main Street, downtown Los Angeles, in 1903. Tracks cross at this intersection, where streetcars mingled with horse-drawn carriages. Security Pacific National Bank Collection/Los Angeles Public Library.

leading positions in the city's banking community. Over a span of six years, he moved up from bank messenger to clearinghouse clerk to receiving teller at the Illinois Trust and Savings Bank. His restlessness continued, though, as did his lung problems. One night in his boardinghouse room, a hemorrhage almost choked him. Find a milder, dryer climate, a doctor ordered. Billy's eyes turned to the West. Boosters in Southern California had been extolling the great life out there: the fertile land, the burgeoning commerce, the waves of tourists, and—most important—the healthy Mediterranean-type climate. Billy boarded a Southern Pacific train and arrived in Los Angeles in the winter of 1890, with twenty-three dollars in his pocket. He moved into a boardinghouse on Olive Street, where he paid nine dollars a month for a room and breakfast. He was all of twenty-four and more than ready for his future.

He had an inexorability about him, an air of fate. When he entered a room, often with a British "Fortunate Hits" cigarette in hand, people would gravitate toward him. What lured them was something impalpable, a certain flair. He had an infectious personality, abundant enthusiasm, unflagging energy, and a powerful handshake. On top of that, he projected composed, eye-on-the ball certitude. Those around him could see that he believed in himself and believed also in the future. Sensing he would always prevail, people wanted to follow him, wanted to climb on his bandwagon.

Billy first found work in LA as an auditor for the Pacific Cable Railway Company, earning seventy-four dollars a month. But he couldn't stop looking out his window at this new world he inhabited. Citrus, wine grapes, and other fruits were growing everywhere. Bean fields covered what would become Beverly Hills; fig orchards covered the future Hollywood. In downtown LA, Billy could still see unpaved roads, with horses and buggies hitched in front of stores. Open water ditches—the *zanjas*—ran down Figueroa Street to Jefferson and along West Adams, delivering irrigation water to homes. Yet Los Angeles was evolving. The population had reached 50,000, after a sharp growth spurt in the 1880s fueled by promoters, the arrival of the transcontinental railroads, and a furious rate war between the Southern Pacific and Santa Fe lines, culminating in fares of one dollar for a journey from Chicago to LA. (It didn't hurt that California's oranges and lemons had taken first prize at the New Orleans International Exposition in 1884–85, suggesting Southern California as a Garden of Eden.) In just one year, 1887, the Southern Pacific brought 120,000 people to Los Angeles.

All this fueled a spectacular real estate boom between 1885 and 1887, lifting the price of an acre in Los Angeles County from one hundred dollars in 1886 to fifteen hundred dollars in 1887. It was sheer madness, a stampede, shot through with frenzied speculation. People were buying lots one day, then selling them the next day at a profit. Soon the developers stepped in, building whole new towns—more than sixty in 1887, each launched with auctions, barbecue parties, and brass bands. In that year alone, Southern California realized a dizzying one hundred million dollars in land sales, well beyond what was understood to be the region's net value.

The boom collapsed suddenly (and inevitably) in the summer of 1888, as banks grew nervous, promoters went bust, and everyone tried to sell property simultaneously. By the time Billy arrived in 1890, real estate prices had plummeted, wiping out $14 million (nearly $355 million in 2018 dollars) of assessed valuation in one year. Millionaires had become indigents, and most of the sixty new towns had turned to grain fields. The bust shocked many residents of Los Angeles, with some fleeing, some questioning the future, and some jumping off bridges. But where others saw a debacle, Billy, as he looked around, saw only opportunity and possibility.

The boom, he reasoned, had lasting positive effects: The influx of population and capital had energized the city and generated the development of hotels, churches, schools, and new industries. The city had expanded half a mile in every direction from the central plaza, developing water service, rapid transit railroads and fifty-seven irrigation companies. Where there'd been only dirt roads, there now were eighty-seven miles of paved streets and seventy-eight miles of cement sidewalks. A number of educational institutions had also sprung up, among them the University of Southern California, Occidental College, and Pomona College. In the fall of 1888, urged on by General Harrison Gray Otis, the owner of the *Los Angeles Times,* the business community had formed the city's first chamber of commerce and launched a spectacularly effective propaganda campaign, luring not fly-by-night investors but farmers and other well-off migrants from the Midwest. Given all this, Billy believed the situation to be far less discouraging than it seemed. No banks had failed. The climate and the fecund soil hadn't gone away. Nor had the transcontinental railroads. Realty would surely rebound, he believed, . . . as it always does.

The descendent of farmers, Billy considered real estate the basis of all wealth. This represented a kind of religion to him. Since the beginning of time, he would later preach, "land has been the source of that which man calls wealth." Real estate—the soil with its fixed improvements—"is very clearly fundamental in the makeup of the universe. It is the granite base upon which we build everything material in life." Banks weren't the only storehouses of wealth: "Before the time of banks, man loved the soil."

With some of the earnings from his job, Billy bought a city lot. As his health improved he considered returning to Chicago. Then he found that his lot had increased $500 in value (the equivalent of $13,058 in 2018 dollars). He decided to stay in Los Angeles. What's more, he decided on a new career. In 1894, after three years as an auditor at Pacific Cable, Billy at age twenty-eight quit to form his own real estate business, W. M. Garland & Co. His first important deal was the subdivision of the Wilshire Boulevard Tract, which he marketed in 1896. It was then a district of the city wholly unimproved and remote, but Billy kept urging its merits. Because he truly believed in what he was selling, so did buyers: the Wilshire tract would eventually become, for its time, the finest residential section of Los Angeles. Billy, regrettably, didn't himself buy in the Wilshire tract (he expected LA to grow to the south). But he was on his way.

So were others, all newly arrived just as the boom went bust. Billy came to know them well. There was Harry Chandler, twenty-five in 1890, already five years into a job he'd landed in the *LA Times* circulation department. There was E. L. Doheny, thirty-four, a struggling frontier prospector just two years away from striking oil near the corner of Second and Glendale Boulevard—with pick and shovel, digging the first producing well in LA after finding this site by retracing the path of a wagon dripping tar. There was Henry Huntington, forty, already convinced Los Angeles would become "the most important city in this country, if not in the world," and already planning the sprawling Pacific Electric Railway, the celebrated "Red Cars" mass transit system that, from 1901 on, connected cities throughout Southern California.

Billy soon became Chandler's investment partner, Doheny's neighbor and Huntington's real estate broker, as W. M. Garland & Co. grew to dominate the field of commercial property. The future—whatever it might involve—animated Billy. Growth would shape the future, of that he was certain. Real estate values would rise along with population— the right kind of population. They just needed to promote their region, or rather, their notion of the region. Billy began to imagine a city that did not yet exist.

# LA ON THE CUSP

It is fair enough to describe Billy Garland as a self-made man, but it's also true that he married well. In 1897, at a party in Turnverein Hall on Spring Street, he met Blanche Hinman, one of the princesses in the Fiesta de Los Angeles that year. Her father was the wealthy cofounder of the Brooks Locomotive Works, located in Dunkirk, New York, and their family came west by private railroad car for four months every winter. "My dear Miss Hinman," Billy wrote to Blanche that April on a sheet of W. M. Garland & Co. letterhead, "Will Mr. and Mrs. Solano, Mr. and Mrs. Hinman, yourself with any friends—occupy seats in my rooms in this building during the revelry of 'All Fools' night? . . . Hastily and Cordially yours, Will M. Garland. Kindly respond by bearer or tel. (Main 845)."

That evening and others like it apparently went well, for when the Hinmans returned to LA the following year, Billy and Blanche became engaged. Their wedding, at St. John's Church in Dunkirk on October 12, 1898, was large and lavish, meriting a full-page story in the local *Dunkirk Evening Observer*. The church ceremony, ornamented with a lush banking of palms, ferns, and roses, was followed by a reception at the home of the bride's parents, where electric arc lights "brilliantly illuminated the beautiful grounds" and guests' tables were placed in the home's bowling alley, "a fine apartment 80 feet long and 12 feet wide, with ceiling finished in natural wood." Late that evening, Billy and Blanche departed for New York in a private car attached to the midnight train, accompanied by several friends as far as Buffalo.

Returning to Los Angeles in mid-November 1898, the young couple resided at the Van Nuys Hotel while building their house at 815 West Adams Boulevard, just west of downtown. Billy by then was already among the best known of the younger generation of LA businessmen, recognized for his prophetic signs, adorning vacant lots all over town, predicting the ever-expanding population of Los Angeles in 1900 and beyond. He was also a conspicuous figure in social circles, which made the Van Nuys Hotel just the place for him. Built by the Southern California pioneer Isaac Van Nuys on the northwest corner of Fourth and Main, the six-story hotel, even before it opened its doors in January 1897, garnered early acclaim from the *Los Angeles Times* as "the much needed first-class tourist hotel that was to be a credit and glory to Los Angeles." Sunny rooms abounded, for "the peculiar situation of the lot makes it possible for the sun to shine on three sides of the house." All bedrooms faced to the outside, all had private baths and telephones. There were richly appointed reception and lounging rooms, a grillroom and dining room, a billiard-room and barbershop, a grand staircase of iron and marble, and interior finishings of hand-polished oak, ash, and white cedar.

At the same time, despite all its fashionable elegance, the Van Nuys Hotel remained in its way very much part of the raucous frontier town it anchored, bedeviled by fatal elevator accidents, inexplicable deaths, thieving bellboys and more than a few angry fights. Interwoven with the laudatory stories hailing the new hotel were other *Los Angeles Times* headlines, such as "Bell Boy Killed" . . . "Charles Gamble Killed in an Elevator Shaft" . . . "Van Nuys Guests Robbed by Bell Boy" . . . "Guest of the Van Nuys Robbed of His Property While at Dinner" . . . "Hotel Waiter Accused of Larceny from Van Nuys and Beating his Wife" . . . "Wealthy Mining Man Expires Suddenly While Going to His Room in the Van Nuys" . . . and—most memorable of all—"Carved With Bread Knife; Bloody Fracas at Van Nuys Hotel; Steward Slashes Baker and Butcher" (this over an argument about a cook's white coat).

Billy and Blanche certainly would have been happy to move into their home on West Adams when it was ready in 1900. With appreciation, Billy had been documenting its construction by taking many snapshots. They were in the newest, best, chicest area of the city, even though it still received its water from an open-ditch *zanja*. Billy didn't mind. He lived now in a spacious, two-story stone-and-wood-frame gabled mansion with an expansive portico, formal dining and living rooms, and abundant grounds. This would be Billy's home for the rest of his life.

Still, even there, he could not avoid the rowdy wide-open village around him. The town he moved through was a rich stew of real estate capitalists—developers, bankers, salesmen—operating not far from centers of prostitution, gambling, and other forms of vice run by the underworld but sanctioned by city hall and the Los Angeles Police Department. To advance their particular interests and obscure the region's seedier elements, Billy's circle had already united to form the Los Angeles Chamber of Commerce and the Merchants and Manufacturers Association, two powerful groups that counted among their chief missions a boisterous promotion of Southern California, an intense campaign to lure migrants, and a fierce opposition to trade unions—an "open shop is our best asset," their leaders liked to proclaim. They had already gained federal funding and started construction of a deepwater harbor at San Pedro (after a battle in which *LA Times* publisher General Otis prevailed over Collis P. Huntington, president of the Southern Pacific, who wanted to locate the harbor in Santa Monica, under his exclusive control). An elite, with Billy at the helm, was rising and congregating in newly formed private associations, among them the Jonathan Club and California Club, both destined to become ever more exclusive enclaves of white, Anglo-Saxon men. (Prominent Jewish families responded by forming the downtown Concordia Club and, years later, the Hillcrest Country Club.) Los Angeles did not yet look like a city—many streets were still unpaved, with horses and a few early automobiles kicking dust and mud on passersby. But LA, like Billy, was on its way.

The year 1903 would prove pivotal, trying, and perilous for Billy Garland. By then he was a public figure and de facto politician, openly promoting the Republican Party and its causes. He'd been a delegate to the Republican National Convention in Philadelphia the summer of 1900, and a member of the committee that afterward visited President William McKinley at his home in Canton, Ohio, to notify him he'd been nominated for reelection. Returning to LA, he'd reported, "I have always had a very high estimate of the character and ability of President McKinley, and my visit to Canton . . . served to intensify and increase that estimate tenfold." At the end of October 1902, this time after a tour across the country to assess business conditions, he had again returned to LA bearing his by now familiar upbeat news: The East was prospering, as was the South, with real estate in good demand, money plentiful, and large crops assured. By comparison, Los Angeles property values had room to grow, but "I predict we shall have more people in

FIGURE 2. La Fiesta de Las Flores Parade on Broadway in downtown Los Angeles, 1903. Security Pacific National Bank Collection / Los Angeles Public Library.

Southern California this season than ever before. . . . You hear of Los Angeles in every direction, and in no place is her fame lessened."

In April 1903, to prepare for this deluge, Billy presided at a meeting in his offices where a small group of men developed a proposal to organize the real estate brokers of Los Angeles. Here was a gang of go-getter civic boosters, eager to plan a city free of labor strife and class conflict, and eager as well to refine the image of the real estate broker, so tarnished by the unprincipled dealers who had bilked buyers in past booms. Out of this meeting came formation of the hugely influential Los Angeles Realty Board (LARB). Billy and eight others signed LARB's incorporation papers and filed them with the state of California in early June. The next month, some one hundred real estate men and their prominent guests, among them Harry Chandler and Los Angeles mayor Meredith Snyder, gathered at the Del Monte Tavern for the first LARB banquet. A cascade of speakers spoke until well past midnight, offering prophecies and odes to the city, as well as a pledge, by LARB president Byron Erkenbrecher, to "make the real estate business as legitimate as any other in existence." The night closed with a rousing speech by Mayor Snyder, who declared, "It is the real estate men who have made this city the metropolis of Southern California . . . and who, by their energy and brains, have enabled men to start large enterprises."

Billy should have been quite pleased. But this evening's event and the founding of LARB came at a difficult moment for him. On April 22, in the very month that Billy helped form an organization aimed at refining Los Angeles real estate brokers' professional image, a "sizzling . . . sensational lawsuit" (the *LA Times'* words) was filed against him by prominent former clients who claimed he had defrauded them. The clients, the heirs of Julia A. Crocker of San Francisco, included Henry J. Crocker, the nephew of the railway magnate Charles B. Crocker. The Crocker family, seeking $50,000 in damages (more than $1.3 million in 2018 dollars), claimed that Billy, while acting as their agent, bought their property at Sixth and Main in downtown LA for himself at a below-market figure by using his wife's relations as dummies, then sold it for much more to another buyer.

Legal documents and accounts in the *Los Angeles Times* spelled out specifically what the Crocker heirs alleged: That in October 1901, they were owners of property at Sixth and Main Streets. That Garland was their agent. That they resided in San Francisco and had no means of knowing the value of the property themselves, so relied on Garland's good faith and fidelity to get them the best possible price. That on July 11, 1901, he wrote that he had an offer of $25,000, and a higher price could not be obtained. That on August 21, Garland told them the purchaser was W. H. Schweppe—but neglected to say Schweppe was his blood relative and an intimate associate who made Billy's office his headquarters. That after the Crocker family deeded the property to Schweppe, Schweppe in turn deeded the property to Billy's father-in-law, M. L. Hinman, who then deeded it back to Schweppe, who then deeded it to the real purchaser, one E. T. Earl, who paid $60,000 for the Crocker property and an adjacent building Billy had also acquired. Garland's representations were "false and fraudulent," the Crocker heirs argued, since Schweppe had never in fact made an offer for their property, which they believed was now worth $70,000.

The filing of this lawsuit would have been no surprise to Billy. He had earlier been visited in his offices by representatives of the Crocker heirs, including Judge W. C. Van Fleet, formerly of the Supreme Court of California, who had appeared without advance notice to interrogate him about the real estate transaction. Billy had vainly tried to escape the interview, but his visitors persisted, and eventually he claimed to them that Schweppe had given him a $2,500 deposit for the property, paid "in $20 gold pieces, done up in a sack, which was placed in my safe." Billy, better prepared now, had ready a formal, angry, typewritten answer.

The sale to his father-in-law, he claimed, was a bona fide transaction. To the best of his recollection, he never told the Crocker heirs he couldn't get more than $25,000. Nor did he tell them it was Schweppe who made the offer. Schweppe was acting as agent for Marshall L. Hinman, his father-in-law. Hinman was the real purchaser of the property, with Schweppe merely acting in trust for him. Billy himself had no interest in the transaction. After the sale to Hinman, his father-in-law had employed him to find a purchaser for the property, and he sold it to E. T. Earl. Yes, he and Schweppe were intimate associates, but neither Schweppe nor Hinman acted as his dummies. The Crocker heirs knew, or had reason to believe, that Schweppe was not the real purchaser. They knew that the real purchaser was someone living at or near Dunkirk, New York (the home of Hinman). They did not care who the purchaser was, as long as they got $25,000 out of it ($694,584 in 2018 dollars).

The trial began in Los Angeles Superior Court in early October of 1903, inspiring daily headlines that must have troubled Billy greatly. He was thirty-seven then, newly a father, with two young sons, three and a half and one and a half years old. Already a prominent figure in LA, he was on the cusp of even greater achievements. Yet here he was, pinned to just the type of Los Angeles scandal he wished didn't exist. From the lips of witnesses in this case, testifying in a public courtroom, Billy repeatedly heard himself being called a liar, cheat and fraud. In the local newspapers, he regularly found himself top-of-the-page news: "Garland Forced to Confess Deception" . . . "Garland's Stories Didn't Hang Together" . . . "Garland Says the Sale Was Made in Good Faith" . . . "Garland Kept on Stand Another Day." When Billy took the witness stand for that second day, on October 7, he was "as gloomy as the melancholy Dane," the *Los Angeles Times* reported. "He had a perfectly horrid time." Closing arguments came in mid-October and, with them, one headline, finally, that Billy must have valued: "Masterful Argument Made by George Denis in the Famous Garland Case" . . . "Character of Defendant at Stake."

George Denis was Billy's lawyer. *The Times* summarized what he told the jury on October 14: "Opening with an eloquent panegyric upon character, as the most valuable asset that a businessman can have, and decrying the utilization of the courts to wreak vengeance upon an adversary . . . he contended that Garland had acted throughout in a bona fide manner. . . . The attorney aimed to show that the vital point of the effect of a verdict against his client would be the blasting of his character as an honest man and fair dealing real estate agent. 'William Garland,' he went on to explain, 'is a young, active, successful business man. The trouble which threatens him is infinitely more than a mere monetary demand. He could readily pay the sum which these plaintiffs seek to recover. But in signing a verdict against Garland, gentlemen of the jury, you sign the death warrant of his good name in this or any other country. . . . This is not a suit for mere money. Money is a trifle in the case to both plaintiffs and defendant. But this defendant is not able to pay his character as the price of his dealing with these plaintiffs.'"

The jury began deliberations the next morning, October 15, at 10:30 a.m., after receiving instructions from Judge N. P. Conrey. Billy, watching the jurors file out of the courtroom, understood his fate would turn on their verdict. There was nothing he could do but wait and contemplate all that had transpired in this matter. Clearly, there'd been some funny business involved, some gamesmanship. That would not have been entirely unusual in 1903 Los Angeles. Over at the *Los Angeles Times* building, not far from the downtown courtroom, Harry Chandler was busy in those days secretly buying up circulation routes and creating dummy operations in order to starve out competing newspapers. Billy himself had used his relative William Schweppe as a go-between in another transaction involving Main Street property, for which he'd drawn a second lawsuit, filed by a widow named Kate Manning. The business community, city hall, the Los Angeles Police Department, the underworld—at this time in Los Angeles, they all operated in a free-for-all, as if the law didn't apply to them. Whatever he'd done in the Crocker deal, Billy still seemed a respectable member of this community, worthy of the citizens' faith.

That's precisely what the jury concluded, unanimously, after just two hours of deliberation. "William M. Garland's Conduct Promptly Vindicated by a Jury," declared a *Los Angeles Herald* top-of-the page headline on October 16, above a photo of Billy encircled by what appears to be a wreath. "Not a Single Member of the Panel Hesitated to Affirm his Faith in the Defendant." The article under this headline began: "William M. Garland can walk down the street holding himself erect, in the knowledge that his actions have been justified in the suit of Henry J. Crocker and other heirs against him. His standing in the business community of Los Angeles has been certified to by the verdict rendered yesterday by the jury. . . . At 10:30 the jury retired to the jury room and at 12:30 made a return into court with the verdict as set forth above. It had taken the jury only two hours to discuss a case full of intricacies and make answer to a number of special questions. . . . And more striking still was the fact that the verdict returned was unanimous when a two-thirds majority would have sufficed."

This verdict, however, did not end the Crocker case. The jurors, besides their general finding in favor of Billy, had provided answers to a number of Judge Conrey's interrogatories. Among other issues, they'd decided that Marshall L. Hinman's money paid for the Crocker's lot; that the lot was worth $25,000 at the time of the sale; that Garland did not conceal from the plaintiffs the name of the real purchaser; that W. H. Schweppe had made a bona fide offer to Garland to purchase the property; that the real purchaser was W. H. Schweppe. In early March of 1904, in response to an appeal filed by the Crocker heirs, Judge Conrey found that the evidence was insufficient to support these answers, that the answers in fact were contrary to law. He particularly saw no basis for the jury to find that Garland had not concealed the name of the real purchaser (his father-in-law, Marshall Hinman). Nor did he see a basis for the jury to find that Schweppe was the real purchaser. Billy's acts were of such a character, Judge Conrey ruled, that the law imputes fraud. He set aside the jury's verdict and ordered a new trial.

News of this ruling did not draw nearly the coverage given to Billy's initial vindication—the *Los Angeles Times* printed a brief, four-paragraph item on March 6, 1904, with the headline "Garland Hard Hit By Court: Jury's Verdict Set Aside and New Trial Ordered." And then the case appears to have disappeared entirely from local newspapers, as did so many other unfavorable events unfolding in LA in this era. The story continued only in court records of the day, which reveal that Billy Garland appealed Judge Conrey's ruling to California's Second District Court of Appeal, where, on July 9, 1906, a unanimous three-judge appellate panel upheld Conrey's ruling, saying he was justified in setting aside the jury's verdict and ordering a new trial.

There was no new trial, though. At least, there was no news coverage of one, and there exists no accessible record of one in the court system. (There is also no subsequent appellate history.) The case of *Crocker v. Garland* seems to vanish at this point. The lawsuit was for financial damages. Presumably, the parties reached a settlement, and Billy moved on, unscathed, ready to join the other Los Angeles boosters in their ever-mounting campaign to lure migrants to an idyllic city of dreams.

Los Angeles by 1905 had 350 miles of graded roads, a growing abundance of autos and telephones, and the country's first movie theater.

FIGURE 3. Looking north across the San Fernando Valley, circa 1909, soon after Harry Chandler's syndicate started construction of the Owens Valley aqueduct. C.C. Pierce, Los Angeles Photographers Photo Collection / Los Angeles Public Library.

Traffic clogged Spring Street in downtown LA, a mix of horse-drawn carriages, electric railroad cars and early automobiles. Land values once again rose, in the boom of 1906. The first movie studios opened in 1907. A throng of winter tourists fueled the construction industry. Huntington's Red Car lines expanded, adding hundreds of track miles. From 1890 to 1900, LA's population had more than doubled, from 50,395 to 102,479. From 1900 to 1910 it would more than triple, to 319,198. On October 1, 1908, with Harry Chandler pulling the strings, construction of the Owens Valley aqueduct began, auguring the coming development of the San Fernando Valley (where Chandler owned thousands of acres). LA's boosters saw growth as the way to achieve prosperity. They had a vision and meant to make it a reality.

Billy operated at the heart of all this promotion, and his fellow boosters warmly embraced him. On January 25, 1907, just half a year after the final ruling in *Crocker v. Garland,* he hosted LARB's annual banquet for 125 men in a private room at the Angelus Hotel, serving as "the genial toastmaster and prophet," as the *Los Angeles Herald* put it. Everyone in the room called him Billy, and they were a raucous bunch. "Water! Water! Water! was the theme of one man's song," the *Herald* reported, "and cheers were the response. When the tune changed to Roads! Roads! Roads! some rose to their feet and shouted. . . . Band lots, subdivisions and population proved subjects equally inspirational." After a multicourse two-hour meal, accompanied by popular tunes played by the Kammermeyer Orchestra, Billy introduced LA mayor Arthur C. Harper, whom he had dragged away from a business meeting—apparently for good reason. "The real estate men are the men who make things go in Los Angeles," the mayor told the LARB crowd. "Without the real estate men and the politicians—don't forget the politicians—Los Angeles would not exist. I used to know a verse from the Bible which said, 'The earth is the Lord's and the fullness thereof.' But when I walk down the streets of Los Angeles it does not seem that the Lord has much to do with it."

Not long after, on May 3, 1907, Marshall Hinman died at his home in Dunkirk, New York. Billy's wife was his only child. *Big Bequest Comes Hither,* announced a *Los Angeles Times* headline the next month. Billy Garland would never have to dabble in dubious real estate deals again. "Los Angeles heirs of the late Marshall L. Hinman . . . ," the *Times* reported, "are to profit extensively in the distribution of his estate." This involved vast holdings, including much property, "many securities and other valuables," and the "valuable Hinman Block on the west of Spring Street in this city," appraised at $150,000 or more ($3.8 million in 2018 dollars). The bulk of the estate would be held in trust for the benefit of Hinman's widow and daughter, the *Times* reported, with Billy's wife receiving one-fourth of the returns until the death of her mother. That demise occurred less than a year later, on March 29, 1908, in Los Angeles. From then on, Billy and Blanche Garland were enthusiastic world travelers.

What kind of man was Billy now? By all accounts, he was, as before, genial, upbeat and enthusiastic. He still had that big strong handshake. (When introduced to Billy years later, American Olympic Committee president Avery Brundage, impressed, asked, "How did you get a hand like that, handball?" Billy replied, "Nope—politics.") He was a joiner, and it seemed he became president of every group he joined. In December 1907, his colleagues elected him president of the exclusive California Club. In July 1908, he took a seat on the Los Angeles Athletic Club's board of directors. Three times, he would serve as president of LARB, twice as president of the National Association of Real Estate Boards. He gave public speeches and wrote columns in the local newspapers. He regularly offered assurances about future prosperity. He bought more and more property in downtown LA. The Los Angeles elite in his era have often been called a hidden "shadow government," but Billy wasn't hiding in the least.

Not all of his activities involved empire-building. There he was, treating orphans to long rides to the Venice and Ocean Park beaches in his new Pierce Arrow (a "horseless vehicle"), part of an Automobile Club of Southern California weekend expedition. There he was, appearing as "good old St. Nick" at Christmastime for 650 poor children. There he was, being named lieutenant colonel and aide de camp by California's governor James Gillett (he'd retain that "colonel" title throughout his life). And there he was, in late June of 1907, protecting a little boy and his puppy from a dogcatcher.

This last, curious, item merits particular attention. "Realty Dealers Show Humanity," read the *Los Angeles Herald* headline on June 30. The story continued: "[Dogcatcher] Harry Dye who already has a battery charge against him . . . added another to his list yesterday morning when some of the largest real estate dealers in the city appeared in the city prosecutor's office and asked for a complaint against Dye on a charge of battery. William M. Garland, Frank Garbutt, Robert Marsh, Robert A. Rowan and Howard Paget filed into Guy Eddy's office one by one and after them came: a deputy dog catcher, a little Mexican boy, his father and Patrolman McLain. The august assemblage ranged themselves around the wall and all began their stories at once. At last W. M. Garland was elected spokesman and he told the story. Garland said the little Mexican boy was leading his pup down Main Street yesterday morning. The chocolate-colored long-eared dog was holding a tiny tin pail in his jaws and the boy was leading him by the ears. The dog catchers [Dye and a second man] spied the harmless pet and the equally harmless boy. They lassoed the dog in true Arizona fashion and hauled him, yelping and whining, to their cart. The boy's father, Jose X Estrado, grabbed at the rope. One of the dog catchers hit Estrado on the head and a fight started. The humanity and chivalry of bygone days surged up in the hearts of the real estate magnates, and even though the little boy was a Mexican, with a dirty face, they did not intend to see him robbed of his dog by the city pound men, nor did they intend to see the lad's father pounded by the dog catchers. Regardless of creased trousers, the men jumped from their auto and grabbed the dog catcher Dye. [Patrolman] McLain came up and the crowd went to the police station.

[Prosecutor] Eddy issued the complaint. . . . Dye was told to appear for trial on July 2 at 3 o'clock. Cigars went the rounds and happy over their kind act, the smiling real estate men departed."

Billy, despite his privilege, did not linger in the elite's protected corridors of power. He embraced what was new or about to come, and thrived on adventures. It's no surprise that he was among those who raised a hundred thousand dollars to stage, in January 1910, the pioneering Los Angeles International Air Meet at Dominguez Field, set on a ranch in present-day Carson. This was the second air meet in history and the first in the United States, held just four years after the Wright brothers lifted off near Kitty Hawk, North Carolina. Drawing some 254,000 spectators over its eleven-day run, most arriving via the streetcars of the Pacific Electric Railway, it included monoplanes, biplanes, balloons and dirigibles and featured a one-hour, forty-five-mile flight by famed French aviator Louis Paulhan, the longest to date in aviation's six-year history. (The Wright brothers didn't participate but were there with their lawyers, trying to stop Paulhan and the American aviation pioneer Glenn Curtiss from flying, owing to a patent dispute.) Billy recognized this air show would demonstrate to the world that Los Angeles was the city of the future, with a climate and terrain ideal for flying. He saw also that airplanes would in time enhance land values in their region by making Los Angeles and the far west more accessible.

But beyond all that, flying looked like a lot of fun to Billy. In late December of 1910, less than a year after the air meet, he prepared to glide through the skies above Dominguez Field, a passenger in the biplane of aviator daredevil Walter Brookins. Billy had made Brookins promise he would "cut out" all the "dips and curves" he often tried while flying. Clad in cap and goggles, Billy climbed into his seat beside Brookins "without a smile on his face," the Los Angeles Herald reported, and "glanced anxiously over his shoulder" as the motor purred and the propellers began to turn. "It's all right," Brookins reassured him, "that's just the buzzer." Billy threw himself into the moment. "Good-bye, boys," he cried cheerfully to his friends. "If I don't come back, keep up the good work." With that they were off, Brookins soaring into space without a hint of a spiral dip or curve, gradually climbing and circling, providing Billy a spectacular view.

This flight temporarily halted "a merry tea party" being given by Billy's wife in a private box in the grandstand, as she and the crowd watched closely until the biplane landed safely. "It was fine." Billy said, setting his feet back on Dominguez Field. "Flying is a fine sport without the dips and spiral curves. Brookins gave me his word as a man he wouldn't do any high diving while in the air. . . . He did not abuse my confidence, but sailed along with me as though he were on a smooth sea. It was fine. I can't say too much for it and of it. Indeed, words fail me when I attempt to express my keen enjoyment of the whole flight. It does not seem as though you were flying. The earth just moves from under you and drops away and you seem to be floating. Brookins appeared a master hand at the game of handling his machine and made no fuss over it. He just simply ran it along as though he had run one all his life."

Of course, Billy could not help but also talk as a booster: "You can never realize Los Angeles' geographical situation as it relates to commerce and expansion until you see the city and the country surrounding from an airplane. The scenery was magnificent and inspiring, from the mountains to the sea. The harbor I never saw to better advantage and it shows up great. . . . Allow me to add one thing more. Anyone who sees this city and its surrounding country from an airship cannot fail to see its future. When I got up there and looked down on the city, I said to myself, 'It's a million in population for Los Angeles in 1920.'" He was a little off: The city of Los Angeles' population would be 576,673 in 1920. But perhaps he meant Los Angeles County . . . where the population would be 936,455 in 1920.

Billy embraced the original automobiles even more than he did the early airplanes. The first he'd owned had been a 1904 Winton, a five-passenger tonneau-equipped touring model with a twenty-horsepower, twin-cylinder engine that sold for twenty-five hundred dollars. Next, he owned a 1906 four-cylinder, forty-eight-horsepower Pierce Arrow known as the "Gee-Whiz"—fire-alarm red with canary-yellow wheels and all brass metalwork. (A photo exists of Billy driving it past his West Adams home, clad in suit and bowler hat, looking intently engaged.) By July 1906 he was president of the state association of automobilists and, in that role, wrote a sarcastic letter to the board of supervisors of Ventura County, complaining about autos getting stuck in dredged streams created by farmers looking to make a business of pulling them out at fifteen dollars each. For the most part, he advised the supervisors, you have good roads, "but you have one or two streams flowing with cold, crystal water that are rightfully hard to ford in a machine, and made more particularly so by the acts of enterprising and energetic people of your county, who—it is reported to me—have repeatedly shoveled out the dirt in the natural wagon rut in these streams so that a heavily loaded automobile would sink down in these soft places and be unable to proceed . . . compelling the owner . . . to disrobe and wade ashore, where, behind the trees, could be found a pair of horses harnessed to a whiffletree, with a man with rubber boots and all paraphernalia convenient for immediately taking the automobile out."

Eventually, Billy's driving ambitions grew beyond the bounds of Southern California. In the spring of 1911, he began developing plans for a cross-country, 4,319-mile journey from Los Angeles to Moosehead Lake, Maine, in his new 1911 Pierce Arrow, a large tourer with six cylinders and a sixty-six-horsepower engine. He intended to make this journey, with three colleagues, at a time when the few roads that existed in the country were rudimentary at best. "Four Prominent Men to Make Hazardous Trip," reported one *Los Angeles Times* headline.

On June 10, 1911, the night before his departure, Billy and Blanche hosted an elaborate farewell banquet at the California Club, complete with dancing to a string orchestra. The slogan of the evening was "Maine in Thirty-Three Days," and the banquet table was a papier-mâché map of the route to be traveled. Billy, recognizing the future of the automobile as clearly as he saw what airplanes would bring, was then president of the Southern California Automobile Association, a promoter of the "good roads" movement, and advocate of building a highway from coast to coast. Those joining him on the journey, all fellow "clubmen and capitalists" as one newspaper account put it, included Robert I. Rogers, vice president of the National Bank of California; Harry Gray, director of the Southern Bank of California; and Richard J. Schweppe, a banker, cattleman, and Billy's first cousin. Billy's expert mechanic, Harry Sarvar, would also be on board, and Pierce Arrow representatives would meet them at points along the route to assist. The party would take no camping equipment, relying instead on a good supply of blankets to make beds in the desert. They'd also bring both provisions for meals en route and an extra gasoline tank. Billy made sure all of these facts were well known to the residents of Los Angeles: A major story, complete with a map and a photo of the touring party sitting in the Pierce Arrow, appeared prominently atop a page of the *Los Angeles Herald* on the morning of their departure.

By all accounts, the 4,319-mile cross-country drive—twenty days of actual driving over thirty-six days, averaging nine hours a day and twenty-two miles per hour—went well despite the limited roads . . . and a near mishap in Iowa on July 3. Billy was to meet Blanche in Chicago that night, she having traveled there by train, but he was running late, so he floored his Pierce Arrow. The fast pace on country roads generated lots of jolts, which caused Billy's wallet to pop out of his pocket and fall unseen on the road. It was, not surprisingly, a thick wallet, containing $6,500 in cash and bank drafts ($165,738 in 2018 dollars). Soon after Billy lost his wallet, a local farmer, Vance C. Orr of Iowa City, found it on the road, opened it and saw Billy's identification cards. Orr telegraphed officials in LA, only to learn that Billy was speeding toward Chicago. Orr set out after him, but Billy was still flooring it, so Orr, realizing he wasn't going to win this race, telegraphed again, this time to Chicago. Eventually, Billy retrieved his wallet, happy to have found it and an honest man in Iowa.

The touring party arrived at Moosehead Lake on July 16. From Maine, Billy reported in a letter to a LARB colleague that "we had a wonderful trip overland. . . . Every foot on our own power, and never raised the hood to look at the engine or spark plugs. . . . No accidents of any sort. We found hot weather galore, but the trip was one grand and glorious dream." This despite the fact that "the roads between Rock Springs and Laramie, Wyoming, 250 miles, were terrible. It was almost impassable for any car."

Again, Billy couldn't help but take the opportunity to play the booster, both for his city and the good roads movement. Upon returning to LA in mid-August by train, after visiting East Coast cities, he declared that "Los Angeles is absolutely and unqualifiedly the liveliest city in the country." He also predicted that "fully 2,000 automobiles will attempt transcontinental trips from New York to Los Angeles during 1912." What's more, "ten times that number will come the first year that a national highway is in use."

By now, Billy had become something of a celebrity in Los Angeles, right up there with the earliest movie stars. He inspired newspaper headlines regularly as he boosted, predicted and hosted. The term *prophet* appeared next to his name on occasion. On June 23, 1915, he topped himself by helping organize one of the most lavish parties Los Angeles had ever seen.

With the National Association of Real Estate Boards in town for its annual convention, Billy and his neighbor E.L. Doheny (they lived around the corner from each other, two minutes apart) were among the hosts who invited five thousand delegates and guests to their tony, exclusive West Adams neighborhood, taking full advantage of Doheny's lavish grounds and conservatory in the gated Chester Place complex, just off West Adams. "Gardens of Magic," the *Los Angeles Times* called the setting in a prominent headline. Visitors danced, dined, and partied from early evening to dawn as four different sixty-piece bands played under an array of one hundred thousand electric lamps and "light-toed, gossamer-garbed maidens gamboled over the greensward beneath a spreading rubber tree." Vehicles were barred from Chester Place, so limousines lined the curbs of West Adams for half a mile. Guests wandered among great bowers of flowers and ferns, discovering booths tucked away among the rose arbors, coral trees, jasmine and honeysuckle, all offering "refreshments of liquid character." Chester Place had been the center of fashionable gatherings before, but nothing like this. "The boulevards of Paris," the *LA Times* reported, "with their scintillating, laughing, dancing crowds on the night of the anniversary of the fall of the Bastille, would prove tame by actual comparison."

Of course, Billy was boosting as he entertained: This party allowed him to introduce five thousand visiting real estate men to an elite, exclusive neighborhood in LA—Billy's notion of, or at least hope for, the city's future. "It was indeed a paradise for the select and elect for a few hours," the *LA Times* reported. "Introductions in this night of nights were unnecessary. There was none to intrude who had no right to do so. The gates were guarded and every ticket and invitation was closely scanned."

Still, even as he promoted Southern California as the Anglo-Saxon's fated home, Billy's eye-on-the-ball pursuit of growth sometimes set him apart from others in his circle. His response to the arrival of movie studios and movie stars in Los Angeles provides one example of this. The first small-scale studios were operating in LA by 1907 and soon were capturing an ever-growing audience—by 1910, ten million Americans were regularly attending movies, and between 1910 and 1912 that number doubled. Yet the LA Chamber of Commerce remained leery of movie people, and a *Los Angeles Times* editorialist in 1911 feared that "the motion picture people may be something of a pest." Billy thought otherwise: He could see clearly how the movies were helping advertise and promote Los Angeles. Gorgeous weather, broad sandy beaches, deep-blue skies, towering mountains, lush gardens, pristine single-family homes on spacious lots—what Americans saw of Los Angeles in movie theaters beckoned them to a land of endless happiness and possibility. Billy did not miss the fact that the moviemakers were accomplishing what he, LARB, and the chamber of commerce had all been attempting for years: to portray Los Angeles as Eden. No wonder he supported the movie studios.

Harry Chandler, straitlaced and reserved, also recognized the studios' promotional value but felt conflicted by the Hollywood bacchanal culture. Others, Hollywood's most vocal opponents, went further, objecting to the content of movies, and they convinced the LA City Council to create a local moving-picture censorship board. Billy was having none of this. In January 1916, as the city council prepared to hold a public hearing concerning the censorship board, he put LARB firmly on record as opposing movie censorship and urging dissolution of the board. The movie industry, Billy pointed out, had invested $100 million in Los Angeles and Southern California (almost $2.4 billion in 2018 dollars) and spent approximately $30 million a year here (more than $718 million in 2018 dollars). All hindrances to the industry should be removed, and censorship abolished. "I am in favor of completely abolishing the censorship board for the moving pictures," Billy said. "Every encouragement should be given the picture producers. This industry has been an immense thing for all Southern California and of incomparable value to Los Angeles. It has invested millions here, advertising California indirectly in every picture that is taken. . . . We have placed detrimental influences, stumbling blocks and annoyances in the way of the picture industry, and I think the time has come to remove them all and get together to encourage the movies. . . . They have advertised and will continue to advertise Los Angeles, and now Los Angeles should . . . help them in every possible way."

That same year, Billy formed and became president of the California Prosperity League, a group of prominent LA businessmen whose mission would be to fight "every measure inimical to California." Their first and central target: two proposed amendments on the state ballot that would impose prohibition in California. Billy enjoyed his cocktails and glasses of champagne—the Uplifters, an offshoot of the Los Angeles Athletic Club, maintained a high-end drinking club in the conveniently isolated Rustic Canyon on the far west side of town—but he had larger reasons to oppose prohibition: A desire to save the state's grape and wine industries from annihilation . . . and a desire to keep liquor available to tourists from the East who came to vacation or linger in California. He was in New Orleans at a realty convention when the California Prosperity League announced its plans, so Watt Moreland, a vice president of the group, spoke for him: "These people are bent on pleasure and they are going where they can find pleasure with personal liberty. . . . If we want to turn our business over to Florida, the best way to do it is to adopt prohibition. . . . The wine industry of the state has done as much if not more for the prosperity of California than any other single thing. There is no reason why this industry should be made to suffer from a law that will hurt the state and the industry and will do no one any good."

The year 1917 would see both Billy Garland and Harry Chandler rise to new positions of power. Harry had married Marian Otis, the daughter of *Los Angeles Times* publisher Harrison Gray Otis, in June 1894, and by 1898, at age thirty-four, had assumed ever-increasing responsibility for running the paper (even while investing in myriad real estate ventures in Southern California and Mexico). Now, in 1917, at the death of his father-in-law on July 30, Harry succeeded him as president and publisher of the *Times*. That same year—in fact, just two days before Harry became publisher—Billy was unanimously elected president of the National Association of Real Estate Boards at the national convention in Milwaukie. On August 23, back in Los Angeles, some two hundred leading businessmen hosted a luncheon in his honor in the men's grillroom of the Broadway Department Store, where those making addresses hailed him as a "real live wire," a "human dynamo," and "an expert in planning municipal advancement."

One year later, on August 23, 1918, the same group again hosted a luncheon in Billy's honor, after he was reelected president of the National Association of Real Estate Boards at the national convention in St. Louis. "Applause and cheering lasting several minutes greeted William May Garland," Harry Chandler's *Los Angeles Times* reported. "It was the greatest demonstration ever seen at a [LARB] board meeting, and was participated in, not only by realty men, but by many prominent in the local business and financial world."

The next week, the directors of the Los Angeles Athletic Club—among them Harry Chandler—unanimously elected Billy president of the club. Billy had been deeply involved in the organization for more than a dozen years, helping raise funds for the purchase of land at Seventh and Olive, where the club's impressive skyscraper home now stood. Opening in 1912, it featured unparalleled meeting, dining, residential, and athletic facilities, including a mammoth indoor swimming pool and running track. In 1913, with Billy already one of its directors, the club had first launched a program of competitive athletics, providing coaching for young athletes, and this program had continually improved over time. The business and social establishment congregated at the Los Angeles Athletic Club, but film stars also were members, among them Douglas Fairbanks, Charlie Chaplin, Rudolph Valentino, Al Jolson and Fatty Arbuckle. This was the place to be.

All the elements were now aligned: with Billy and Harry in esteemed positions of power, and the Los Angeles Athletic Club under Billy's leadership, the city was poised for a burst of unprecedented growth that would make the 1887 boom look puny by comparison. How to get there, though? Los Angeles, after all, remained just a big village. An idea began to percolate: like Billy, Harry worshipped real estate. Like Billy, he dreamed about the commercial future of Southern California. The path to that future, they both would come to believe, involved bidding for and staging the Olympic Games in Los Angeles.

# 3

# THE QUEST

One day in late 1918, Billy Garland ushered five visitors into his office at 729 South Spring Street in downtown Los Angeles. The men were all familiar to him as publishers of the city's major newspapers: F. W. Kellogg of the *Evening Express,* Guy B. Barham of the *Herald,* M. H. Ihmsen of the *Examiner,* H. B. R. Briggs of the *Record,* and—easily the most powerful—Harry Chandler of the *Times.*

"Certain Signs of Dawn" promised a recent headline on his newspaper's business page—a typical example of Harry's trademark "Sell 'em Sunshine" approach to news about his city. But the opening sentence of the article told another story: "There is a temporary lull in financial and business activity in Los Angeles just at present." A nationwide quarantine to combat the growing Spanish flu pandemic, coupled with uncertainty about the Great War (fighting still waged, though an armistice was near), "is all having its effect, and as a result there is considerable lethargy in financial circles."

*Considerable lethargy.* Looking out Billy's windows, they could literally see the lethargy. The streets were virtually deserted. The flu pandemic had claimed more than 115,000 lives in California so far. Since mid-October, all schools, colleges, churches, theaters, and motion picture houses in Los Angeles had been closed by order of city health officials. Public gatherings of any sort had been banned, retail promotional sales discouraged, Christmas shopping restricted to the phone. The movie industry and scores of other businesses were losing millions of dollars daily. Even worse was the severe decline in tourism. By itself a lucrative industry, tourism more importantly sold the advantages of Southern California and induced visitors to return, buy homes and start businesses. To the public, the *Los Angeles Times* might call it a "temporary lull"—once "politics and germs are out of the way things will hum"—but the men sitting in Billy's office were not so positive.

To counter their qualms, they needed Billy's energy and can-do optimism. That's why they'd come to his office. Harry, particularly, had been turning to Billy in this way for years. He'd propose plans, then Billy would convert the plans to reality. He'd get it done.

Harry was then fifty-four, Billy fifty-two, and their years in LA had been good to them. The population explosion resulting from their successful promotion of the region had produced exceptional windfalls in real estate—windfalls that had hugely benefited them. They were partners in a realty syndicate that had picked up numerous parcels throughout downtown LA, and both still considered land the source of all wealth—*everything springs from the soil,* Billy even now liked to say. As part of the region's private business elite, they regularly did deals together, sat side by side on assorted boards, and shared memberships in exclusive private clubs (some of which they'd founded). On this day in 1918, Harry had already assembled one of the largest real estate empires in the country.

Billy studied his colleague. He knew something was brewing. Harry, a big, husky man who stood six feet two, as always seemed more reticent than ruthless. He spoke softly. For the first time in the history of LA, Harry explained, the five newspaper publishers in Billy's office had determined to work together "as a unit on everything that had to do with the upbuilding and advancement of Los Angeles." They reserved the right to exercise their individual judgment politically and in the fundamental conduct of their newspapers, but "in everything that had to do with the upbuilding of Los Angeles, we will work in unison." They had in mind creating a nonprofit organization of businessmen to further this goal, and they wanted Billy to serve as its president.

Of course they did. They knew Billy could lead. They knew Billy could, with ease, step into the spotlight. Above all, they knew Billy recognized the importance of image in swaying opinion and making things happen.

Billy stood about as tall as Harry and had the same type of broad, open, resilient face. Despite that and their shared interests, they weren't entirely alike. Harry avoided public appearances and speechmaking and, by choice, lived a relatively Spartan existence: the food served in his home was simple, alcohol rare, the house modest. Harry likely walked to Billy's office this morning—his preferred method of transport. Automobiles confounded him; rather than use the brakes, he would simply yell "Whoa" and hope for the best. Billy, on the other hand, enjoyed—relished—the good and public life. His many extended tours of Europe included visits to the most important museums, galleries and monuments, as well as stops at the Continent's finest hotels and restaurants ("the Garlands did not eat fast food" a granddaughter would later observe). He and Blanche journeyed well, with a lady's maid, a valet, a driver and a stack of wardrobe trunks. New Pierce Arrows kept showing up on their driveway. Billy wasn't showy or boastful in the least, but he didn't hide what it was that pleased him.

Still—Billy and Harry were both descendants of "second-boat" seventeenth-century immigrants to America. Like Billy, Harry as a young man, in 1883, had come west from New England, suffering from lung problems that had caused him to drop out of Dartmouth College before ever starting classes. Like Billy, he'd had to scramble during his first years in Los Angeles. Just nineteen when he arrived, with little money and a severe cough, he rented a room in a cut-rate boardinghouse and began searching for work. His landlord soon evicted him after other lodgers objected to his cough. Jobless and ill, he roamed the streets, lost, without direction. In time he met a man who shared his lung problems and either owned a farm in the Cahuenga Pass or was a squatter there (accounts vary). Harry reached a deal with him to break horses and pick fruit in exchange for a share of the crops, which he could sell to nearby ranch crews. Within a year, while camping out in a tent on the farm, Harry saved $3,000 ($69,545 in 2018 dollars). He returned to Dartmouth in 1884 but soon was suffering lung hemorrhages again, so he came back to Los Angeles. In 1885, he landed a job in the circulation department of the *Los Angeles Times*, which General Harrison Gray Otis, then the editor, was about to purchase.

Like Billy, Harry engaged in certain dubious dealings during his early career. Independent contractors then managed the daily distribution of most newspapers, and Harry quickly opted to get into that business. He launched a small company that in time became responsible for delivering many of the city's morning newspapers. (In the early going, his carrier boys rode saddle horses, then later, bicycles.) This eventually allowed him to control—as a subcontractor with various dummy connections—the circulation lists of the *Times* and several other local papers, including the *Herald.* That control came in handy when the publisher of the *Herald* started scrapping with General Otis: Harry hired a big horse-drawn carriage and shipped the entire *Herald* circulation and carrier crew to the San Bernardino Mountains for a five-day holiday; during the resulting confusion, the *Times* launched a campaign that wooed away half of the *Herald*'s subscribers. "That kind of thing made life exciting," Harry would reminisce late in life. "We used to pull all kinds of tricks on one another in the newspaper business in those days and think nothing of it. . . . As it might be the other fellow's turn the next day, hard feelings did not last long."

Next he helped General Otis kill off another rival paper, the *Tribune,* once again through his control of the circulation lists. "My scheme was to starve out the Tribune," Harry recalled. "With two of the three morning paper distribution systems under my control, it would be simple to play them together against the Tribune. . . . If a Times subscriber quit, we could swing him to the Herald, whereas he might have gone to the Tribune if left alone. If a Herald subscriber quit we could swing him to the Times. Of course, no one but General Otis would know of my connection. The Herald routes were to be handled through a dummy." The *Tribune,* staggered by this scheme, folded within two years. Secretly, Harry then bought the *Tribune*'s assets for five cents on the dollar. Otis, concerned about this unknown new competitor, asked Harry to learn the name of the buyer and cut a deal with him. When Harry allowed that he was the buyer, Otis had no choice but to make him a top manager at the *Times.*

Billy looked at the five men sitting before him. It certainly was odd to see these five publishers banded together, when normally their papers, especially the *Times* and *Examiner,* were waging war against each other, less over journalistic supremacy than the selling of real estate advertising (often to shady land promoters who ducked paying their bills for the ads, but later became leading citizens). That Harry Chandler sat with them was a particular hoot, given how he'd launched his career by shrewdly squeezing out competing newspapers. How could this team of publishers work together? If we formed such a group, Billy asked, what exactly would it do?

They all fell to talking and imagining. They understood that tourists and a sharply rising population had fueled the city's extraordinary financial and business activity. They also understood this condition couldn't continue indefinitely. To prevent a future business depression, they had to intelligently develop their one most productive natural resource—the appeal of Southern California to travelers and homebuyers.

Billy loved this idea of overriding the natural cycle of things. *Growth always—perpetual growth*. But could they really do it? The men talked on. One idea, not yet fully articulated, hung in the air, as it had in LA ever since Fred Kelly of USC won gold in the 110-meter hurdles at the 1912 Olympics. What if Los Angeles bid for the Olympic Games? If they won it, wouldn't that raise the city's prestige, generate a pile of publicity, and have a lasting impact?

Billy saw nothing peculiar in this notion, even though their city was remote and unknown to the great capitals of Europe. He'd instantly grasped the grand scope of the games and the full significance of their meaning to Los Angeles. He was already strategizing. As the publishers rose to leave, Billy said, "Yes." He would be happy to serve as president of this new committee.

At first they called their nonprofit organization the California Fiestas Association, a group Billy envisioned as sponsoring a range of events: "Of music and drama, of Olympian Games, aviation meets, horse shows, motor races, flower and fruit exhibits, or Spanish celebrations showing the fascinating charms of early California life." All aimed at demonstrating the "world famous old-time California hospitality, good-fellowship and cordiality."

Billy in this way was starting to put in motion the perpetual "upbuilding" of Los Angeles, a term he would use more than once in the coming months and years. He'd spent most of 1918 in Washington, DC, serving as a "dollar-a-year" volunteer, supporting the government's war effort by leading a team of real estate men who did appraisals for various federal departments, helping them save hundreds of thousands of dollars in the purchasing and leasing of private property. Now back home, speaking on March 5, 1919, at yet another luncheon in his honor, this one attended by public officials, businessmen, LARB members and out-of-town guests, he first explained that *realtor* had come to be the term used nationally to designate men engaged in the real estate business. He then plunged into discussing local conditions. With the war finally over, he said, everyone in Los Angeles must look to the "upbuilding of the peace-time prosperity of the city." First and foremost, the city needed "a great hotel commensurate with the size and importance of the city."

This would do more than anything to advance the general interests of the city, for visitors could not understand why Los Angeles, "the most advertised city in the world," should be without a big hotel comparable to those in other communities.

A great hotel, however, was not Billy's only—or even chief—concern at the time. The country just then was caught up in the first Red Scare, driven, in the wake of the 1917 Russian Revolution, by a widespread fear of Bolshevism and anarchism. Billy shared those fears. Most particularly, he worried about the effects of radical political agitation in American society and the suspected spread of communism in the American labor movement. He saw everywhere challenges to the social order. So after calling for a "grand hotel" at this luncheon, he also declared that the real estate men of Los Angeles should be among the first to rise against "Bolshevik agitation" of any kind and to insist that disturbers in the community be deported. There can be no prosperity in any community, he said, in which these "foreign trouble-makers are allowed any latitude."

Three days later, a headline appeared at the top of the *Los Angeles Evening Herald*'s front page: "Broad Policy For L.A. Urged by Garland: Realtor Asks Immediate Campaign of Expansion in Lines of Business." Billy here was sounding very much like a politician campaigning for office—one clearly affected by his year in Washington spent watching the "whole world enflamed in the horrors of human conflict." And one also concerned that workers were stirring, that "Bolshevikism is again afoot." His solution: improve the workers' conditions.

This time he'd conveyed his thoughts not at a business luncheon but in an interview with an *Evening Herald* reporter. The resulting article began: "Urging upon Los Angeles a program of expansion of business in all lines, a progressive financial policy, a substantial movement in public and private building and improvements, and sounding the slogan, 'Wage earners should own their own homes,' William May Garland, prominent Los Angeles realtor and president of the National Association of Real Estate Boards, declared today that the time is here for a constructive community cooperation."

Billy urged business and financial men of LA to start building and expanding, rather than keep waiting for an era of lower prices and wages. He asked, "Are we ready to quit business or are we ready to go ahead?" He said, "Something must be done to stabilize the buying power of the people. Wage-earners must be able to feel a security in their employment, and this condition cannot prevail unless business and finance increase their own activities. Wage-earners should own their

**FIGURE 4.** The Fairfax and Wilshire Boulevard intersection, Los Angeles, in 1920, featuring undeveloped land with many oil derricks. C.C. Pierce, Los Angeles Photographers Photo Collection / Los Angeles Public Library.

own homes, and they cannot and will not buy homes with a feeling of uncertainty prevailing. . . . One never sees a red flag waving over the roof of a contented homeowner." Billy concluded by sounding his signature theme, one he would echo often over the years: "Why be afraid of the future? Let us play the game as the cards are dealt."

He continued his ceaseless "upbuilding" campaign all through 1919. There he was on June 24, at the annual convention of the National Association of Real Estate Boards in Atlantic City, declaring that the country needed one million new homes—and a network of "good roads." There he was on September 5, at a luncheon for officers of the California Fiestas Association, saying, "The need of a great auditorium [in Los Angeles] to seat at least 20,000 is more apparent than ever now." There he was on October 26, in the LA Chamber of Commerce directors' room, sitting among other members of a newly appointed committee, among them Harry Chandler, discussing plans to provide financial underwriting to new industrial firms. There he was on

November 11, with other California Fiestas Association officers, again including Harry Chandler, launching a campaign to raise $588,888 (more than $8.6 million in 2018 dollars) from the business community, in support of the association's drive to stimulate tourist traffic year around. There he was on November 26, joining the California Fiestas board in calling for the building of a seventy-five-thousand-seat stadium—"essential for Los Angeles." And there he was on November 28, predicting Los Angeles would be "a city of 2,000,000 in 30 years." The prophet was pretty close this time: In 1950, thirty-one years later, the city's population stood at 1,970,358.

Early in 1920, the California Fiestas Association changed its name to the Community Development Association and whittled the roster of members from one hundred to twenty-two, with an eight-man executive committee chaired by Billy. Others in this "Big 8" included the newspaper publishers Harry Chandler, Guy Barham, Max Ihmsen and F. W. Kellogg; former US senator Frank P. Flint; Edward A. Dickson, editor and owner of the *Evening Express;* and businessman Henry McKee.

Together they represented a vivid sample of the men who shaped Southern California in the early years of the twentieth century. Guy Barham, who, after migrating from Oregon in 1883, had invested profitably in LA real estate and joined all the prestigious private clubs, was considered "close in the inner circles of all important matters pertaining to the welfare of the local order." Max Ihmsen had helped an ambitious developer promote the agricultural potential of the newly named Apple Valley, where he owned 320 acres of prizewinning apples and pears. F. W. Kellogg, who'd married Florence Scripps in 1890, was a member of the philanthropic family that founded the Scripps Research Institute, Scripps Institution of Oceanography, and Scripps College; he would later purchase and expand the La Jolla Beach and Yacht Club. Frank Flint, who like Billy and Harry had migrated from the Northeast to California in the 1880s because of lung issues, was a fruit grower, banker, prosecutor, developer (La Canada Flintridge) and politician; as a US senator from California, he played a major role (along with Harry Chandler) in bringing Owens Valley water to metropolitan Los Angeles. Edward Dickson was a cofounder of UCLA who would serve as a University of California regent for forty-three years. Henry McKee was a local banker and president of the Business Men's Association, organized by "several prominent commercial leaders."

In the spring of 1920, at the Big 8's first meeting (in offices leased from Billy), they tossed about ideas, as they'd been doing for months. It was here that the *Examiner*'s publisher, Max Ihmsen, formally proposed what before had just been floated as a possibility: that Los Angeles bid for the Olympic Games as a means to raise the city's prestige and generate unbounded publicity for the region. The only Olympic Games previously held in the United States—in 1904 at St. Louis as part of a World's Fair—had proved to be such a disaster (virtually no foreign athletes participating, virtually no coherent organization) that it is considered the worst in history and often is not even counted as an Olympic Games. Games held in Los Angeles did not promise to be any better. Few Europeans had even heard of Los Angeles or knew where it was. Still, the Big 8 were intrigued—though they had no idea how to bid for the Olympics or what it would cost the city. Their ignorance did not stop them from taking on this challenge. It's no surprise that the Big 8 delegated to Billy the task of starting a process aimed at bringing the Olympic Games to Los Angeles. At the same time, building off an idea first voiced the previous November, they began pushing the notion of a huge public sporting facility that could host major events, such as conventions, meets and festivals (and, of course, the Olympic Games). LA had no such facility in 1920 and very few existed anywhere in the country, but the Big 8 now declared that a seventy-five-thousand-seat stadium was essential. They commissioned the noted architect John Parkinson to draw up tentative stadium blueprints, and on August 10, 1920, the LA City Council approved putting a bond measure on the local ballot as a means to finance the project.

By then, Billy had sailed (on July 8) for Europe with his two sons, Jack and Marshall, aboard, of all ships, the SS *Olympic*. They were on holiday, visiting London and Paris and touring World War I battle sites. But Billy also had some work on his schedule: once he and the boys had completed their tour, they took the train to Antwerp, arriving on August 14, just as the 1920 Olympics were to begin. Joining them was Robert Weaver, president of the Southern California branch of the Amateur Athletic Union, whom the LA City Council had delegated to convey the city's invitation. Weaver, though, seems to have operated in Billy's shadow and eventually shifted his attention to managing the US Olympic team.

Billy soon was learning all about the Olympics protocol and how to bid for the games. Armed with what he called a "very beautiful Morocco bound" invitation signed by California's governor, LA's mayor, and a half dozen prominent businessmen, Billy met first with the two American members of the International Olympic Committee, Professor William Sloane and Judge Bartow Weeks. "I must say," Billy would later write to Blanche, "they received my invitation [for the 1924 Games] with a smile and informed me that they thought it would be difficult to bring the Games to America, and certainly not to California, which was three thousand miles beyond New York." Still, Sloane arranged a meeting with the International Olympic Committee (IOC) four days later at the Hotel de Ville.

There, at ten in the morning, Billy for the first time met the IOC president and legendary founder of the modern Olympic movement, Baron Pierre de Coubertin. The baron, a bantam five feet three, was a decidedly formal and fussy man, aristocratic in bearing, dressed in a gray formal cutaway and sporting a big bushy mustache. He and Billy together entered a remarkable building. The Hotel de Ville, Antwerp's town hall, had been built by Cornelis Floris in 1564. Its long façade (249 feet) was a striking mixture of Flemish and Italian Renaissance styles. Billy particularly appreciated the building's skylights and gables. He appreciated Baron de Coubertin, as well.

Born in Paris to a wealthy aristocratic family, Coubertin had first floated the idea of reviving the ancient Olympic Games (a Greek religious ritual) at a jubilee in 1892. After meeting disinterest and rejection there, he had more formally proposed it to an international congress at the Sorbonne in June 1894. Driven by the notion that physical education could have protected his country from military disgrace by the Prussians in the late 1800s, Coubertin had fought a difficult battle to realize his dream. The first modern Olympic Games, held in Athens in 1894, had not gone well; nor had the 1900 Paris games or the 1904 St. Louis games. Not until the 1912 games in Stockholm did Coubertin see his ideals fully realized. He paid a high price: By the time Billy met him in 1920, Coubertin had spent most of his sizable inheritance to promote the games. Penurious, he had sold his home and discharged his servants. Still, in 1920 he remained firmly in control of the Olympic movement.

Billy, three years his junior, forged a bond with Coubertin, despite their disparate origins. Though an American without pedigree, Billy somehow left the baron feeling he was talking to a fellow aristocrat with high civic ideals. Billy forged bonds as well with most members of the IOC, once the baron led him into their dimly lit meeting room. Billy was in an unfamiliar setting, facing forty strangers from all sections of the world—strangers also dressed in formal cutaways, who rose in a dignified manner when he entered the room. Billy was struck by the solemnity of the occasion. This was not how transplanted Yankees conducted business in California. Yet he did not hesitate. For some twenty minutes, Billy eloquently addressed Coubertin and the forty committee members. It was a bravura performance, full of Billy's signature certitude; the IOC minutes for that day say: "Mr. Garland from Los Angeles made a brilliant presentation of the city's candidacy." Standing erect, speaking without notes, Billy told them, "I represent a country that has shown its good will and sympathy toward Europe by sending two million soldiers to Europe to preserve the autonomy of your different nations and restore peace throughout the Continent." He told them (with a straight face) that "I represent the bone and sinew of America, not the wealthy classes whom you are more familiar with." He told them that "our people, far from remaining isolated, would like to touch flesh with the people of Europe and the world." He told them that, in Los Angeles and California, "there are representatives of most every nation in the world." Then he presented LA's formal invitation—along with blueprints of the planned Coliseum.

Billy felt he'd been received most graciously. Nonetheless, he did not prevail. Just what he heard in response that day remains murky. As Billy recalled it years later, Coubertin promptly informed him that the games for 1924 had already been awarded to Paris, and that the games for 1928 had been promised to Amsterdam, and that several cities were clamoring for the games of 1932. But IOC minutes and Coubertin's memoirs suggest only that the decision about the host city for 1924 was "postponed until later," with no less than fourteen cities still contending, including three American cities besides LA—Boston, Chicago, and Atlantic City. Whatever the IOC response, Billy certainly heard nothing encouraging in Antwerp. All Coubertin could offer him after his "brilliant presentation" was a heartfelt invitation to attend the reception that evening at the palace of King Albert and Queen Elizabeth. Billy had to regretfully decline, since he and his sons were traveling only with business suits, without the expectation of being entertained socially at a palace.

What Billy did next speaks volumes about the methods he was willing to employ in order to achieve his goals. On August 28, from Antwerp, he and Bob Weaver sent a cablegram to the "Coliseum Committee" in LA, meant for public release. It read: "Have presented our city's very cordial invitation for Eighth Olympiad in 1924. Decision of selection next meeting place postponed to meeting later in Geneva. Feel confident that if Los Angeles Coliseum is approved by voters on the 31st [August 31], its unequalled facilities for carrying on this great international event will land it. . . . Urge voters to insure world prominence for their city."

"Olympiad Here if Bonds Carry" read a headline the next day in the *Los Angeles Times*. "Cable from Antwerp Tells of Committee's Attitude: May Select Los Angeles if Facilities Are Certain." The story continued, with more fiction than journalism, likely showing Harry Chandler's hand: "Los Angeles has a chance for the Eighth Olympiad in 1924. . . . Only one condition remains in the way of a favorable decision. The Olympiad committee has agreed to withhold its decision until it meets in Geneva, and until it has learned whether Los Angeles can be expected to take care of the enormous throngs attracted by such events, and whether athlete contests of this magnitude can be staged here satisfactorily. The appended cablegram from Robert S. Weaver and William May Garland shows that the decision rests with the voters, who will decide Tuesday what is to become of the Memorial Auditorium and the Coliseum."

Wily as it was, Billy's ploy didn't work. Three days after sending the cablegram, Billy, having returned to his holiday, was dismayed to learn that in Los Angeles, voters had narrowly defeated the bond measure to finance the Coliseum. Needless to say, he chose not to disclose this information to members of the International Olympic Committee. Once back in LA near the end of that month, Billy reported to the Big 8. Clearly fuming about the bond measure vote, he told his colleagues that "active steps must be taken to construct a Coliseum," because "otherwise I would not care to again extend an invitation to hold the Olympic Games in Los Angeles."

# 4

# A FOOT IN THE DOOR

What followed Billy's return to Los Angeles showed just how effectively he could make things happen. He arranged for the Big 8 to meet with the mayor, the LA City Council, and the LA County Board of Supervisors. At that meeting, they turned to a plan they'd first conceived in June 1920, before Billy left for Antwerp. It was an alternative to the bond issue: The Community Development Association would lease a parcel of land from the city, build the stadium, and rent it to the city and county for ten years, each public agency paying a total of $475,000, with the revenue used to pay off one million dollars in construction financing provided by a syndicate of private bankers. At the end of ten years the development association would turn over the stadium to the local governments to own and operate.

From the start, they all had favored this plan over the bond issue; but the bankers had worried about its legality, so they'd arranged a test case in the legal system and, meanwhile, had kept the bond issue on the ballot. Now, with a failed bond issue and a favorable May 1921 state supreme court ruling, it seemed obvious what to do. They sealed the deal in the fall of 1921, with the bankers requiring no collateral. That November the city and county leased to the development association seventeen acres in Exposition Park near the University of Southern California. Here was a pivotal moment in the city's history, even if its provenance stirs some ambivalence among sports historians. In moving to build and manage a public stadium that Los Angeles citizens had voted down, Billy Garland's Big 8 demonstrated both great vision and the arrogance of power. Despite being an unelected elite, their insistence on building the Coliseum carried Los Angeles into the future.

Construction of LA's coliseum—which was to be the largest sports arena in the United States, made entirely of concrete and steel—began in late 1921, and Billy shrewdly sent news stories and photos about it to Baron de Coubertin, along with the architect John Parkinson's initial plans, which featured a classic Roman peristyle and seating for seventy-five thousand, about 13 percent of LA's population at the time. (Parkinson's other iconic buildings in Los Angeles would include City Hall, the Los Angeles Athletic Club, Union Station, and Bullock's Wilshire.) Billy and the baron by then had been corresponding for months. In late March of 1921, Billy had learned from William Sloane, a member of the US delegation to the IOC, that "protests against assigning the next Olympiad to America have been received from substantially every European country. . . . [T]he decision will be either Paris or Amsterdam." (Sloane added, "To me, it is appalling that Europeans so bitterly dislike America, but so it is. They are too deeply our debtors. They were terrified by the ease with which we put an invincible army in the field.") The very next day, March 24, Billy wrote to Coubertin, still campaigning for the 1924 games. In fact, insisting: "We believe that the United States is entitled to the international recognition that will accompany its selection as the country in which will be held the VIII Olympiad. From a competitive viewpoint we believe that, of all American cities, Los Angeles is entitled to the selection, very largely because the Olympiad has never been held in the West and because Los Angeles can extend a bid replete with the greatest number of advantages. Principal among these are climatic and similar features, as well as an abundance of the essential accommodations. . . . But probably most important of all is the great Memorial Coliseum, which the people of this community are pledged to erect. . . . This structure will be the greatest of its kind in existence."

In truth, when Billy wrote this letter in late March of 1921, they were still months away from closing the deal to build the Coliseum with private financing, and the "people of this community," rather than being "pledged to erect" the stadium, had voted down the bond issue. Coubertin, at any rate, wasn't persuaded. He had, in fact, already notified IOC members that he wished to award the 1924 games to Paris, and the 1928 games to Amsterdam. On April 22, he wrote Billy, offering a sympathetic but discouraging response that carefully hid his role and the decision he'd already made: "The hate of the world is such that the

California plan for 1924 seems very hard now to put up[,] and in Europe almost all the [national] Olympic Committees seemed to agree that the games of the 8th Olympiad and even the 9th (1928) should be celebrated within their reach." Instead, Coubertin suggested holding, in LA in 1923, "a great meeting of an Olympic character" to inaugurate the new Coliseum, "although of course not to be called the Olympic Games."

Billy chose not to respond just yet. They both were crafty maneuverers. The battle was joined.

"It was a masterly coup d'état!" Coubertin would enthuse in his memoirs, thinking back to what he pulled off in 1921, ahead of the IOC's annual congress in Lausanne in early June. (He titled this section of his memoirs "The 1921 Maneuver.") In a letter to IOC members on March 17, he revealed his intention to step down as IOC president in 1924. His final wish, he said, was for his colleagues to vote for his native city, Paris, to host the games in 1924, as a means to celebrate the thirtieth anniversary of the modern Olympic Games, which he'd revived. (As he put it: "At this moment when the reviver of the Olympic Games judges his personal task to be nearly at an end, no one will deny that he is entitled to ask that a special gesture should be made.") At the same time, though, he also insisted that Amsterdam should have the 1928 games. He wanted the IOC to vote on both years at the Lausanne congress. Coubertin well understood this to be a radical presidential intervention, but he knew few of his colleagues could refuse—it would, he believed, be morally impossible. As it happened, the vote did go his way at Lausanne; but for the first time ever, it wasn't unanimous (four countries opposed), and the Italian delegation, which favored Rome, stormed out in protest.

Only after this vote, on June 3, did two delegates representing Los Angeles belatedly arrive at the IOC session, held at the Casino de Montbenon, to speak for LA's candidacy. They were Gustavus Kirby and Fred Rubien, president and secretary of the American Olympic Committee, who were filling in for two ill American IOC members. Kirby and Rubien were upset, in fact furious, to learn that the voting had already taken place and apparently expressed their frustration to Coubertin. "This was reason enough," the meeting minutes report, "for [Coubertin] to give them a long lesson in the principles of the IOC and expressed his concern that the Americans did not know more about the IOC even after 27 years of existence."

That, at any rate, is how it all unfolded according to the IOC minutes. A later report by the American Olympic Committee offered a decidedly different account. "The International Olympic Committee is a self-perpetuating, non-representative body," the AOC report observed. "Great as the work of the IOC has been and is . . . both the IOC and its president are none the less not without criticism and apparently sometimes lacking in those business-like methods and courtesies which make for success." It also "has no stenographer present at its meetings and it is generally understood that the minutes are made up by the president from his memory and notes."

What really happened, according to the AOC: Los Angeles had authorized the representatives of the AOC to renew LA's invitation for the 1924 games, and to relay LA's offer to take over the games if Paris won them but proved unable to host. Gustavus Kirby had conveyed this, and also LA's interest in the 1928 games, to Coubertin immediately upon his arrival in Lausanne, and Coubertin had promised him an opportunity to present LA's invitation before the IOC took any action. But some ten days later, without formal notice, and without notifying the Americans, the IOC met and voted for Paris in 1924, Amsterdam in 1928. The AOC's Kirby and Rubien called upon Coubertin after hearing "rumors" of this meeting, asking what had happened. Coubertin replied that the matter had been considered already at Antwerp in 1920. "Concerning the candidacy of Los Angeles," he added in a written statement, "it appeared that owing to the distance of that city, the expense to Europeans was incompatible with their present economic condition, of which there was no prospect for an early improvement."

When the American Olympic Committee publicly released this report, it triggered stormy headlines ("Steam Roller Methods Seen in Grant of Olympic Games . . . American Bid Receives Scant Courtesy") and drew Coubertin's animus—he strenuously objected to what he called its errors and "willfully misleading insinuations." Gustavus Kirby stood firm, welcoming an investigation. The AOC, he said, had nothing to add or retract. The offer on behalf of Los Angeles had not been treated by the IOC and Coubertin "with the respect and courtesy due such an invitation."

What's most striking about this unruly sequence of events is how little it affected Billy Garland's outlook or his relations and communications with Coubertin. On June 6, just as the Lausanne congress was closing, Coubertin wrote Billy to report, from his perspective at least, what had transpired: "I do not think I have ever since thirty years, more deeply regretted not to be allowed to answer favorably a friendly call than when, three days ago, I had as President of the IOC, to decline the invitation to hold the games of the VIIIth Olympiad in Los Angeles. I trust you have been told what my feelings were personally." Though he greatly appreciated "the delights and the magnificent future of California" and felt "nothing could have pleased me better than the celebration of the Olympics Games of 1924 under your auspices," it had been certain since the previous January "that the votes would be in favor of a European city and circumstances led me to propose Paris." Coubertin again begged Billy to kindly consider instead "the possibility of holding in 1923 a big meeting in Los Angeles for the inauguration of the Stadium," an event he would "do my best" to attend.

Coubertin made clear he had an underlying reason to push this idea: He feared that the "political and social troubles" brewing in Europe might make it impossible for Paris to host the 1924 games. Beyond the general postwar devastation and territorial claims, these troubles included the rise of nationalism, imperialism, and socialism; the advent of a Bolshevist government in Russia; and, particularly in Germany, a mounting resistance to the Treaty of Versailles, disarmament, payment of reparations, and trials of war criminals. If Paris couldn't host in the face of all this, Coubertin reasoned, LA could postpone the 1923 meet for one year and convert it into the 1924 Olympics. "Thus in one way or the other," Coubertin explained to Billy, "Los Angeles would be associated with the VIIIth Olympiad celebration."

Billy, who surely knew from Kirby and Rubien what had really happened in Lausanne, chose not to respond to Coubertin right away. It was not in his nature to argue in such a situation. He'd rather rely on his charm and geniality . . . and the passage of time. He understood he had leverage, given the roiled, war-inflicted devastation in Europe and the United States' emergence as the world's dominant economic power. He was right: Coubertin grew anxious waiting for a response. Finally, in mid-September, he wrote to both Billy and Los Angeles mayor George Cryer, saying, "It seems impossible" that his letter of June 6 could have gone astray, "yet no answer came." Given the situation in Europe, he now seemed to particularly value—even need—the offer Los Angeles had extended in Lausanne: "It was a very great comfort to know that if the difficult circumstances through which the world is struggling made it impossible to hold the games of the VIIIth Olympiad (1924) in the old world, Los Angeles would be ready to take it up in place of Paris. I sincerely hope that no such step may have to be taken but if it had we should rely on the offer officially made at our Lausanne meeting." He trusted that this offer still stood.

Billy finally responded to Coubertin on October 18. What he said, and did not say, in this letter is revealing. He began by thanking Coubertin for the "fine and complete letter" he'd sent in early June, at the close of the Lausanne congress. He had been traveling for a large part of the last few months, Billy explained, making it impossible to send a prompt response. "We later decided to withhold our communication to you in the hope that we would, in the meantime, be able to consummate the final details for constructing the great Los Angeles Coliseum and then be able to convey this happy information to you at time of writing. Therefore, it is with the very greatest of pleasure that we now inform you of the virtual completion of our plans and the success of the Coliseum project."

They were still a month away from concluding the Coliseum deal, but Billy's use of the word *virtual* acknowledged that much. What he didn't address was Coubertin's idea of Los Angeles staging an inaugural meet in 1923 that could possibly be converted into the 1924 games. For Billy, it would be the games or nothing. "We will not take occasion at this writing," Billy concluded, "to discuss the possibilities or the uncertainties that surround the holding of the next Olympiad . . . inasmuch as this great event has been awarded to Paris. But Los Angeles, as you know, possesses a great desire to receive the honor some day of staging the great world Olympiad and should your plans meet with difficulty this City holds itself in readiness for the event."

Less than a month later, on November 12, a thankful Coubertin wrote back, saying "My colleagues were very much gratified to hear that the interest for Olympic matters was by no means going down at Los Angeles. In fact, I can say it was for many of us a sense of real sorrow that we had to vote for Paris and Amsterdam first." He was led to believe, from what Billy indicated, that LA would prefer to wait for the 1932 games, "rather than to have in 1923 games which, brilliant as they may be, would not be included in the great international series." He could assure Billy that it is "very probable" that the IOC would give LA the 1932 games, "especially when you act so nobly in repeating your offer of taking up the 1924 games in case the state of things in Europe would make it impossible to assemble in Paris that year."

Billy had effectively won over Coubertin. There might be considerable "hate in the world" that prevented awarding the Olympics to America, there might be simmering tensions between Coubertin and the

American Olympic Committee, but the IOC and its president liked Billy. They warmed to his energetic enthusiasm. They enjoyed this vibrant, self-made, self-educated American, so unlike them yet still able to connect with them. Billy, by force of personality, had managed to transcend political and cultural tensions.

This became clear when Coubertin, at the end of his letter of November 12, raised a matter that Billy had only heard about unofficially and tentatively, from William Sloane. The International Olympic Committee, it seemed, wanted to invite Billy to fill a vacancy and become a member of its group, representing America. Awhile back, Sloane had asked Billy: Would you accept? Billy hadn't answered, uncertain whether he could arrange his affairs in a way that would allow him to devote the needed time and effort. Now Coubertin pressed the question again: "I think I may say that we had looked forward with delight—and will do so—to electing you as a member of our Committee for the U.S. . . . Prof. Sloane was to consider this question with you. Did he do so?"

One month later, on December 12, Billy responded. "Relative to your suggestion that I become a member of the International Olympic Committee . . . I assure you that I very greatly appreciate your invitation and will deem it a high honor to accept the same." The IOC might be a "self-perpetuating, non-representative body," but Billy now had a foot in the door.

# 5

# THE HAND OF MAN

The formalities and patrician prose that fill the letters between Billy Garland and Baron de Coubertin appear to rise out of a vanished, long-ago world. In his letters, Billy would bend over backward to avoid using the first person "I" ("The writer had the pleasure and honor of appearing before the International Olympic Committee in Antwerp last year . . ."). Coubertin, particularly in his valedictions, would do a lot of throat-clearing ("With renewed thanks for your letter, I am, Sir, Yours very truly . . ."). Even when he was fuming at Billy, something he did more than once, Coubertin would close with a bow: "Please remember us all to Mrs. Garland. It will be such a delight to have you both in Rome . . ."

These types of communications seemed particularly archaic for Billy, given all that was happening just then in Southern California and the United States. The year 1920 saw the adoption of both the Eighteenth and the Nineteenth Amendments—prohibition and women's suffrage—and the start of a cultural upheaval: the Roaring Twenties. With prohibition came speakeasies, bordellos, bootleggers, smugglers and gangsters (which, combined, functioned as a strong rival power to the business elite that controlled Los Angeles). With suffrage came women's growing independence. With the Roaring Twenties came short dresses, smoking, drinking, dancing, flappers, and virtually unrestricted sexual conduct, all captured in books and theater, from F. Scott Fitzgerald's *This Side of Paradise* (1920) to Eugene O'Neill's *Strange Interlude* (1923) and Ernest Hemingway's *The Sun Also Rises* (1926). Then there was the growing impact of movies and their enticing focus on the femme fatale. One of the first, Theda "the Vamp" Bara (promoted as "foreign and voluptuous," though she was in fact Theodosia Goodman, a nice Jewish girl from Ohio, the daughter of a tailor), lived just a block and half down the street from Billy Garland on West Adams.

What could Billy have been thinking, looking out at all of this? The revolution underway certainly made him uncomfortable. Yet this revolution wasn't the whole picture, wasn't close to all Billy had before him just then. In truth, he was basking in a period of robust conservatism, a national celebration of Big Business. On March 4, 1921, Warren Harding was sworn in as president of the United States, replacing Woodrow Wilson. The "return to normalcy" had begun. With the war over and the Red Scare of 1917–20 abated, what many people wanted was rest, privacy, and freedom from government meddling. Harding, given his friendly attitude toward business, promised just that. So did Calvin Coolidge when he became president upon Harding's sudden death on August 2, 1923. Cooperation between business and government flourished, with Big Business seen as the savior of democracy. Billy Garland, Harry Chandler, and their fellow clubmen were in their element. This was their decade.

They fully recognized the vast reach of newspapers (the ratio of newspaper copies printed to total population was one to three) and the enormous popularity of radio broadcasting (newly launched in November 1920). They knew also that the country was growing ever more entranced with sports—both as spectators at events and as radio listeners. They saw opportunity everywhere, rather than threats. Realtors, publishers, chambers of commerce—they all could benefit. The field was wide open.

For Harry Chandler particularly, real estate (hundreds of thousands of acres) now formed the center of his domain. By pushing through construction of the Owens Valley aqueduct, completed in 1913, a syndicate Harry led had parlayed a secret $3 million investment in once-dry San Fernando Valley land into an estimated $120 million (more than $3 billion in 2018 dollars). Harry had a sure instinct for this kind of scheme, for transforming cheap land into valuable tracts, often by pulling strings. Though he remained hidden in the shadows, his influence could be seen everywhere in the 1920s, a decade when developers in Los Angeles built some thirty-two thousand new subdivisions.

Since anything that fueled the Southern California economy was good for real estate, Billy Garland and Harry Chandler, looking beyond land deals, worked also to underwrite other kinds of enterprises. When a nearly broke thirty-eight-year-old engineer named Donald Douglas arrived in LA in 1920 with no means to get bank loans to fulfill an order for three experimental navy fighter planes, Harry and nine of his California Club cronies ponied up the $15,000 he needed. Later—after Douglas had delivered his three planes and won a larger navy contract—Billy and Harry together arranged to lease to Douglas, at $42,000 a year, an old Santa Monica studio for use as a factory. So began the Douglas Aircraft Company and LA's foothold in the country's aviation industry. Not long after, at Billy's suggestion, he and Harry underwrote Harris "Pop" Hanshue, founder of Western Air Express. They also, along with other LA business leaders and hotel owners, organized the All-Year Club of Southern California, a private corporation supported by public Los Angeles County funding that would spend some $5 million during the 1920s promoting the region as a tourist resort.

Much to Billy's regret, the All-Year Club couldn't always obscure the more notorious elements of Los Angeles, many of them tied to Hollywood. He tried his best, though, to dissociate himself (and his world) from the most sensational local scandal of the early 1920s—the death of twenty-five-year-old Virginia Rappe after a raucous Labor Day weekend drinking party hosted by the comic actor Roscoe "Fatty" Arbuckle in a San Francisco hotel suite. Billy knew Fatty—by 1920 the highest-paid actor in the movies—both as a fellow member of the Los Angeles Athletic Club and as a neighbor living a block and a half down from him on West Adams (in Theda Bara's old home). Being an auto enthusiast, Billy had spotted the $25,000 Pierce Arrow (not unlike his own) on Fatty's driveway. He also had heard the noise emanating from the wild parties Fatty threw at his home, featuring guests such as Mack Sennett, Charlie Chaplin, Buster Keaton, the Talmadge sisters and Mabel Normand. Not only Billy heard these raucous parties: so did E. L. Doheny at his Chester Place mansion around the corner. On more than one evening, an exasperated Doheny walked over and banged on Arbuckle's door. To rid himself of the disturbance, Doheny even tried to buy Fatty's home, but Arbuckle wasn't interested in selling, despite the oil baron's high offer.

It was far from certain what truly had happened in Fatty's St. Francis Hotel suite. What's known is that Fatty and two friends drove up to San Francisco on Saturday, September 3, 1921, checked into three rooms at the St. Francis, popped open the bootleg liquor, and invited several young women of doubtful repute to join them. After three days of hearty carousing, the partygoers found aspiring actress Virginia Rappe on a hotel room bed looking seriously ill, moaning in pain. She ended up at a private hospital, where Rappe's companion, Maude Delmont, claimed to doctors that Fatty had dragged and violently raped her friend. The next day, Virginia died, likely of peritonitis due to a ruptured bladder caused by underlying chronic conditions, though the police blamed the rupture on Fatty's overweight, 266-pound body. (Later theories, much played up by the Hearst newspapers, had Fatty violating Virginia with a champagne or Coca-Cola bottle or pieces of ice.)

Late on the night of September 10, San Francisco police arrested Fatty on a charge of murder and jailed him without bail. That was enough for Billy Garland and the Los Angeles Athletic Club Board of Directors. Feeling the need to distance themselves from a mounting wave of Hollywood scandals, they were not inclined to wait for a legal resolution. "Roscoe Arbuckle has been dropped from the club's membership list," Billy announced on the evening of September 12, forty-eight hours after Fatty's arrest. "I have little to say regarding the action except it was the unanimous belief of the directors that such a step should be taken. We do not want that kind of men in the club, for we do not care to associate with that class." Billy, careful to not lump all of Hollywood into "that class," added, "There are many righteous and splendid men and women in motion-picture work and we honor persons of that sort for they reflect great credit on their profession. Every effort should be made, I believe, to encourage the profession whose art means so much not only to this generation but to those of future years." Billy also emphasized that he was making no attempt to pass judgment on Fatty's guilt or innocence: "My position is that events as far as they have gone show that Mr. Arbuckle is not a proper person to be a member of the club. Therefore he ceases to be a member."

The next day, a grand jury indicted Fatty on a charge of manslaughter, rather than murder. Two weeks later, a Superior Court judge in San Francisco bound him over on the manslaughter charge and released him on five thousand dollars bail. First one, then a second trial resulted in hung juries. On April 12, 1922, jurors at a third trial unanimously acquitted him after only six minutes of deliberation. They spent five of those minutes writing a formal statement of apology to Fatty, which the jury foreman read in court: "Acquittal is not enough for Roscoe Arbuckle. We feel that a great injustice has been done him. We feel also that it was only our plain duty to give him this exoneration . . . for there was not the slightest proof adduced to connect him in any way with the commission of a crime. . . . The happening at the hotel was an unfortunate affair for which Arbuckle, so the evidence shows, was in no way responsible. . . . We wish him success and hope that the American people will take the judgment of fourteen men and women who have sat listening for thirty-one days to evidence, that Roscoe Arbuckle is entirely innocent and free from all blame."

That night, Fatty issued a statement: "This is the most solemn moment of my life. My innocence of the hideous charges . . . has been proved by a jury of the best men and women of San Francisco. . . . For this vindication I am truly grateful to God and my fellow men and women." But the damage had been done. By then, Fatty's films had been banned and newspapers had been filled for the past seven months with stories about the Hollywood scandal. With Fatty publicly ostracized and blackballed by studios, his career never recovered. Nor did the Los Angeles Athletic Club restore his membership. In time, needing to downsize, Fatty finally conceded to his neighbor: He sold his West Adams home to E. L. Doheny, who bought it for his in-laws.

Despite the Fatty Arbuckle drama and others like it, Hollywood scandals were not what most troubled Billy Garland just then. Looking about, he saw the greatest danger in an overheated real estate market. He feared another speculative boom in Los Angeles—particularly one fueled by a stampede of developers and real estate men from other parts of the country. He bided his time during much of 1922 but finally decided he must speak out. "Boom Danger Threatens City," read a headline in the *Los Angeles Times* on December 24, 1922, over an article written by Billy Garland himself. The subdecks of the headline continued his theme: "Build on Sound Basis, Urges Dean of Realtors . . . Enough Lots for Three Great Cities on Market . . . Oversubdivision Brings the Curse of Speculation."

Billy seemed concerned over a confluence of events. Recalling the "great boom crisis in 1887–8," where "speculation in town lots was feverish," where "men and women stood in line all night and all day to be the first purchasers in any new tract," he urged restraint: "We want the growth of Los Angeles to be at all times healthy and justified by our advancement in population, industry and business generally." He wanted growth to be "built on the solid foundation of prosperity." He wanted citizens to be aware that cycles of depression "are bound to come." Most of all, he wanted his city to condemn "every semblance of an attempt to stampede Los Angeles into a speculative boom"—an attempt he believed was being made just then by a horde of outsiders. "It is reported that 2000 real estate men have appeared in Los Angeles during the last six months, mostly from other sections of the United States," he warned. "All . . . [are] engaged as subdivision promoters or as salesmen." They were welcome, Billy insisted, and they were all "advocating Los Angeles." But "as a prime guarantee of safety," he suggested that buyers should ask whether their agent is a member of the Los Angeles Realty Board—LARB. In other words, Billy wanted to assure that his inner circle of realtors maintained control of the market.

He desired this not just for their personal gain but also because he believed he and his LARB team knew what was best for LA. There'd been an average of twenty-two new subdivisions opened every week during 1922 in the three-mile-wide zone surrounding the city, he pointed out, a good number of them so lacking in "artistry and refinement" that they suggested "prairie dog villages." LA now had enough lots and subdivisions for sale "to accommodate the cities of New York, Philadelphia and Detroit." He wrote, "I am not an alarmist—I am absolutely an optimist. I welcome, in common with all of Los Angeles, every honorable man who comes to Los Angeles, either to visit or abide. But I cannot refrain from calling the attention of every citizen who loves Los Angeles to what I believe to be the one great outstanding danger in the future growth and prosperity of Los Angeles confronting us—an epidemic of frenzied speculation boom fever."

One other element of the situation seemed also to concern him. Billy began his article with these words: "There is a great question today confronting those Los Angeles citizens who have long dwelt in Los Angeles, and who have consistently, during that period, striven by all honorable methods to build here a splendid progressive city, populated by an ideal citizenship, socially, commercially and industrially." It's hard not to see some code in this. The speculative boom might not just heat up the real estate market; it threatened to draw to Los Angeles newcomers who did not fit the profile, or share the open-shop outlook, of those long settled there.

Billy's broadside, which appeared atop page one of the *LA Times'* Sunday "Real Estate, Industrial and Development Section," drew a heated, widespread response from businessmen in Los Angeles, with some offering praise, others leveling protests. Both the *Times* and Billy received many letters and phone calls. "Warning From Garland Stirs Hot Discussion," read another page-one *Times* headline, a week after

Billy's article appeared. In a community so inclined to give Billy standing ovations at honorary luncheons, it was unusual to hear anyone take exception to his views. In truth, though, not many of his critics were heard, for the follow-up *Times* story quoted only one of them. The story instead gave voice to a slew of Billy's supporters, including Frank Ryan, then the president of LARB.

They and Billy look prescient, from a perspective of time, despite the underlying motives and messages: The early 1920s would see all manner of worthless subdivisions pop up on Southern California's stark, desiccated pastures. One, named Girard (later, Woodland Hills), in the southwestern San Fernando Valley, included a fake Moorish-style town center at the corner of Topanga and Ventura Boulevards, an utter illusion composed mainly of false storefronts. Promotional materials described marvelous views, ocean breezes, and "small hillside country estates," which translated to 6,828 lots sliced out of 2,886 acres. Billy likely knew of its developer, a witty charmer named Victor Girard, for Girard years earlier, in 1907, had opened his first subdivision—in the vicinity of Billy's West Adams neighborhood.

In the spring of 1922, Billy received official notification that he'd been unanimously elected a member of the International Olympic Committee. Coubertin wrote him with the news, telling him it would be "most desirable" that he attend the IOC annual meeting to be held in early June, in Paris—not just to meet his new colleagues, but also to settle "the 1923–24 problem." Coubertin, still worried about Paris's ability to host in 1924, and knowing the French Olympic Committee might abandon the project, was back to lobbying Billy about an inaugural meet in LA's Coliseum that could become the 1924 Olympics: "We shall therefore be able to make arrangements for the preliminary games of 1923 or for the 8th Olympiad Games if Paris is led to give up, owing to the topsy-turvy state of things." In his memoirs, Coubertin claimed he had "come to a tacit agreement" with Billy about this, an agreement that "enabled me to watch what was going on in Paris with seeming serenity." But Billy never directly confirmed this deal; he was too careful a chess player. We see only Coubertin, at the end of his letter to Billy, saying, "Until the Paris meeting we must keep the whole thing strictly private."

Though their agreement might be private, Billy's quest was not. "Angeleno Seeks International Meet for Great Coliseum," read an *LA Times* headline on May 10. The subheads: "World Events For This

City . . . Garland Aims to Bring the Olympic Games . . . Off to Paris Sunday." The story began: "There is a fine chance that the Olympic Games . . . will be held in Los Angeles in 1924 or 1928. William May Garland . . . will leave for Paris Sunday to attend a meeting and present the claims of this city."

Billy certainly was maneuvering here, with Harry Chandler behind the scenes providing the spotlight. Billy was also feeling his oats. On May 28, while he was en route to Paris aboard the SS *Paris,* an article written by him ran in the *Los Angeles Times.* "California development is a tribute to the hand of man," it began, sounding one of Billy's familiar themes. "Ties and rails laid by human initiative first proved the stimulus for the making of the State." Billy continued, building his claim that men—individual men—shaped LA's history: "Nowhere can be found a metropolis of like size which owes so much to the human equation as Los Angeles. Five decades or so ago there was an almost motley collection of habitations in which lived 5,000 souls. It was stretched over a level piece of terrain between the mountains and the sea and was an uninspiring settlement giving little promise of the future. . . . Nowhere in the early history can be found any portents of future greatness." Agriculture, industry, motion-picture making (by then the fifth-largest industry in the world), all had contributed, but there was another element, often unnoticed by the visitor: "I speak of the spirit of 'never say die' cooperation of the civic and business leaders of Los Angeles." And one more thing: "In this remarkable development of California and of Los Angeles, naturally the realtor has a feeling of pride because he believes he has played a prominent part." As evidence, Billy pointed to recent words in an eastern real estate publication: "Yet the great achievement in the West would not have come so quickly without the real estate men. . . . The city of Los Angeles is a monument to the real estate men." Billy liked that. "This praise," he wrote, "is appreciated."

Billy arrived in Paris on June 1, taking up residence in the Hotel de Crillon on the Place de la Concorde, and on June 6 attended the opening ceremony of the IOC's annual session at the Automobile Club de France. When the meetings themselves began the next day, Coubertin formally introduced Billy as a new member of the IOC. Billy, deeply impressed with Coubertin's gracious reception, reported to the gathering about the "big athletic competition" scheduled to take place in Los Angeles in 1923, to inaugurate the Coliseum. He asked for the IOC's "patronage," which was granted.

"It was an entirely new experience for me," Billy later reported to Blanche. "The continental language, being French, was used at these Congresses. I could not understand everything that was said—though many of the important matters were presented in both French and English. Baron de Coubertin translated much of the business under consideration to English." Billy knew enough to again assure Coubertin that LA was willing on short notice to host the 1924 games if Paris faltered, or the 1928 games if Amsterdam "retired from the field." This offer pleased Coubertin, Billy reported to Blanche, "but I was reminded that the first open date was for the Xth Olympiad in 1932—which would not be considered until the next IOC meeting in 1923."

After the IOC meeting adjourned on June 10, Billy and Blanche, joined by their son Jack, departed on an extended chauffeur-driven motor tour of Europe that can fairly be described as lavish. The five-week excursion would take them to Tours, Bordeaux, Bayonne, Biarritz, St. Jean de Luz, Lourdes, Carcassonne, Avignon, Nimes, Nice, Monte Carlo, Turin, Milan (where they motored out to see Leonardo da Vinci's *The Last Supper*), Bellagio, Lake Como, Lausanne (where they lunched with Baron de Coubertin and his family at the Hotel Bon Sejour), Geneva, and Dijon. They returned to Paris and the Hotel de Crillon on July 18 and departed for Cherbourg on July 22, where they boarded the SS *Aquitania,* sailing for New York.

Once back in Los Angeles, Billy exchanged a number of letters with Coubertin during the rest of 1922. Whatever Billy heard at the IOC meeting about Paris hosting the 1924 games, the matter clearly remained uncertain to Coubertin, who kept circling around their "tacit agreement" concerning LA's plans for a meet in 1923. In one letter, he proposed calling this event the "Los Angeles Inaugural Games," which would be "under the patronage of the International Olympic Committee." He continued: "It remains settled that if the state of things in Europe made it necessary, these games should at the last moment be postponed until the Spring of 1924, in order to become the Games of the VIIIth Olympiad." He clearly wished to keep Billy and LA on the hook, given the unstable political, financial and social conditions in Europe: "I want to make Los Angeles the center of Olympism for half the world. Let old Europe go its own way but the rest of the world is wanting an 'Olympic metropolis.' That should be Los Angeles." He added, "Of course this letter is not meant for publication, but you can read it to your LA Committee and friends."

In mid-July, Coubertin wrote three more letters to Billy, all dated July 14—one he designated "official," one "semiofficial," the third "private." "On behalf of the International Olympic Committee," the official letter began, "I request that you will kindly tender to the City of Los Angeles . . . our warmest and most sincere appreciation of the help they are ready to give by offering to celebrate in 1924 the Games of the VIIIth Olympiad if circumstances made it impossible to hold that year such games in Paris. . . . In the meantime, the International Olympic Committee has been pleased to solemnly place under its official patronage the Inaugural Games that are to be held in Los Angeles for the opening and dedication of the great and beautiful Stadium the city is putting up."

The semiofficial letter underscored that the LA Inaugural Games "are not to be called 'Olympic,'" but should still adopt a program equivalent to the regular Olympic Games, "so that if needed, their postponement until the Spring of 1924 and the transfer from Paris to Los Angeles of the VIIIth Olympiad ceremonies might be easily arranged."

In the private letter, Coubertin reminded Billy that "I want very much to make Los Angeles the center of a permanent action in favor of Olympism." He had in mind calling a "big Congress" to convene in LA at the time of the Inaugural Games, assembling, above all, "the Canadians, Australians, Chileans, Peruvians, Japanese, Chinese." He was sure Los Angeles "will prove ready to take up with us such a big plan."

Billy played Coubertin's overtures in two ways. First, he went public with them. "International Games of 1923 May Develop Into Olympics," read an *LA Times* headline on August 22, 1922. "Affair May Be Staged Here . . . France Still Dubious About Holding Big Games . . . William May Garland Has Not Given Up Hope . . . Believes Los Angeles Can be Athletic Center." The article continued: "Los Angeles will have a series of International Games next year in the new stadium in Exposition Park duplicating the program of the last two Olympic contests if the suggestion of M. le baron Pierre De Coubertin . . . is carried out. William May Garland . . . received a letter from M. Coubertin suggesting that the contest be held as late in 1923 as possible so that in case Paris cannot entertain the next Olympiad it can be held in Los Angeles in 1924. It is thought by Mr. Garland that this brilliant Frenchman with his keen insight into the international drama that is now being enacted realizes that possibly dark times are ahead for France. . . . It is believed here that should the conditions abroad—financial and otherwise—prevent the holding of the 1924 Olympic Games in Paris, then they can logically be held in Los Angeles by simply postponing the dedicatory event planned for next year." Coubertin, the article added, had advised Garland that "he believes this half of the globe should have as its Olympic capital the city of Los Angeles." So Garland thought "it is within our grasp to establish that capital of Western Olympic activity here in this forward looking city we call home." Billy, certain as always, embraced the role of prophet: "It is difficult for the average citizen of Los Angeles to grasp the great scope of these games and the full significance of their meaning to this city of ours, which is rushing onward in its development faster than any other metropolis in the world."

Privately, though, Billy entertained other thoughts and responses to Coubertin's plan. The LA Inaugural Games were not to be called "Olympic," he reasoned. So if Paris did finally hold the VIII Olympiad, then Los Angeles would forfeit all rights to a regular Olympiad. This did not sit well with Billy.

"After several months of careful consideration . . . ," he wrote to Coubertin on November 13, 1922, "the Community Development Association has been enabled to act definitely regarding staging of the proposed 1923 World Games in Los Angeles." Billy paused for a moment to offer deep appreciation for "the very kind consideration" given LA's bid for the 1924 games and for the IOC's granting of "official sanction" to the proposed Inaugural Games in LA. Then he got to the point: "After giving the matter very serious thought for some time . . . our Association, at its meeting a few days ago, found it advisable to not attempt a staging of this 1923 event. We feel that, because of the unsettled conditions prevailing over a large portion of the world at this time, anything short of the Olympic Games would be very hazardous from a financial standpoint as well as from the standpoint of successful staging of the same in the matter of interest." He continued: "We wish again to set forth the ambition that we have cherished for holding the Olympic Games in Los Angeles and to say that we are, at least tentatively, prepared to accept the same if conditions should arise that made it advisable for them to come to Los Angeles in 1924. This is, in effect, a repetition of the invitation that I extended . . . at the last meeting, to the effect that if Paris should decide to abandon the games, Los Angeles stood ready to accept them."

Billy, though, now had one requirement: "Our Association . . . desires to express to you the request that if such action became necessary, Los Angeles be given at least one year's advance notice . . . in order to provide this city with sufficient time. . . . Our request for the games necessarily embodies this condition." Billy knew well he was by these words precluding Coubertin's plan for a last-minute, emergency transfer. "In closing," he wrote, "I repeat again that we do sincerely hope that nothing will arise to prevent Paris from being the scene of the 1924 Olympiad."

Before receiving this letter, Coubertin on November 19 wrote one of his own to Billy, their messages crossing in the mail. It signaled how little he'd welcome the news that Billy had just sent him. "Several months have elapsed since we parted here in Lausanne," he began, "and with the exception of a few lines . . . I have heard nothing from you. What have you been doing? What about the 1923 'Inaugural Games'? . . . Things are getting worse and worse daily." Coubertin must have been dismayed when he learned, days later, that there would be no 1923 meet in LA, and so no backup plan for the 1924 Olympic Games. "Baron de Coubertin did not enthuse over our position" is how Billy later recalled it, "but felt resigned finally and went ahead and organized Paris."

Their next round of correspondence reflected something of Coubertin's capacity for anger, and an apparent tension between them. It began with a seemingly supportive statement Coubertin made on December 10 in an interview with the Associated Press. He did not believe, he said, that Europe had the right any longer to monopolize the Olympic Games. "There is something astounding in the way we on this side constantly ask the Americans to come to us without facing the possibility of ever going to them. . . . It will be the International Olympic Committee's duty to make the Olympics henceforth a much more American affair than ever before." Billy wrote him the very next day, enclosing a copy of the AP story with the comment "If you had only said that in 1920!"

Coubertin did not take kindly to Billy's letter, which seemed also to discount the troubles in Europe while repeating LA's decision not to hold a 1923 inaugural meet. Coubertin wrote back on January 9, 1923, labeling his letter "private" and "strictly confidential." He began, "I am not astonished to hear that the Americans do not believe Europe is going wrong. Ignorance is everywhere the vogue nowadays. On the other hand, it seems no less clear that the Los Angeles people do not understand what Olympism is or means and see it only as the occasion of big quadrennial meetings with as many athletes and spectators as possible. Well, I am sorry, I will do without them." He wasn't finished: "You are sending part of an interview published all over the U.S. by the Associated Press and you add: If you had only said that in 1920! Well, dear friend, if I *had* said that in 1920 I would have done wrong not only to my work but to you all in California, for there would have been an immediate *secession* of the games and nobody would have come from this side to *your* games. I know what I did and why I did it. . . . I am working for the future and not to suit the wishes of hurried and quickly passing people."

Five weeks later, on February 14, Coubertin was still fuming as he wrote another "private" letter to Billy, whom he even now addressed as "My dear colleague and friend." Apparently, Billy had started angling for the 1928 games. "There is no question of 1928 being given to anybody else than the Dutch," Coubertin advised. "The celebration of the IXth Olympiad has been awarded to Holland by a regular and nearly unanimous vote. . . . The question was about 1924. If your countrymen had understood and heeded me and arranged the 1923 meeting, I would have led France to give up and the celebration of the VIIIth Olympiad would finally have been turned to Los Angeles. But they proved unable. . . . I had nothing else to do than to try and revive the Paris interest in the coming games. . . . As to the calling of a world Congress and creation of a permanent Center, the Los Angeles people did not even answer my proposal, which is therefore totally withdrawn by me. No promise whatever has been given to Los Angeles for the holding of future games by the IOC. . . . I advise you to secure the Xth Olympiad (1932) without delay for many are asking for it."

Through his customary charm and wile, Billy had somehow managed to stay distanced, in Coubertin's mind at least, from the choices and conduct of his colleagues in Los Angeles. He endured the IOC president, never taking the bait when Coubertin bristled, never showing signs of rancor. Billy always kept his eye on the goal line. Come to the 1923 IOC meeting in Rome, Coubertin had advised. Nothing is guaranteed. Make your bid for the 1932 games. Billy understood. On March 4, 1923, he and his wife sailed from New York aboard the SS *Paris*, bound for Europe.

# 6

# ROME, 1923

After a stay in Paris, Billy and Blanche reached Rome by train on April 5, checking into the Hotel Excelsior. There Billy prepared for his presentation and greeted fellow IOC members, who were arriving daily from around the world. Their annual meeting convened on the morning of April 7 in the main hall of the Old Capitol Building bordering the Roman Forum, with the king of Italy, Victor Emmanuel III, opening the session, accompanied by the president of the chamber and the senate, the secretaries of state for foreign affairs and for fine arts, and the prefect of Rome.

Two days later, Billy rose to make his pitch. He knew well the task at hand: to sell a conservative, aristocratic, Europe-controlled IOC the unprecedented idea of holding the games eight thousand miles away. Once more standing in a dimly lit room full of solemn men in formal cutaways, Billy politely but firmly threw down the gauntlet: "America," he told the group, "has been sending a large number of athletes to Europe for many years, so you must be convinced we are athletically minded. . . . If the Games are to be truly international in character, they must also be held in other parts of the universe." The New World, he declared, should organize one Olympiad every third year in the future. He continued: "In extending to the committee an invitation to come to Los Angeles, I extend it in behalf of the whole United States. The welcome of the entire country is contained in this invitation and we promise you the greatest hospitality ever witnessed at any Olympics."

To the IOC members that day, Billy must have had the feel of an irresistible life force. With his boundless vision, he made everything seem possible to them—largely because that's how everything seemed to him. His faith enlivened the room. Yet there was more going on than Billy's personal charm. "In addition to the keenness and enthusiasm of W. M. Garland," Coubertin would later write, "Los Angeles held three powerful trumps. First of all, the state of progress of its Olympic preparations, which represented an invaluable pledge of success; then its privileged situation, from the point of view of political and social events, far removed from the trouble that I felt brewing. . . . Finally, the time had really come to show some gratitude to the sporting youth of the United States . . . for its always brilliant and numerous participation in past Games."

These three considerations, especially the brewing trouble, would heavily influence the IOC members. "The voting took place at the Capitoline Hill in Rome, during our 1923 Session," Coubertin later wrote. "Nine years ahead of time! If the proposed site had been a city in Europe, I would not have agreed to any decision made so far in advance, because of the obvious imprudence of such a move. But absent some seismic catastrophe, California was not subject to any of the threats looming even then in the eyes of observant Europeans. I would not have wanted to end my third ten-year period as president of the IOC without underscoring, in a gesture of this kind, the ambition I had expressed from the start concerning the new form of Olympism: that it should encircle the globe, and thus not be subject to the chance events in a particular region or to narrow, nationalist views."

After Billy finished his initial pitch, he next spoke specifically about the appeal of California and Los Angeles, warning that "much rivalry and perhaps bitterness" might result if the contest were thrown open to all cities in America. He told the group that "California was sometimes called the 'Italy of America,'" that "almost every language was spoken in LA," that "every country in the world had a share in its development." He told them that his city was just completing "one of the finest Coliseums in the world," that they would receive a royal welcome, that LA was the largest metropolis in the United States west of Chicago, that its citizens were "familiar with the history of the Olympics and well versed in the work accomplished by Baron de Coubertin." In the "interest of harmony," he concluded, "I think it would be wise to select a particular city at this present moment so that America could know where it would be holding its Olympic Games." Billy said he hoped someone would move that the games be allocated to Los Angeles, California, U.S.A.

For a moment, no one spoke. Then, out of the silence, a gentleman unfamiliar to Billy rose—and so moved. Someone else seconded, and the motion carried unanimously, without debate. Billy had done it.

Two days later, on the evening of April 11, he and other IOC members were invited to the Quirinal Palace (then home to Italy's royal family) for a wedding reception given in honor of Princess Yolanda. The Quirinal, which sat on Quirinal Hill, the highest of the seven hills of Rome, was the ninth-largest palace in the world, with twelve hundred rooms contained in 110,500 square meters, all built around a regal courtyard and a renowned set of gardens laid out in the seventeenth century. A celebrated fresco, the *Blessing Child* by Melozzo da Forli, hung over the central stairway. Rare tapestries lit by magnificent crystal chandeliers filled the rooms. As Billy watched, the royal parade began: the king of Italy, Victor Emmanuel III, and his wife, Princess Elena of Montenegro, he just five feet tall, marching stiffly; the retinue of ladies-in-waiting; and Princess Yolanda herself, a dark-haired beauty of twenty-two, who had married Giorgio Carlo Calvi, Count of Bergolo, two days before. Everyone was wearing the most beautiful jewels, an absolute rampage of glitter. Billy, not the least intimidated, moved through this new world with his customary confidence.

After the parade of the king and queen ended, he noticed a large group surrounding and talking with animation to a bald, intense man who was posturing proudly in a fancy military uniform. Who is that? Billy asked a colleague. Why, his colleague told him, that is Mussolini. Have you never met him? Come with me.

A moment later, Billy found himself shaking hands with Il Duce. The king had handed over power to Mussolini just six months before, installing him as prime minister after thirty thousand Fascist blackshirts had gathered in Rome to demand the resignation of the liberal prime minister Luigi Facta. Since Mussolini did not speak English and Billy did not speak Italian, their exchange was limited, but Billy impressed Mussolini by comparing him, in looks, to Napoleon. "If he had only had one or two locks of hair over his forehead," Billy later told Blanche, "I would have deemed him a replica of Napoleon."

The next day, Billy and other IOC members had the pleasure of an audience with Pope Pius XI, at noon in the Vatican. It began with guards ushering them into the anteroom next to the pope's suite. There, without any notification, a gentleman came through the door from the pope's quarters and put out his hand in the direction of General Reginald J. Kentish, one of the British IOC members, who immediately grabbed the man's hand in a firm grasp and said, "How are you?" Billy and all the others, realizing the pope had entered the room, went to their knees. Lord Cadogan (Gerald Cadogan, the other British IOC member), kneeling next to Billy, leaned over and whispered, "I say, Garland, did you notice what that ass, Kentish, did?" The pope quickly left Kentish and moved toward the ladies, who knew enough to kiss the ring on his right hand. Billy thought, *When you are in Rome, do as the Romans do.* So he too kissed the pope's ring. In return, he heard the pope praise the Olympic Games as a means of furthering goodwill among nations.

Days later, while in Brussels on an extended motor tour of Europe, Billy received a welcome letter from Coubertin. "My dear Colleague and Friend," the baron wrote on April 28, "I am glad my colleagues followed my advice in giving America the Xth Olympiad and . . . accept[ed] my suggestion, one Olympiad out of three for the New World. . . . With the Rome meeting back of us, we are prepared to face any difficulties."

From his hotel room in Houyet, Belgium, Billy, already focused on promoting, wrote back to the baron, asking him to send a letter to the citizens of California "stating in your splendid phraseology . . . that the 1932 Olympics have been awarded to LA. If you care to speak of this Pacific Coast as one of the future centers of New Olympism, so much the better." Billy knew just how to coax the baron: "It will create interest because of its writer, the 'Father of Modern Olympism.' I'd like photos as well."

After a total of seventy-one days in Europe, the Garlands sailed for New York on May 23 and arrived in Los Angeles in early June. There Billy found to his delight that the Coliseum had been completed (the first football game in the stadium would be played that November between USC and Pomona College). On June 6, the Los Angeles Realty Board welcomed him home at a banquet held in his honor both to celebrate his achievement in obtaining the 1932 Olympic Games and to recognize the twentieth anniversary of LARB's founding. There, he, as principal speaker, regaled the realtors with stories of his first real estate trades in Los Angeles (though probably not the Crocker transaction in 1903). Two hundred realtors rose to give him a roaring ovation. Two weeks later, on June 19, no less than four local civic groups—the Los Angeles Chamber of Commerce, the Realty Board, the Clearing House Association, and the Merchants and Manufacturers Association—

named Billy the "most useful citizen of 1923." Harry Chandler had won the same award the year before.

They were both on a roll. In early October 1923, the Coliseum officially opened, as did the grand downtown hotel Billy had long desired—the Biltmore, built and financed by a syndicate of businessmen led by Harry Chandler, at a cost of ten million dollars. On the evening of October 2, more than three thousand of the city's elite—including Douglas Fairbanks, Theda Bara, Myrna Loy, Dolores del Río, Cecil B. DeMille, Jack Warner, Cornelius Vanderbilt Jr., and Jack Dempsey—thronged the hotel at Fifth and Olive, overlooking Pershing Square, to celebrate its opening at a lavish banquet and ball. Speeches by William Jennings Bryan and William G. McAdoo (secretary of the treasury in Woodrow Wilson's cabinet and a future senator from California) were broadcast on the Chandler-owned radio station KHJ. Within a year, the Biltmore's great success would lead the syndicate to expand the hotel, adding five hundred new guest rooms, a swimming pool, and the world's then-biggest ballroom, the Sala de Oro. This allowed Los Angeles to boast of having the largest hotel west of Chicago.

A month after its opening, in late November 1923, the LA Chamber of Commerce held a luncheon at the Biltmore to celebrate the rise of the city's population to one million. Billy had predicted they'd achieve that level in 1920, so he was three years off. Still, the *Los Angeles Times,* in reporting on this event, once again called him a "local prophet." Soon Billy had his own monument: in the spring of 1924, the W. M. Garland Building opened on the corner of Ninth and Spring in downtown Los Angeles.

With years to go before the 1932 games, Billy had time to savor the fruits of his efforts. In 1924, for *The Realty Blue Book of California,* he wrote an extended essay, "Real Estate, the Basis of All Wealth." It was an unabashed ode:

> As far as history and legend penetrate into the recesses of time, land has been the source of that which man calls wealth. . . . Real estate is very clearly fundamental in the makeup of the universe. The chair you are sitting in as you read this may be made out of mahogany which was grown in the jungles of the tropics. The cushion may be stuffed with a product from Ecuador. Nevertheless, the soil somewhere is responsible directly or indirectly for the existence of these materials.
>
> The paper on which this book is printed was once wood pulp, the product of soil fertility. The printing presses were originally iron ore extracted from rich deposits. That clear Havana which you are quietly puffing owes its growth to kind old Mother Earth.

As you glance at your watch to see how long you can read this book you can reflect for a second on where the materials for your timepiece came from and there is just one answer to each query: "From the ground."

Learned economists have made the statement that real estate values underlie all values. . . . The amount of soil is stationary, while there is an ever steady accumulation of people. Because of the growing demand it has been estimated that there is an increase in value of average land of 10 percent a year. . . . Present day values that may seem high are in reality in full accord with sound, conservative economic laws. There is no inflation—speaking generally—just a new economic era.

That same year, for the magazine *Southern California Business,* published by the LA Chamber of Commerce, Billy wrote another article, "Mixing Games and Business Profitably." California has many assets, natural and acquired, he pointed out. "Among these acquired assets is an international event, the magnitude of which is as yet little comprehended even in this forward looking, progressive commonwealth. I refer to the 'Tenth Olympiad, Los Angeles, 1932,' as it is officially known. This meeting of the brain and brawn of the many nations of the world is an enormous asset because of its advertising value. We can capitalize this value in many ways." From the "remarkable harbor" Los Angeles built to the "motion pictures . . . greatly in vogue in foreign countries," LA had a "budding international reputation" that could "pave the way for a publicity campaign which will carry [LA's] name again and again into the countries where it will do this city an inestimable amount of good—a dollar and cents good." But beyond that, Billy also saw and welcomed a "general effect upon California in an intellectual and artistic way . . . for we will have the inspiration of meeting, knowing and learning from the best young men and women produced by other nations of this earth. It is truly an event fraught with deep and intense interest to all of us in ways other than the mere pecuniary profit."

Billy had been urged more than once to run for mayor but had always declined, and why not? He had considerably more influence than any mayor. If anyone at that time merited the title "Mr. Los Angeles," it was Billy Garland. Only time would tell just what that meant for the city.

# THE GREAT MIGRATION

While Billy had been pursuing the Olympic Games, the city had been changing in dramatic ways. Though still more a sprawling village than a metropolis, it was expanding rapidly, driven by the boosters' extraordinary promotions. Earlier population leaps paled in comparison: in the decade 1920–30, more than 2 million people would move to California, nearly three-quarters of them settling in Southern California, with LA County growing by some 1.2 million and the city of Los Angeles by 661,375, tripling its population. Oil, tourism, and motion pictures were major reasons for this deluge, which inevitably—and not incidentally—fueled a huge appreciation in real estate values. The number of building permits skyrocketed, with the real estate salesmen leading the charge, just as Billy had envisioned. Here was the hand of man at work—Billy's hand.

Yet the city's elite, even while celebrating, perceived threats to their dream of Southern California. On June 24, 1923, a strange but revealing editorial appeared in Harry Chandler's *Los Angeles Times*. Bearing the title "The Soul of the City," it began, "We are living in a day of great things. We are playing with immensities. We are walking in a world of wonders. . . . The progress of our fair municipality has become one of the seven sublimities of civilization." It continued: "In population we are making a progress that almost baffles comparison. Our numbers are being swelled by trainloads every day. The highways of the nation are congested with eager pilgrims. . . . Last year they bought more than fifty thousand lots. . . . New subdivisions provided more than 80,000 additional sites. . . . Our swelling bank clearings and deposits prove that we have become one of the great financial centers of the country. . . . We have achieved greatness in every department."

Despite all this, something worried the editorial writers: "But if our material greatness is worthy of world comment are we keeping pace in spiritual progress? Are we building character as we are building homes? What of the soul of the city? . . . It is one thing to be prosperous and enterprising; it may be another to be morally clean and mentally just."

And that brought the editorial writers to the heart of the matter: "The conditions which exist here should make for the finest character-building in the land. . . . We should have more than the ordinary proportion of patriotism because our citizens are mainly the descendants of American pioneers. As a city we have no vast foreign districts in which strange tongues are ever heard. The community is American clear to its back-bone." Which provided the editorial writers considerable relief: "Therefore it may be seen that we have here a splendid foundation upon which the superstructure of civic character may be built. . . . For a long time the country was torn by financial and industrial depression. Commerce lagged and there was a grievous lull in most human activities. During that period the Los Angeles district was the only white spot on the 'money map' of the country. Business was still good and factory fires were burning in this territory. People came from every section to taste these activities and share in the prosperity. Los Angeles is still the white spot on any industrial map. . . . May it also prove to be a white spot when character-building is being charted."

This editorial, it's fair to say, reflected certain deep strains rippling through Los Angeles and the country at the time. Class conflict, labor unrest, cultural and social tensions, the Red Scare, fears over the influx of immigrants—all of this would concern someone in Billy's and Harry's positions. They and other city leaders fought the threats with more than newspaper editorials. In 1919, the LA Chamber of Commerce and the Merchants and Manufacturers Association had lobbied hard for the California legislature to pass the Criminal Syndicalism Act, which made it a felony to advocate violence as a means "of accomplishing a change in industrial ownership; or control or effecting any political changes." The new law was chiefly aimed at the radical Industrial Workers of the World, which in April and May of 1923—while Billy was in Rome before the IOC, winning the Olympic Games—launched a waterfront strike in the San Pedro Harbor. The chamber and the Merchants and Manufacturers Association began pressing city hall and the Los Angeles

Police Department to invoke the new act. The authorities readily obliged, arresting more than one thousand strikers after a rally of five thousand at Liberty Hill on May 13, including the writer Upton Sinclair, his offense being to rise and read aloud from the Constitution.

The year 1923 also saw a National Association of Real Estate Boards committee, chaired by Frank Ryan, the former LARB president, codify a new national policy on class and racial segregation. "A realtor," the revised code read, "should never be instrumental in introducing into a neighborhood a character of property or occupancy, members of any race or nationality, or any individuals whose presence will clearly be detrimental to property values in the neighborhood." By then, LARB members had already segregated Los Angeles in this way, along both racial and class lines. In Billy's own West Adams neighborhood, restrictive covenants had long been in place that prohibited homeowners from selling to African Americans.

Blacks weren't the only target. Jews, too, were being excluded—not just from the downtown and country clubs, but also from positions in law firms and corporations. Catholics as well found it hard to enter the city's inner sanctums. Everywhere across the country, the kind of nativism expressed in the *LA Times'* "The Soul of the City" editorial enjoyed wide support, driven in part by an ascendant Ku Klux Klan. A policy of favoring the interests of the "American clear to its back-bone" led first to the 1921 National Origins Act, which created immigration quotas set at 3 percent of the total foreign-born population of each nationality in the United States as recorded in the 1910 census. Then came the Johnson-Reed Act, signed by Calvin Coolidge in May 1924—legislation that set even stricter 2 percent quotas designed to support immigrants from western Europe, bar most from eastern and southern Europe (especially Italians, Slavs, and Jews), and ban entirely those from Asia. While slashing overall immigration levels, the law assigned quotas to each country based on the number from that country living in the United States as of the 1890 census, before the flood of immigrants began from beyond the borders of western Europe. The bill's chief author, Senator David A. Reed of Pennsylvania, explained, "Each year's immigration should so far as possible be a miniature America, resembling in national origins the persons who are already settled in our country."

Billy largely avoided comment on all this. We get only oblique references. On November 14, 1924, he wrote to Baron de Coubertin, just days after Calvin Coolidge had been reelected president of the United

States, an event that greatly pleased him (Billy had headed Coolidge's campaign in Southern California). His pleasure was such that he brought it up in his letter: "We have had a very satisfactory National Election and the Republican Party—Mr. Coolidge, President—remains overwhelmingly in power, representing the conservative, safe and sane element of our citizenship."

Coolidge's reelection was not, however, the focus of Billy's letter. He had other matters on his mind. That morning, an Associated Press report out of Paris had appeared in the *Los Angeles Express* concerning the 1928 Olympic Games in Amsterdam. The International Olympic Committee, the article revealed, "is much exercised over the prospects for the 1928 Games. . . . Several letters of an imperative character have been sent to Holland. . . . The Dutch Olympic committee and government have been requested to give their final answer before March next. . . . If the IOC does not receive a satisfactory reply . . . the Games will automatically go to the American Olympic Committee and the city of Los Angeles." This news surprised and troubled Billy. Immediately writing to Coubertin, he enclosed a copy of the article. "All this material explains itself," Billy observed. "Do you know anything authentic concerning the matter? . . . I really hope nothing will transpire to prevent the celebration of the Olympic Games in 1928, for we do not seek them prior to 1932."

Coubertin wrote him back, oddly in French for a change, and wasn't reassuring about the Dutch. Europe's post–World War I devastation, deprivation, and strife had only deepened, leaving the continent even more impoverished and destabilized politically. Given this environment, the entire modern Olympic movement was foundering. They'd managed to stage the 1924 games in Paris, but now, in late 1924, Coubertin was feeling increasingly uneasy about Amsterdam's ability to organize the 1928 games, not least because internal conflicts in Holland had led the Dutch government to withhold guarantees and financing. The 1928 games, Coubertin advised Billy, are in serious danger. He asked if Los Angeles would step in if Amsterdam could not host them.

Billy replied on December 9. "Difficult as it is for me to translate French," he began, "I was pleased to translate that portion of your communication. . . . Regarding your inquiry concerning the allocation of the IX Olympiad to LA, in the event Amsterdam fails to accept the responsibility . . . I can only reiterate my feeling stated to you in a previous communication: that I would much prefer adhering to our original resolution and commitment to have the X Olympiad in 1932." Here he made a prediction that later would haunt him: "I believe that the financial situation in Europe in 1928 would prohibit the visitation to this country of the large number of visitors we would like to have come to America, and I believe in 1932 we shall be in a far better position to help the athletes in a material way than we would in 1928. . . . I would like to have it settled permanently in our minds that we can look forward absolutely to the 1932 event without any fear of change in the program. . . . It would perhaps be the greatest Olympiad ever held."

Billy could not hold back the drumbeat. On December 27, an Associated Press story out of Paris, with the headline "Next Olympics in California?" asked, "Will Holland pass up the 1928 Games? Such is the question which is agitating European athletic circles since the close of the eighth Olympic games." Should Amsterdam bow out, "there will be little objection to Los Angeles being the seat of the Ninth Olympiad."

Coubertin was still imploring Billy two months later. "My dear colleague and friend," he wrote on March 12, 1925. "The E.C. [executive committee] of the I.O.C. met this morning and I was asked to inquire . . . whether in case of Holland failing to fulfill her engagement, would Los Angeles be willing or not to take up 1928 instead of 1932 . . . ?" There was obvious urgency now in his request: "An answer must be given immediately," Coubertin instructed. "Therefore we ask that you shall consider without delay . . . with the mayor of Los Angeles and the organizing committee. But we want you to do it in such a way that the press be kept aside of it and no public discussion brought in." Coubertin therefore suggested that Billy telegraph a simple "yes or no" answer.

Within a week, Billy sent his reply: "No." He recognized the turmoil abroad, but still saw no advantage in rushing at this stage. California was booming, and merchants were clamoring to join his "Garland's Group" organizing committee—one had offered a ten-thousand-dollar donation to be on their board. It would be better, he reasoned, to take their time. By waiting, they would realize the greatest Olympiad in history, with the largest number of athletes ever and five hundred thousand persons flooding the region. About that, Billy remained certain: Europe would be in much better financial shape by 1932, much more able to send athletes and spectators to California.

Of all the decisions Billy made over the years concerning the LA Olympic Games, this one would prove most fateful. Though his expectations seemed reasonable at the time, his choice would leave Los Angeles facing unimaginable difficulties. Of course, Billy, with his abiding faith in the future, could not foretell the coming Great Depression.

# 8

# PROTECTING THE IMAGE

By the time the International Olympic Committee gathered in Prague in late May 1925 for its annual meeting, Amsterdam Olympics organizers were able to announce "satisfactory news" about their progress. Order had been restored there after a "general subscription" secured the financing for the games that the government had hesitated to provide. The Dutch were now eager to host the 1928 games.

Relieved, Billy resumed his promotions and predictions about the 1932 games, though he tried to throttle back a bit, allowing Amsterdam the spotlight. That he found hard to do: In the summer of 1926, returning from yet another IOC meeting and tour of Europe, he once again enthused about the "bright outlook" for 1932. Every nation, he told the *LA Times,* is looking forward with pleasure to sending its athletes to California. Good feeling and cooperation abounded. Even President Coolidge had wired him, Billy reported, to express his gratitude. Billy was certain—Los Angeles would be the scene of the greatest Olympiad ever held.

Yet for the games to succeed, Billy understood he needed to keep protecting the image of Southern California. That often presented a challenge. Leave aside for a moment the Hollywood scandals: local politics alone, with its snake pit of fixers, double-dealers and influence peddlers, habitually seemed beyond the repair of a can-do optimist.

This likely is one reason why, in October 1926, Billy reacted so publicly and vehemently when an extraordinary "warfare of unprecedented proportions" (as the *LA Times* put it) broke out in Los Angeles County political circles. It was both messy and, in its way, hilarious: First, LA County district attorney Asa Keyes filed felony charges against all five members of the LA County Board of Supervisors and three other top county officials. The supervisors, in turn, brought criminal charges against Keyes. All of them—supervisors and prosecutor—were arrested and hauled into court. Misuse of public cash was the ostensible issue in both cases, with the supervisors accused of building private cabins on public property near the Big Pines county park in San Bernardino County, and the district attorney accused of exceeding his authority in paying attorneys and appropriating five thousand dollars. The charges were dubious all around. This fundamentally was a battle over control of the county government, and it revealed the kind of shady politics saturating Los Angeles at the time. Behind it, argued an ominous-sounding editorial in the *Los Angeles Times,* was "a powerful organization that dispenses patronage and controls public officers for private gain. It has its ramifications all through the invisible government of Los Angeles."

The reference here was to Kent Kane Parrot, a behind-the-scenes power broker for the administration of Mayor George Cryer. Parrot ran the political machine in Los Angeles during the 1920s and came, over time, to be one of Harry Chandler's main rivals in city politics. In a front-page editorial in April 1925, the *Times,* in opposing Cryer's reelection, had attacked Parrot, saying, "There should be no one attached to the office of Mayor whose peculiar genius runs to the business of controlling patronage, of fixing cases in police court, of interfering with police activities, of ordering the affairs of the gambler, the bootlegger, the bookmaker and other breakers of the law. Los Angeles does not need a boss." The voters nonetheless had reelected Cryer, and Parrot now was clearly trying to extend his influence to county government by ousting the supervisors, with the cooperation of prosecutor Asa Keyes—whom the board of supervisors had not favored for the district attorney's position.

Billy was appalled. This certainly was not the image of Los Angeles he wanted projected to the world, especially since it involved his allies on the board of supervisors. He normally avoided public recognition of LA's sleazier side but felt obliged now. "It was with a strong feeling of indignation that I read of the criminal charges recently filed against the members of [the] Board of Supervisors," he wrote in a letter to the editor, published in the *Los Angeles Times* on October 24. "Here is the ablest board that has ever conducted the great public business of the Los Angeles county government. It has done so with particularly marked efficiency and absolute honesty." The supervisors had enabled "the wealth and prosperity of Los Angeles County" to be "advertised to the world by the Chamber of Commerce," and yet they are "being pilloried in the courts." Billy objected to using "the people's courts and the people's money" to prosecute the supervisors over "some cabins in the mountains in San Bernardino County." Regarding the "particular matters of the cabin sites . . . I have no concern." But he did care about "the larger principle involved, of this constant badgering and persecution of our public officials." His biggest fear: "By cases of this kind . . . we give notice to the world that . . . our public officials are to be rewarded for their efficiency . . . by being dragged through the courts as defendants in criminal cases filed against them on trivial grounds." He didn't believe the public supported this. "I know that this is not the true, broad-minded California go-ahead spirit."

Not long after, the prosecutions of Asa Keyes and the supervisors both petered out, with a municipal court judge dismissing the charges against the supervisors. The *Los Angeles Times,* in an editorial on December 9 titled "The Plot That Failed," celebrated "the total collapse of the sinister conspiracy of Kent Parrot . . . to extend to the county the boss control which has so long disgraced the city of Los Angeles." Billy must have winced at that phrase "disgraced the city," despite the favorable outcome in court.

This would not be the only time he winced, for the region at that time, even more than in earlier years, was percolating with seedy corruption, spectacular trials, political shenanigans and sexual scandals. A good number involved Hollywood characters, often undone by drugs, lust and liquor. There was the mysterious 1920 death in a Paris hotel room of Mary Pickford's sister-in-law, the beautiful young actress Olive Thomas, ruled an accidental poisoning though widely rumored to be a suicide, possibly the result of heroin addiction, syphilis infection or her husband's philandering. A year later came Virginia Rappe's death at Fatty Arbuckle's hotel-room drinking party in San Francisco. On the night of February 1, 1922, a person unknown murdered the prominent director William Desmond Taylor in his tony Westlake Park home, some two miles from Billy's, in a never-solved homicide involving movie studio cover-ups and revelations that Taylor was someone else entirely, working in Hollywood with a false identity. Not long after, the actor Wallace Reid died, likely the result of a morphine addiction.

Hollywood scandals, though, weren't all that needed obscuring in order to maintain Los Angeles' image. In fact, a particularly intriguing and unusual cover-up of that era involved not a murder or transgression of any sort but a rat-borne pneumonic plague outbreak—the last such outbreak ever in the United States. Billy and his colleagues found this much more alarming than Hollywood bacchanalia, for it threatened to bring financial ruin to Los Angeles if not handled properly. Even the suspicion of plague, they quickly realized, would lead not just to bad publicity but to a quarantine of the harbor, with boats blocked from docking, goods rotting in warehouses, and businesses going bankrupt. Walter Dickie, secretary of the California State Department of Public Health, warned them, "There is no disease known that has such an effect upon the business world as plague."

The outbreak began on October 29, 1924—a clear, ninety-one-degree day—in an East LA ghetto called Macy Street, home to some twenty-five hundred Mexicans. First two, then thirteen more patients, fell critically ill, with three dying within a day. City officials, linking the disease with the community's ethnic makeup, quickly quarantined the eight-city-block district, setting up a military parameter and placing special sentries at the front and rear of houses hit by the plague.

Authorities moved just as quickly to quash news about the epidemic, which they had first thought to be bubonic plague. Brief stories reporting on the deaths were relegated to back pages of the *LA Times'* second section. These stories, for cause of death, vaguely referred to "Spanish influenza" or "severe pneumonia" or "a strange malady," though by then officials knew the true cause was pneumonic plague—far deadlier than bubonic plague, in fact the most contagious disease on earth. Not until November 6, when the epidemic appeared over, did Los Angeles newspapers use the term *pneumonic plague*.

Only Los Angeles imposed this news blackout. Other newspapers, in California and across the country, provided accurate accounts, and the state board of health discussed the epidemic on its weekly radio show. The *New York Times* and *Washington Post,* happy to strike back at Harry Chandler's "Sell 'em Sunshine" approach to local news, were particularly direct: The *New York Times* on November 2 quoted LA's acting city health officer, Dr. Elmer Pascoe, as saying, "There is little doubt that the illness which caused the sudden deaths of these people is pneumonic Plague." For that candor, Pascoe would lose his bid to become the permanent city health officer.

On November 3, all the key players gathered together at an emergency meeting in the office of LA mayor George Cryer. There, federal, state, county and city health officials conferred with several directors of the LA Chamber of Commerce, the business and financial interests of the city, and the local publishers, including Harry Chandler of the *LA Times* and George Young, managing editor of the *Examiner*. What a group: in this room sat the storied "shadow government" of Los Angeles. The concerns they expressed spoke volumes. George Young assured everyone that no paper in the Hearst empire would print anything "we didn't think was in the interest of the city." Harry Chandler made a similar pledge. Added a member of the LA Chamber of Commerce, "If we formally recognize an epidemic, Eastern papers will exaggerate it and our summer tourist business will be ruined." Was Billy Garland present? The records don't indicate, but it's hard to imagine Billy not knowing of, and monitoring, the unfolding developments in the outbreak.

Those attending this November 3 meeting agreed that plague control would be coordinated by an advisory committee consisting of state, county and city health officials, with the state health department's Walter Dickie in the lead. The chamber of commerce also appointed its own committee composed of physicians, health officers, businessmen, newspaper editors and local publishers, who met regularly to discuss, investigate, recommend, and coordinate. Others jumped in as well. The Los Angeles County Board of Charities provided a week's rations for each household in the quarantine zone. Public health nurses made house-to-house inspections. County General Hospital admitted and isolated every person who lived in a home where pneumonic plague had occurred—114 in all.

On November 13, with the quarantine still in place, Harry Chandler and *Los Angeles Herald* editor George Young were guests at a meeting of the LA Chamber of Commerce Board of Directors. Again, the concern was how to handle news of the plague and protect the city's image. The board thought it time to make "a frank statement" to the members of the chamber of commerce about the plague epidemic "in order that this statement might be used by the members in combatting unfavorable publicity in the East." The board felt that members should "write their friends and business acquaintances in the East, telling these people the facts to offset a great deal of unfavorable publicity." Board members asked Chandler and Young for their opinions, and both thought such a statement "would be desirable immediately after the quarantine had been lifted."

"I am now satisfied in my own mind the danger is past," George Young said. "I had the good fortune to see that as far as our chain of papers, nothing went out over the wires emanating from our place excepting some official statements on the third and fourth days to the effect that [the] pneumonic epidemic was under control. They assured us by wire, the various editors, that they would print nothing we didn't think was in the interest of the city."

Harry Chandler added, "The doctor [Walter Dickie] . . . told me he thought the state board would put out a bulletin in a day or two in which they would officially say it is wiped out. He suggested we might get together and issue a statement based on their report. . . . When that comes, I have no doubt the Associated Press and all the press representatives if approached properly would be willing to put out a statement that could be telegraphed all over. But of course it won't reach everybody and it would seem to me after that comes, or when it comes, would be time for the Chamber to take action and make a statement." Harry couldn't help but add a clenched-jaw complaint: "There has been a campaign as you all know of lies going on all over America as to conditions in Los Angeles. It has been systematic."

A chamber director asked, "Your idea would be to let the matter rest as it is until that official declaration?"

Harry said, "It would be much more effective to then take prompt and strong action."

With that, the chamber's board of directors voted to follow the suggestions of Harry Chandler and George Young. They would send nothing to chamber members until the official state board of health statement came out.

By mid-November, health officials believed the epidemic over. So at the chamber of commerce's next board meeting, on November 20, the directors, having considered the matter further, decided that apart from the official state board of health report, they should give the outbreak "no more publicity," not even "publicity to the report." The consensus of the publicity committee was: "The less we said about it the better." They would only send to chamber members "a carefully prepared form letter which they can use as a basis of writing to friends and business acquaintances in the East" in order to "offset unfavorable propaganda."

In the end, the city's swift, harsh quarantine worked effectively: Fewer than fifty cases were reported, fewer than forty people died, and none outside the immediate infection area. Within four weeks, health officials had the plague outbreak under control. The story soon disappeared from the local newspapers.

Yet another matter would also have been troubling Billy Garland just then. In June 1924, his neighbor and colleague E. L. Doheny was indicted on multiple charges of bribery and conspiracy for his role in the Teapot Dome scandal. This began when President Warren Harding, less than three months after taking office in 1921, signed an executive order transferring three tracts of government oil reserves (one in Teapot Dome, Wyoming, two in Elk Hills, California) from the custody of the secretary of the navy to the custody of the secretary of the interior, Albert Fall, a onetime Old West prospector with ties to big oil interests. In April 1922, Fall had secretly leased the Teapot Dome Reserve on favorable terms to one such interest, Harry Sinclair's Mammoth Oil Company. In December 1922, he had secretly leased the Elk Hills Reserve to Doheny's Pan-American Petroleum Company, also on favorable terms. Soon after Harding unexpectedly died on August 22, 1923, the Senate Committee on Lands began to investigate.

It emerged that Doheny's son, Edward L. "Ned" Doheny Jr., at his father's instruction, had on November 30, 1921, withdrawn $100,000 in cash (nearly $1.3 million in 2018 dollars) from his personal bank account in New York, boarded a train to Washington, DC, and there, in a Wardman Park Hotel room, handed the cash in a satchel to Secretary Fall. Doheny called it a loan to an "old prospector friend," while the government's criminal indictment, naming Fall as codefendant, thought otherwise. In September, the government filed a separate civil lawsuit against Doheny's company, seeking to cancel the Elk Hills oil leases because they were gained through conspiracy, fraud and bribery.

With Democrats in Congress sensing blood over Republican cabinet-level corruption, the civil trial began in the Los Angeles federal courthouse on October 21, 1924—precisely as the pneumonic plague hit the city. To represent him, Doheny had hired LA's most prominent attorney, Henry W. O'Melveny, who counted Harry Chandler among his clients, and Frank Hogan, a noted Washington, DC, trial lawyer. The courtroom was packed, with US District judge Paul J. McCormick presiding over a case that had attracted global attention. With their criminal prosecution looming, neither Doheny nor Fall testified, both invoking their Fifth Amendment privilege against self-incrimination. The trial, heard without a jury, ended after ten days. Judge McCormick took months to reach a decision. In late May 1925, he finally ruled—finding against Doheny and his company on every charge, labeling Doheny's $100,000 bribe a "colossal infamy." By October 1926, Doheny had exhausted all appeals. The next month, on November 22, 1926, his criminal trial began in Washington, DC, with Albert Fall again as codefendant, both facing charges of having conspired to defraud the government.

Doheny was not in Billy's inner circle. Being a Catholic and the son of a lowly Irish immigrant made it difficult for Doheny to crack the elite that governed Los Angeles, despite his great wealth. Still, that wealth was hard to overlook—he was worth an estimated $300 million (well more than $4 billion in 2018 dollars). What's more, he and Billy did have an alliance. They'd staged the "Gardens of Magic" party in Chester Place for the National Association of Real Estate Boards in 1915; they'd sat together that same year on a host committee when Thomas R. Marshall (then Woodrow Wilson's vice president) visited LA; and they'd cosigned a petition to have West Adams converted into a boulevard with parking down the center of the street, adorned with ornamental lights.

Beyond these connections, there was Billy's fundamental unease about the consequences of the Teapot Dome scandal, which threatened to undermine the Coolidge administration and all it represented. When details of the oil lease scandals first claimed front-page newspaper coverage in early 1924, some in the business community seemed to censure, not those who had swindled the government, but those who were exposing the swindlers. Various business leaders around the country thought it "unpatriotic" to condemn the men involved and thereby "cast discredit on the Government." An investigation, they feared, would upset the status quo, which was not what they wanted to happen in the prosperous Coolidge era. Billy certainly shared this feeling. He wanted "safe and sane" normalcy. He wanted government to leave business alone, supported but unregulated. What he did not want was any kind of scandal—be it local government corruption, big-business swindling, or a pneumonic plague outbreak—to tarnish the image of Los Angeles or the country.

It helped considerably that Harry Chandler and the other local newspaper publishers shared his interests. In Los Angeles, only the liberal *Record* gave the Teapot Dome scandal major page-one attention. Elsewhere, newspapers roundly condemned the Democratic investigators in Congress; even the *New York Times,* in a March 31, 1924, editorial, labeled them "scandal-mongers" and "assassins of character."

Doheny and Fall's criminal trial continued for three weeks, stretching into mid-December, with the courtroom packed every day by lawyers, aides, and journalists—only a handful of the general public could land seats. That the defendants were two old-time prospectors who'd first met in the mines of New Mexico's Black Range, one now a cabinet member, the other a multimillionaire, made for compelling theater. Midway through, as the government hammered home its case, the prevailing opinion among spectators had the jury highly unlikely to acquit

**FIGURE 5.** E.L. Doheny waves in celebration after being acquitted of bribery charges connected to the Teapot Dome scandal. Everett Collection Historical / Alamy Stock Photo.

them. Doheny was anxious to testify, according to news accounts on December 7, but his lawyers likely would not allow that. Yet there he was on December 9, walking slowly to the witness stand, an infected arm in a sling, at age seventy looking pale and tired.

The image was misleading. Over the next two days, he delivered what most observers regarded as a bravura performance. Speaking softly and earnestly, mincing no words, his arm resting on a pillow, he recounted the story of his early life, from his time as a "shave-tail mule driver" in the Old West to digging his first oil well in Los Angeles in 1892 with a pick and shovel. He talked about his patriotism in lending his fleet of tankers to the government in the Great War and building Pearl Harbor storage tanks after hearing stories of an impending war with Japan. He once again described his hundred-thousand-dollar payment to Fall as a loan made to help an "old prospector friend." He drew laughter from courtroom spectators when he wryly suggested that his son Ned, in delivering the cash to Fall, would have learned something "even if he had been held up on the way." He explained that he'd taken the Fifth at his civil trial on the advice of his lawyers, who'd warned him of the pending criminal case. The prosecution's cross-examination did not crack him—news accounts reported that he "fenced skillfully with the cross-examiner," his voice "low and cautious."

On the afternoon of December 16, 1926, after deliberating for nineteen hours, the jury returned with a verdict: Doheny, not guilty . . . Fall, not guilty. Doheny wept as he listened to the judgments being announced. His son, Ned Doheny, rose and wrapped his arms around him. By that afternoon, more than six hundred congratulatory messages had reached Doheny in his hotel room. Back in Los Angeles—so telling of the city and the era—he was treated as something of a conquering hero. A cheering crowd of several hundred led by a welcoming committee of fifty prominent bankers and businessmen—including Billy Garland— gave him a tumultuous welcome at the Santa Fe station when he stepped off the train on December 21.

Soon after, on January 10, 1927, more than four hundred of the city's elite—including the mayor, Hollywood celebrities, and top businessmen—attended a banquet in his honor at the Biltmore Hotel, where Doheny's attorney Frank Hogan, the featured speaker, drew a wild standing ovation when he called Doheny one of "our greatest patriots." Positioned at the head of a receiving line, a beaming Billy Garland presented each guest to Doheny personally. For good reason: Billy had made this event happen. He served as toastmaster for the evening and chairman of the banquet's organizing committee.

# A BOLT FROM THE BLUE

In the summer of 1928, aware that the Olympics movement was still foundering amid mounting international tensions, Billy sent Zack Farmer, the general secretary of the LA Olympic Organizing Committee, to Europe on a scouting mission. Farmer, a focused, intense former newspaperman, returned to LA in late August after also attending the 1928 games in Amsterdam. On August 27, he met with the board of directors of the Community Development Association (who also constituted the newly formed California Tenth Olympiad Association) at the Los Angeles Athletic Club, where Billy still was president. Sitting before the directors at a conference room table, Farmer delivered his eight-page report—which proved to be a shock to all present.

Farmer's assessment abroad had left him full of misgivings and pessimistic observations. Conditions in Europe and in the IOC community had deteriorated since LA won the right to host the 1932 games, Farmer warned. Despite the IOC vote for LA, there was "little enthusiasm in Europe for holding the Games so far away," and "little likelihood European countries would participate." The core "Olympism" spirit did not seem to be working, given that a brutal world war had just ended and another appeared to be brewing. Olympism had for a long time been "failing to achieve the purpose and results originally expected." Baron Coubertin having retired in 1924 (he was replaced by a Belgian, Count Henri de Baillet-Latour), the IOC now "was comparable to a ship drifting without a rudder, a mutinous crew aboard and the officers in a state of indisposition." This placed Los Angeles "entirely at the mercy of the many national and international sports federations and athletic organizations," which themselves were "at loggerheads with each other and beset with bitter politics and dissension." There were "bitter international feelings evidenced, rivalries and uncontrollable politics." There were a few individual IOC members supportive of LA, "but looking beneath the surface, there is not a unified friendly attitude toward staging the games in Los Angeles."

Farmer feared there was "a good chance for Los Angeles to be harmed" in staging the games. Though "we undoubtedly could guide publicity to our advantage" better than other cities had done, "there is a good chance for unfavorable publicity regardless of how well we might perform our task." Despite the "praiseworthy work of the Dutch" in preparing for the 1928 games, "the world has been told in recent weeks all about the unfortunate incidents occurring to mar the Ninth Olympiad. . . . If an athlete had his pocket picked the story went out that Amsterdam was full of pickpockets and the government had failed to protect the athletes." Amateur athletics, particularly in the United States, "have become so accentuated, over-organized and commercialized . . . that it is utterly impossible to merge all of the athletics of the world, with the added difficulties of various temperaments, nationalities and languages, without having a flood of criticism." Los Angeles would have to finance and create the games, "without ever being certain in the preceding four years that the cast and show will be what it should be, as definite commitments from nations entering probably will not be obtainable very far in advance." In fact, he considered it a "silly situation" that cities begged for the Olympic Games, since "precedent indicates" the games have been "of little tangible constructive value to the cities." What's more, Farmer added, uncertainty remained about LA's own financing for the games—they had no guarantee the public would approve the one-million-dollar bond measure that the Community Development Association (CDA) had placed on the coming November ballot. Given the deteriorating conditions, he felt the CDA was obliged to present to voters "a careful but frank statement" before Election Day—only then will "we have not practiced deception." The bottom line for Farmer: "Los Angeles and California stand to lose far more than either might gain from the Olympic experience."

The committee members were stunned by Farmer's report. As it happened, Billy Garland was not present—he had remained in Europe after also attending the 1928 games in Amsterdam—and Harry Chandler would arrive late for this meeting. Those in attendance knew that Farmer, far from being an alarmist, always had a steady hand, so his report sounded particularly ominous. What to do? Here was a room full of bold, confident leaders—around the table sat such men as Frank Barham, publisher of the *Los Angeles Herald Express;* Henry M. Robinson, entrepreneur, philanthropist, and chair of Security Trust and Savings Bank; Dr. Robert Millikan, Nobel Prize–winning physicist and chair of Cal Tech's executive council; Harry J. Bauer, president of Southern California Edison; and R. B. Hale, president of the Hale Brothers department store chain. An august body indeed—but almost immediately they folded, passing a resolution to abandon the Tenth Olympiad. Fearing the possibilities, they just could not go forward with this. The prospect of holding the Olympic Games in LA in 1932 appeared dead.

Then Harry Chandler showed up. Dumbfounded but nonconfrontational, he urged his colleagues to rescind their resolution, and reconsider the matter upon Billy's return to the city. Harry knew that only Billy could persuade this group. With relief, he watched as the committee, after some debate, voted to wait.

Billy arrived home ten days later. What a city he walked into as he stepped off the train at the Santa Fe station. Los Angeles in early September 1928 was seething (even more than usual) with intrigue and wrongdoing. Above all else, the messy Julian Petroleum Corporation scandal had been roiling Los Angeles for months, sharing notoriety with the Teapot Dome affair. But this one was local: Through a massive swindle involving the overissue and manipulation of Julian Petroleum's stock, and the company's eventual collapse, some 40,000 LA residents had been bilked of $150 million (more than $2 billion in 2018 dollars). This in turn had inspired a grand jury, on June 23, 1927, to hand down the largest indictment in the history of Los Angeles, targeting fifty-five men, including many leading financiers and businessmen, some in Billy's circle. "The Julian Mess" is what the *Los Angeles Times* called it on the morning of the indictment, in a strident page-one editorial that blasted company founder C. C. Julian (Harry Chandler's bitter enemy). That hadn't buried the scandal, of course, despite Chandler's wants—Billy had to read headlines about it regularly as the trial unfolded for four and a half months, finally resulting, on May 23, 1928, in not-guilty verdicts for everyone still standing. LA County District Attorney Asa Keyes, who had prosecuted the case—and had testified as a character witness for E. L. Doheny at his criminal trial—did not fare as well: The trial judge publicly suggested he had thrown the case, and evidence eventually emerged that he'd accepted bribes of one hundred thousand dollars from principals in the Julian Petroleum Corporation. Soon after Billy arrived home, Keyes was indicted, convicted and sentenced to San Quentin prison, where he resided for nineteen months before Governor James Rolph pardoned him.

This was not all that disturbed Los Angeles just then, and not all that drew Billy's attention. On March 10, 1928, Walter Collins, a nine-year-old, had disappeared from his home in Lincoln Heights. On May 16, Lewis and Nelson Winslow, aged twelve and ten, had gone missing in Pomona. The Los Angeles Police Department, already disparaged for assorted fiascos and corruption scandals, was enduring intense criticism for failing to solve these cases. This would have mattered to both Harry Chandler and Billy Garland: LAPD's police chief at the time, the choleric James "Two-Gun" Davis, was a favorite of theirs for his hardnosed positions against crime (he promised to haul in criminals "dead or alive") and labor activism (he cultivated the growth of the LAPD's "Red Squad" intelligence bureau, which gathered information on radicals and labor organizers). Mayor Cryer, advised by chief of staff Kent Parrot, had appointed Davis police chief in 1926 as a means to appease Chandler and the city's business elite. That it did: some three hundred leading figures, including Billy Garland and Harry Chandler, attended a breakfast bash to honor the new chief.

Now, in the spring and summer of 1928, came a wave of negative attacks on the LAPD. Walter Collins's disappearance, particularly, had been receiving countrywide attention as the LAPD vainly pursued hundreds of leads. In early April, police had widened the search into neighboring states, still with no result. A week later, two hundred police, under the command of Captain J. J. Jones, had fruitlessly launched a new hunt in the northeastern section of Los Angeles. All through that summer, the pressure mounted. Then, in early August 1928, a boy claiming to be Walter showed up in DeKalb, Illinois, where state police detained him and contacted LAPD detectives. Aiming to counteract the months of negative publicity, LA police quickly arranged a public reunion between Walter and his single mother, Christine Collins, a telephone operator. But at that reunion—held on August 18, 1928, in downtown LA's Juvenile Hall, just as Zack Farmer was presenting his grim report to the Olympic committee—Christine Collins balked when brought face to face with the boy claiming to be Walter. "I do not think that is my boy" were her first words. She maintained that position for a good long time while she, the boy, and Captain Jones, in charge of the case, talked together. Jones, wanting this case to be solved, finally convinced Christine to take the boy home, at least temporarily.

That didn't resolve the matter. Christine returned to see Captain Jones three weeks later—on Saturday, September 15, days after Billy arrived in LA—again insisting the boy was not Walter. She had dental records to prove her case and statements from people who knew Walter, including his schoolteacher. Captain Jones, rejecting the evidence, raged at Christine: "What are you trying to do, make fools out of us all? Or are you trying to shirk your duty as a mother and have the state provide for your son?" Then he said, "You're insane and ought to be in a madhouse. You're under arrest now and I'm going to send you to the psychopathic ward." That's just what he did—the police captain had her committed to LA County Hospital. There she stayed for five days, until the mystery boy, on September 19, admitted he was not Walter but, rather, eleven-year-old Arthur Hutchins, who'd run away from his home in Marion, Iowa, because he was under probation for a minor theft. "She was nice to me," Arthur said of Christine Collins, "and it's fun to be somebody you aren't."

Collins, demanding an investigation, sued the city, police chief James Davis and Captain Jones. After the Police Commission initially declined to discipline Jones, and Chief Davis defended his captain, more than a thousand angry citizens packed a city council committee hearing on October 24—the largest crowd ever in council chambers. Under subpoena, Captain Jones refused to testify, while Chief Davis, also under subpoena, dismissed rumors that he would soon resign or be removed. A month later, the Police Commission finally suspended Jones for four months, and a judge ordered him to pay Collins $10,800 in damages; but he didn't pay and was reinstated after his suspension. Davis stepped down as chief in December 1929 but was reappointed in 1933, serving until November 1938.

In the end, authorities determined that the real Walter and the other two missing boys had been kidnapped, molested, beaten and killed on Gordon Stewart Northcott's rundown chicken farm in Wineville, a community in unincorporated Riverside County, just to the east of Los Angeles. After investigators found partial body parts near the ranch's chicken coop, Gordon Northcott and his mother, Sarah Louise Northcott, were arrested; following trials, he was sentenced to death, she to life. Thus ended the saga of what came to be known as the "Wineville

Chicken Coop Murders." Fittingly enough, this being a story of Southern California in the 1920s, Wineville in 1930 changed its name to Mira Loma, hoping to shed the adverse publicity related to the murders.

Aware as he was of these unfolding events, they didn't sidetrack Billy, just as nothing he read in Zack Farmer's report altered his optimistic outlook. At a hastily convened meeting that September, again in a Los Angeles Athletic Club conference room, he pressed the Olympic committee to reverse its decision to abandon the games. Why be afraid of the future? he once more asked. Let us play the game as the cards are dealt. Harry Chandler spoke up also, adeptly arguing against a retreat. For an hour, the prominent industrialists and bankers and developers debated while the fate of the 1932 LA Olympic Games hung in the balance. Just days before, they had folded with little discussion, voting to withdraw the city's invitation. Now, though, they had Billy Garland before them. It made a difference. Bowing finally to his will, the CDA directors voted to retract their resolution and move forward with the games. Zack Farmer felt obliged to submit his resignation, but Billy refused to accept it.

For years after, Billy kept secret the CDA directors' vote to abandon the 1932 games. No one outside of the committee room knew what had happened. Not until 1935 would Billy share the story—and a copy of Farmer's report—with Avery Brundage, the head of the American Olympic Committee, emphasizing that "it is strictly confidential . . . and I trust you will, as my friend, hold it inviolate." He recounted how the CDA directors, "so impressed by the dark outlook" portrayed in Farmer's report, had "immediately passed a resolution" abandoning the games. "Had it not been for the arrival, a few minutes later, of one of the most enthusiastic members and sponsors of the Games, Mr. Harry Chandler . . . the Xth Olympiad would never have been held in Los Angeles." Billy added, "I have always desired to tell you this story, but I felt sufficient time should elapse so that no personal feeling of resentment on my part could obtain. It is interesting, isn't it? . . . It strikes me, looking backward, as a classic."

Through all this, through all the scandals and rebellions, Billy kept beating the drums for the 1932 Olympics and the coming one-million-dollar bond issue needed to support it. In early September 1928, in a letter he provided to the *Los Angeles Times,* he reported that the people of Amsterdam have been "reveling in comparative wealth all summer" as a result of hosting the Olympic Games. The Holland government's appropriation to aid the games proved to be "the most profitable single investment ever made by that government." And then to the real point:

"When Californians vote for Proposition No. 2 next November they will be voting themselves the same prosperity Holland is now enjoying—and a great deal more. There will be ten times as many visitors in Los Angeles during the 1932 games as there were in Amsterdam this year. I hope the people of Los Angeles realize the good fortune that came to them when the city succeeded in securing the 1932 Olympiad. All that is needed to make it a tremendous success is to ratify Proposition No. 2, which will make available $1,000,000 as State aid for the games. The $1,000,000 will bring the people $100,000,000."

Billy continued his campaign on September 21, publicly claiming that in Amsterdam "I found the greatest interest in the forthcoming games among athletes and officials, and received assurances of active participation from numerous European, Asiatic and South American countries." On November 3, three days before the election, he once again urged "the sports fans of California" to vote for the bond issue: "We boasted to the world as to what we were going to do and now it's up to us to make good our boast, but we can't make good without the proper funds to carry on the work. If we will all start from scratch Tuesday by registering a 'yes' vote for the Olympic measure . . . we can win a world triumph for California and Los Angeles."

That's just what happened: On November 6, the state's citizens, heeding Billy's call, overwhelmingly voted for the one-million-dollar Olympiad Bond Act. Billy exulted. Not even an attempt by Avery Brundage to take control of the LA Olympics gave him pause. "The hell you will, sir," he advised the crusty head of the American Olympic Committee. "This is entirely our affair."

# PLANTING A SEED

In February 1929, Billy received a confidential letter from Baron de Coubertin. On one level, it was simply amusing and revealing. Coubertin, now retired and struggling financially, warmly thanked Billy for inviting him and his family to be guests of LA at the 1932 games, all expenses paid—but then balked, feeling "the invitation should come not from the Olympic Committee but from the city of Los Angeles . . . to the founder of Modern Olympics." There was more to Coubertin's letter than that, however.

The former president of the International Olympic Committee hesitated to offer his opinion about the 1932 games, since "those who lead now in the IOC are somewhat nervous when they fear some interference of mine." All the same, since Billy had asked for advice, he would give some, "if only in a non-official way." The athletes of other nations should not be transported or housed at America's expense, he wrote, for "this would be contrary to the spirit of Olympism." On the other hand, "It is quite certain that the number of nations taking part in the games will be small . . . if not proper steps are taken toward reducing the enormous expenses of their participation." Coubertin proposed an idea: "That transportation over sea and land and housing and food during the games should be provided for at reasonably reduced prices." Also: "That for nations . . . where the value of national money has gone down very low, the American dollar might be calculated at its before the war standards" (which was 1 dollar = 5 francs, as compared to

1 dollar = 25.44 francs in 1928). Coubertin considered this "the *only way* of securing a fair representation from distant lands."

In this fashion, Coubertin planted a seed that would grow, in time, to be a critical, defining element of the 1932 games. Billy, however, could not have given Coubertin's letter full attention when it first arrived. He had another matter on his mind: just days before, E. L. Doheny's son Ned, and Ned's personal secretary, Hugh Plunkett, had died of bullet wounds to the head at Greystone Mansion, the breathtaking fifty-five-room Tudor-style estate newly built on Doheny's 429-acre ranch overlooking Beverly Hills—a gift from Doheny to Ned.

The Greystone murder-suicide—which is what it appeared to be— happened late on the evening of February 16, 1929, just two years after Billy hosted E. L. Doheny's appreciation banquet at the Biltmore. It would quickly take its place among the most notoriously murky crime stories in Los Angeles lore. The events of that night likely derived from the Teapot Dome scandal, for Hugh Plunkett had accompanied Ned on the fateful day in 1921 when he presented Secretary of the Interior Albert Fall with one hundred thousand dollars in five twenty-thousand-dollar bundles. Fall and E. L. Doheny had been acquitted at their criminal trial for conspiracy, but each still faced trials on charges of bribery, with Fall's scheduled first, for October 1929. Both Ned and Hugh had been called to testify. The stakes were high: the senior Doheny's fate and their own hinged on their testimony. Yet their situations differed— Ned had been granted immunity, Hugh had not.

Hugh understandably was frightened. He had trouble sleeping; his eleven-year marriage was breaking up; he suffered from back and teeth problems. The Doheny family would later say he began showing "signs of a nervous breakdown." On Christmas Eve in 1928, they said, he suffered a complete breakdown and was put in the care of the family physician, Dr. Ernest Fishbaugh. By February 1929, according to the family, Hugh was losing his mind. They and the doctor urged him to retreat to a sanatorium for a long rest (which would, as a side benefit, exempt him from testifying at Fall's bribery trial). On Saturday afternoon, February 16, "We had a conference at the Doheny home," Dr. Fishbaugh would later say. "Mr. and Mrs. Doheny, Plunkett and I were there. We all urged Plunkett to take a rest. He refused. He simply sat there. Almost shaking at times. He said he would come out of it all right. I could see it was no use to push him further and so I left."

Later that evening, Hugh Plunkett drove to Greystone from his Hollywood apartment and let himself in with his own key. He went to a bedroom in the east wing, kept for him. Ned, already dressed for bed, joined him. They poured drinks, smoked cigarettes, and talked. Accounts start to vary from this point on. At around 11:30 pm, according to one version, Ned's wife, Lucy, had Dr. Fishbaugh paged out of a Hollywood theater, telling him she'd heard a gunshot. According to another version, Ned paged him, seeking help with an agitated Hugh Plunkett. Whatever the impetus, the doctor rushed to Greystone in his chauffeur-driven limousine. A night watchman admitted him to the rambling forty-six-thousand-square-foot mansion.

"As I entered," Fishbaugh told reporters the next day, after giving a statement to investigators, "Mrs. Doheny was standing in the middle hallway approximately eight feet back from the door, and greeted me. She said her husband was in a guestroom on the first floor, to the left side of the hall leading from the front entrance. . . . Both Mrs. Doheny and I started down the hall, side by side. A door, which partitions the hall, was slightly ajar, and I saw Plunkett walking toward it. 'You stay out of here,' he shouted at me and slammed the door shut. I then heard a shot. 'You go back,' I told Mrs. Doheny, and she returned to the living room, which was about 75 feet from the guest room. I pushed the door open and saw Plunkett lying on his face opposite the door to the bedroom. . . . The door to the bedroom was open, and when I looked in I saw Mr. Doheny lying on his back, a chair overturned between him and the bed."

Some three hours passed before police were summoned, around two in the morning. Leslie White, the district attorney's investigator at the scene, didn't think the evidence fit with the doctor's story. In fact, the testimonies of all the employees and family seemed rehearsed—they "dovetailed with remarkable accuracy," White would later write. The powder burns around the hole in Ned's head, and the lack of burns on Hugh, suggested that Ned, rather than Hugh, held a gun to his own head—a gun with no fingerprints on it, a gun that felt oddly warm to White's touch, given the elapsed time. Both men had been drinking, and Hugh had been smoking a cigarette (unfinished, in his hand). Leslie didn't think that fit with the notion of Hugh being a hysterical killer fighting to avoid commitment to a sanitorium. It looked more like Ned had shot Hugh, then himself.

On Sunday morning, Leslie White brought his findings directly to the LA County district attorney, Buron Fitts, visiting the DA at his home. "Mr. Fitts," he said, "I don't believe Hugh Plunkett killed Doheny and

FIGURE 6. Edward "Ned" Doheny Jr., son of oil tycoon E.L. Doheny, circa 1920. Los Angeles Herald Examiner Photo Collection/Los Angeles Public Library.

then committed suicide. . . . The physical facts and the testimony of witnesses do not jibe." He added, "I understand, too, that some people believe the Doheny family are too influential to tamper with."

Fitts flared: "There isn't a man in the United States that's big enough to stop me from conducting a criminal investigation." Fitts, indeed, had run for office as a reformer. At the same time, he had political ambitions and close connections to Harry Chandler and the hidden powers controlling Los Angeles. So, a balancing act ensued.

News coverage began the next day, Monday, February 18, with Fitts launching "a sweeping investigation"—but one already focused on "events surrounding the slaying of Edward L. Doheny Jr., late Saturday night by the latter's secretary, Hugh Plunkett, who later took his own life." Over three pages in the *Los Angeles Times,* the narrative flowed almost entirely from the Doheny family and their doctor, who repeatedly emphasized Hugh Plunkett's ever-deepening nervous ailments and his resistance to their urgings that he retreat to a sanatorium for a rest. The stories at no point mentioned Plunkett's ties to the Teapot Dome scandal or his coming duty to testify at Fall's and Doheny's bribery trials. "In order to eliminate any doubts that the tragedy was the result of a mind suddenly gone mad," Fitts reassured, "we will completely push our investigation until we have completely reconstructed the murder and suicide as far as it is circumstantially possible."

That changed within hours: The very next day's *Los Angeles Times* headline read, "No Inquest on Doheny . . . Officials Close Inquiries." The DA had signed death certificates for both men, officially labeling the affair a murder/suicide. Since the man who brought tragedy into the Doheny family was dead, Fitts declared, there would be no inquest. Also, there would be no autopsy on the body of Ned. With that, after just forty-eight hours, the story disappeared from the *Los Angeles Times.*

Rather than drawing connections to the Teapot Dome scandal and Albert Fall's coming bribery trial, later talk focused on a possible sexual drama: Ned and Hugh were gay lovers, one theory went, both killed by Lucy Doheny after she found them in a suggestive situation. Conjecture like that multiplied, with no resolution—the story turned into yet another Los Angeles fable, and yet more evidence that an elite controlled Los Angeles, populated by many of the four hundred exuberant citizens who attended E. L. Doheny's triumphant banquet at the Biltmore Hotel in January 1927.

On March 29, six weeks after the Greystone murder-suicide, Billy sailed from New York en route to the annual IOC meeting, to be held April 6–11 in Lausanne. Aboard ship, he had plenty of time to consider Coubertin's letter. The notion of reasonably reduced prices for transportation and housing resonated in his mind. An idea began to germinate.

Upon arriving at the IOC meeting, Billy delivered a report about progress being made in Los Angeles, including plans to build a swimming stadium next to the Coliseum with two pools, one for diving, the other for polo and swimming. Then he raised, and participated in, a discussion about the costs for transport and lodging. This led J. S. Edstrom, chairman of the International Amateur Athletic Association (which would oversee the track and field events at the games), to present a proposal: that Billy negotiate with the steamship companies, seeking a 50 percent reduction in fares to and from New York; that he negotiate in the same way with the railway companies; that he try to arrange the lowest prices possible with LA hotel proprietors for the lodging and feeding of athletes; and that he inform the IOC "with the least delay possible" about the result of his efforts. Billy agreed to all the terms, and the IOC members voted to accept the proposal.

On his journey back to Los Angeles in early June, Billy stopped in Washington, DC, to visit President Hoover, a fellow Californian and Harry Chandler's close ally. He personally invited the president to open the Olympic Games. Hoover told Billy that he deeply appreciated the invitation and hoped that his official duties might be so arranged that he could be there.

Billy arrived in Los Angeles by train on the evening of June 11, stepping down from the Santa Fe passenger train the *Chief* to be greeted by family members and officials of the Los Angeles Olympic Organizing Committee, including Zack Farmer. He said he was "glad to be back in the land of sunshine and home," but he had more than the climate on his mind. The deal he'd cut in 1921 with city and county officials to get the Coliseum built called for the Community Development Association to turn over the stadium to local governments after ten years. That would require the CDA to give up control of the Coliseum in 1931— one year before the Olympic Games. Billy had been trying to negotiate an extension of ten years, plus a commitment of nine hundred thousand dollars from the city and county for improvements, but LA mayor George Cryer had recently refused to sign the agreement, despite earlier approval by the county board and city council. Though Cryer didn't oppose the CDA's continued management of the Coliseum, or the plans to enlarge the stadium, he did question the terms of a contract handing full control of a public facility to a private corporation. In a message describing his objections, he said, "I do insist that the contract under which the work is to be done should fully protect the interests of the people and insure to the taxpayers the full benefits to be derived from their large investment in the enterprise."

At the railway station, in response, Billy came out swinging. "The only obstacle in the pathway of the Olympic Games for Los Angeles in 1932 is the Mayor of Los Angeles," began a front-page story in the *Times* the next morning. "That was the message brought to Los Angeles last night by William M. Garland. . . . While the entire European world is looking forward anxiously to the California meet, Mr. Garland declared that the only hindrance so far encountered is in the recent action of the Mayor, who refused to sign a renewal of the agreement held by the Community Development Association, which would provide security for the enlargement of the Coliseum to handle the crowds that will certainly throng to the games."

The article continued, sounding one of Billy's familiar themes: "Mr. Garland deplored the possible effect that this policy of the Mayor might have on the enthusiasm of the countries of the world which plan to send large representations of athletes to the meet. It is absolutely necessary that the stadium be enlarged in accord with the plans of the association, he declared. The Community Development Association built the amphitheater, he pointed out, and has managed it successfully since the bowl was opened. This is no time to transfer a pre-eminently successful control for an uncertain political supervision, Mr. Garland believes."

The article had been paraphrasing Billy, but now he spoke directly: "The action of the Mayor created unfortunate publicity for Los Angeles, after the representations I have made to the International Olympic Committee and the countries of Europe, where I found nothing but unbounded enthusiasm for the next Games." Although there'd been no commitments from any countries this far in advance, Billy claimed "more than forty-six nations have announced that they will be represented by athletic teams. California and Los Angeles are in the best advertised places in the world. Everywhere I went in Europe I found numbers of people who want to visit this talked-of place. We cannot let any obstacle remain in the way of making the 1932 Games the greatest that have ever been held."

It took a few months of string pulling and heated debate—and a newly elected mayor, John Porter—but Billy finally prevailed. In November 1929, lawyers drafted a revised contract between the CDA and local agencies that provided financing for improvements, with control of the Coliseum remaining in the CDA's hands until January 1, 1933—four and a half months after the scheduled close of the 1932 games. Mayor John Porter signed the contract on January 9, 1930.

There was little to celebrate, though. By then, Billy had far more troubling matters to address. The Great Depression had arrived.

# THEN CAME THE CRASH

Even in confident and prosperous times, the prospect of holding the Olympic Games for the first time on the shores of the Pacific Ocean, with all that required in extended travel, had posed a daunting challenge. Then came the October 1929 stock market crash and the world's plummet into the Great Depression, which seemed to transform that challenge from daunting to downright insurmountable. Across the globe, devastated countries struggled with mounting bankruptcies, unemployment, financial crises and political strife. Los Angeles, for all its economic prosperity during the 1920s, felt the sting too. Even Southern California's strongest industries, including oil and moviemaking, cut thousands of jobs. In 1930, more than seven hundred thousand were unemployed in California, half of them in Los Angeles and Orange County. LA led the nation in the number of bankruptcies. Long lines wrapped around soup kitchens. A huge Hooverville encampment, holding seven hundred cold, hungry, angry and embarrassed Americans, rose on a five-acre site not far from the Coliseum and Billy Garland's home—one of several in the region, all without power or toilets, all built out of cardboard, tarpaper, canvas, and scraps of metal. An extraordinary epoch of growth seemed to be meeting its demise. The vision and mind-set that inspired Los Angeles' boosters to bid for the games a decade before now starkly conflicted with the particulars of an impoverished, overexpanded region.

No wonder that doubters eventually began calling the whole Olympic Games enterprise "Garland's folly." Billy, though, saw things differently.

From where did he draw his preternatural resolve to persevere? Certainly, one model was his father-in-law, the bearded, gaunt-faced Marshall Littlefield Hinman. Blanche's father had started out his career, in 1861, as timekeeper in the Dunkirk, New York, shops of the Erie Railroad, under the supervision of the master mechanic there, Horatio G. Brooks. Eight years later, in October 1869, he and Brooks founded the Brooks Locomotive Works, where Hinman served as secretary and treasurer, then (following Brooks's death) as vice president and president. At a testimonial dinner in 1901, three years after Billy married his daughter, Hinman recounted a history of Brooks Locomotive that sounded strikingly similar to what Billy was now experiencing at the start of the Great Depression.

Billy well knew that history: The Panic of 1873, coming so soon after Brooks and Hinman founded their company, triggered a major depression in Europe and North America that lasted until 1879—in fact, it was known as the "Great Depression" until the events Billy faced in the early 1930s set a new standard. When the financial storm first broke on "Black Friday," September 19, 1873, Hinman was in New York seeking to close a contract for a few locomotives. That night he sent a telegram to Brooks, reporting on the failure of many important banks, but Brooks, outwardly full of mirth, proceeded as planned the next day with a gala company parade and picnic—not unlike Billy's Rose Parade performance on January 1, 1932.

During the dark years that followed, as Hinman recalled at his testimonial dinner, "many an hour both day and night did Mr. Brooks and I spend together, devising ways and means to continue the Works, and on more than one occasion did Mr. Brooks express himself ready to close up the business. . . . But fortunately during such time of his despondency I had not lost faith in the future[,] and by our united efforts the Works were carried along until such time as activity did come."

Billy realized that what his father-in-law called "activity" didn't always mean earning a profit: In order to keep their workers employed, Hinman would take orders for locomotives at the bare cost of labor and material. "During that period I too became despondent," Hinman allowed. "Mr. Brooks was full of hope upon such occasions when I was despondent, and fortunately for the Brooks Works we were not depressed at the same time. Had we been so . . . the Brooks Works would have passed out of existence in 1880."

Instead, after ten long years of struggle the company began to prosper, making both Brooks and Hinman very wealthy. The continued expansion of Brooks Locomotive Works had another effect as well: by drawing workers and other newcomers to the region, it enlarged Dunkirk from a village into an incorporated city—much as Billy's efforts would enlarge Los Angeles. "My recollection of the struggle during the first ten years," Hinman concluded, "should be told as an incentive to others to persevere and[,] in the words of the naval hero, Lawrence, as he fell mortally wounded on board his vessel—'Don't give up the ship.' This was practically the motto of Horatio Brooks, as well as myself[,] during years through which we struggled for an existence."

It's hard to imagine Billy not thinking of his father-in-law as he faced the mounting consequences of the stock market crash in October 1929. Rather than retreat or fold his hand, he at this moment began a series of shuttle trips to Europe. Opening a bold public relations campaign, he met with the International Olympic Committee in Lausanne, then with a range of individual national committees. Despite his efforts, he drew a response quite different from what he had received in 1923, when he impressed Mussolini and heard Pope Pius XI praise the games. Many interviews were downright discouraging. In Portugal, a government official asked, "Just where is your state?" and, after Garland showed him Los Angeles on a map, added, "That's a very long, expensive way from here." At a meeting at Claridge's in London with Baron de Coubertin and his recent successor, Count de Baillet-Latour, the two IOC leaders brimmed with gloom. "Your 1932 ambitions now do not look so certain," Coubertin advised.

Nonetheless, Billy returned home radiating optimism. In private, he told his committee all about the discouraging meeting in London with Coubertin, but in public he remained upbeat. He kept smiling and insisting that nothing would stop the games. The first department he'd created, weeks after the stock market crash, was—no surprise—a press office. It now in earnest began promoting both the games and Southern California. Feeds to cooperative wire services and newspapers, a twice-monthly news bulletin, an official periodical titled *Olympic,* and advertising through the All-Year Club: the LA Olympic Organizing Committee energetically unrolled what it would proudly call its full arsenal of "press propaganda."

In early February 1930, Billy also mailed formal invitations to sixty-five countries, encouraging their participation in the games. Each invitation, in English on parchment, bore the engrossed address of the receiving nation, the great seal of the Tenth Olympiad Committee, and the signature of Billy Garland. Billy for once had avoided a public show. Rather, for hours he'd sat in his private office, pen on parchment.

A month later, Billy met with President Hoover in Washington, reporting in detail on the work then under way in support of the 1932

FIGURE 7. Billy Garland signing invitations to the 1932 Olympics, to be sent to sixty-five countries, requesting their participation in the games. Security Pacific National Bank Collection / Los Angeles Public Library.

Olympic Games. He explained the expansion plans for the Coliseum and described arrangements for swimming, yachting, and other contests. He told Hoover that he and others representing the United States would be going to Berlin in May to present their proposal at a critical Olympic Congress. All our plans will be determined in Berlin, he said. The Berlin congress will decide our fate. Billy did not seem daunted by that challenge. He reassured Hoover: There will be tremendous world interest in the 1932 Olympic Games.

Even as Billy scrambled to save the 1932 games, groups of young athletes across the country, little noticed at the time, were training and competing, their eyes on the coming Olympics in Los Angeles. In the

Midwest, two African American high school boys, Eddie Tolan (Detroit) and Ralph Metcalfe (Chicago) were climbing out of hard, impoverished childhoods by winning every hundred-meter and two-hundred-meter race they entered. In Pine Bluff, Arkansas, a short, unknown middle-distance runner named Bill Carr was gunning to topple the NCAA champion Ben Eastman of Stanford University, then ranked the second-best quarter-miler in the nation. At USC in Los Angeles, Clarence "Buster" Crabbe—who'd learned to swim in the waters off Hawaii, where he spent his early years—was juggling classes and part-time jobs, including dishwashing at a college fraternity house, as he obsessively trained to improve on the bronze medal he'd won for the fifteen-hundred-meter freestyle at Amsterdam in 1928.

Not only men were fantasizing about the 1932 games in Los Angeles. Those training and competing just then included a number of singularly talented teenage girls. Women had first been allowed to compete, on a limited basis, in the 1928 games, and hopes were high for even more opportunities in 1932. In mid-March of 1930, six weeks after Billy's invitations to sixty-five nations went out, some of these girls gathered at the Roman Pool in Miami Beach to compete in the National Amateur Athletic Union Indoor Swimming Championships for women. Here was a glimpse of what Los Angeles could expect to see if the city managed to stage the 1932 games.

Two athletes represented Billy's Los Angeles Athletic Club in Florida: diving champion Georgia Coleman, eighteen, and star swimmer Josephine McKim, twenty, both medal-winning members of the 1928 Olympic team. From the Crystal Pool Club of Seattle came swimmer Helene Madison, at age sixteen making her national debut, though she already was something of a sensation, having beaten Josephine McKim at a recent Los Angeles Athletic Club meet where she set a new world record in a 220-yard race. From the Women's Swimming Association of New York came Eleanor Holm, just sixteen but considered a certainty to win the 100-yard backstroke event after setting eight new records, at varying distances, in the past two months.

The meet began on March 13. By the time it ended on March 17, Helene Madison had set four new world records and equaled a fifth, in distances ranging from 50 meters to 500 yards. Eleanor Holm, shining as well, had broken the American records for the 100-yard backstroke and the 300-yard medley, her medley record stamping her as an all-around swimmer without peer. Overall, Helene Madison took the individual championship, Eleanor Holm placed second, Josephine McKim third. Of most interest, the winning women's times in many events were not far off of the best men's times in the recent past.

Frank W. Blankley, chairman of the National AAU Swimming Committee, was beside himself after witnessing this meet. He wrote soon after in an AOC report: "It was a study to watch the girls, mostly high school girls, swim and to compare their performance with the championship records made by our best men swimmers only a few years back." Helene Madison, in particular, amazed him—he felt compelled to describe her as "a 16-year-old naiad, standing 5 feet 9½ inches and weighing upwards of 140 pounds." But his eyes were mainly on her scores: "Here is a 16-year-old girl, junior in high school, in her first championship effort creating new championship records for women that are better than those made by . . . recognized men champions of only a few years ago."

Helene had long been aiming for this moment. When she was two, her parents had moved from Wisconsin to Seattle, where her father started a dry cleaning business. Her mother, thinking it good for her health, began taking Helene to Madrona Beach on Lake Washington, some twenty blocks from their home. Helene did more splashing than swimming at first, but then, when she was six, her family moved to a home one block from Green Lake, where Helene's parents could watch her in the water from their front porch.

In grade school, Helene spent hours swimming at West Green Lake Beach, with much of her early training provided by the Seattle Parks Department swimming program, and particularly by Jack Torney, then a University of Washington student instructor who would later become the men's swim coach at the university. At age thirteen, Helene resisted when Torney first urged her to enter a municipal race, feeling she couldn't dive into the water properly. Torney responded by working with her in early morning sessions until she felt more confident. Racing against older swimmers, she lost at first, but by age fifteen she was the Green Lake master of the water. Ray Daughters, an instructor at the Crystal Natatorium in Seattle, noticed and stepped in as her coach, guiding her during hours of training at the Crystal Pool. In 1929, Helene broke the state record for the women's hundred-yard freestyle, then broke the Pacific Coast record. Months later, in March 1930, the Seattle Chamber of Commerce financed her journey to Miami and the national indoor swimming championships.

She'd left home still a relative novice; by the time she returned to Seattle, having won every freestyle event and broken five records, she was, at age sixteen, a superstar. "Why, they had her make her entrance into town in an airplane," her father, Charles Madison, recalled. "They wanted her to fly from Portland, but she hadn't been up before and she didn't quite like the idea. Kind of scared." Aboard a single-winged tri-motor, she landed nonetheless at Boeing Field, where some four thousand people gave her a tremendous ovation. Then, Charles Madison said, "well, there was a big parade. Helene going down the streets in a flag-covered automobile, motorcycle escorts. Everybody cheering. A big community gathering at the auditorium that night." In fact, it was a banquet in her honor, where one thousand guests watched a screening of the 220-yard race in which Helene beat Jo McKim by a wide margin. To show her appreciation for all this adulation, Helene promptly established two new records at a local meet, in the 200-yard and 300-yard swims. She was already dreaming of the 1932 Olympic Games in Los Angeles.

# BERLIN, 1930

When Billy Garland left Los Angeles for Berlin on the evening of May 8, 1930, the stakes could not have been higher. He carried with him the complete if tentative program for the games, which he and Zack Farmer planned to present at a session of the International Olympic Committee, and then, immediately after, at the larger Olympic Congress, which involved the IOC and various national sports federations. The Olympic Congress, held two years in advance of every Olympic competition, had the power to approve—or disapprove—the entire program for the coming games. It could, if the situation warranted, go so far as to recommend the abandonment of the games.

That was a distinct possibility in the spring of 1930. A true, fully realized Olympic Games had never been held outside continental Europe, and the thought of attempting one now, amid a worldwide economic crisis of frightening proportions, was stirring considerable apprehension among European sports organizations. A round-trip journey to and from California would require two weeks of travel each way, plus nearly a month in Los Angeles, at an estimated expense of two thousand dollars per athlete. That kind of cost made participation seem improbable, if not utterly impossible, for many European nations.

Billy and his team, fully understanding this threat, had been working secretly for more than a year on a plan that would dramatically reduce the per-athlete cost. Their plan could be traced back to the IOC session in Lausanne in April 1929, where delegates asked Billy to try to negotiate lower steamship, railroad, and lodging costs. That was just what he had done—and more.

On May 23, Billy Garland rose to address the IOC at its opening day session in Berlin's Neo-Renaissance Herrenhaus building (the old Prussian House of Lords, designed by architect Friedrich Schulze). He'd come well-armed. Besides an exhaustive, comprehensive report, he'd brought with him a letter from President Hoover, a reel of motion pictures about Los Angeles compiled by MGM studios (where Louis B. Mayer was a great supporter), a stack of architects' plans, and a big pile of photographs of the Coliseum and other event venues, among them the two-pool Los Angeles Swimming Stadium, built at a cost of a quarter of a million dollars. Billy began by reading from Hoover's letter, which offered the IOC the president's "best wishes and a hearty welcome." Then he addressed what he knew were the IOC's two chief concerns. First, he announced, Los Angeles was far ahead of schedule, with more than 80 percent of all buildings already constructed two years in advance and the expansion (to 105,000 seats) and upgrade of the Coliseum underway; matters were so well organized they could easily hold the games in six months, if necessary. Second—and this was the bombshell—the total cost of the round-trip for European contestants would be approximately four hundred dollars per athlete, including thirty days in Los Angeles. That was less than one-fourth of the expected two-thousand-dollar cost, a savings gained largely by the efforts of Billy and his team to get sizable 40 percent rate reductions from the railroad and steamship companies. (Billy had pointed out to the companies that they'd otherwise have a lot of empty seats, given the international economic crisis.)

There was more. The savings, Billy explained, would come not only through reduced transportation costs. For lodging and meals, Los Angeles proposed to build an Olympic Village—the first ever in the history of the games—on a site within a fifteen-minute drive of the Coliseum. This village would provide dining, sleeping and entertainment accommodations for three thousand athletes, all living together in one community with a lounge, central dining salon, screening room and information bureau. And yet, every nation would have its own separate quarters and cooking facilities, enabling the athletes of each country to enjoy their native diet. Most important of all, the cost for housing, food and local transportation would be just two dollars a day per athlete.

The village had been Zack Farmer's idea. Despite his gloomy assessment in 1928 of the games' prospects, and his offer to resign, he'd stayed on the job and had come up with a pivotal innovation, one of the most audacious in Olympic history. Later in the afternoon of May 23, after Billy's presentation, Farmer, a cogent and persuasive thirty-eight-year-old, rose before the IOC to lead an extended discussion about the proposed Olympic Village.

Traditionally at the Olympics, nations had lived, dined and trained separately, coming together only in competition. The idea of sharing a communal space struck some IOC members and Olympic Congress delegates as "collectivism." They did not respond warmly. "Some were afraid," Farmer would recall. "Open racial clashes were predicted . . . the idea was shot full of danger, no doubt about that." He added, "You have no idea of the resistance because these different countries were afraid of the political and racial differences. They squawked that they had training secrets and didn't want to live so close together."

All the same, the IOC agreed to accept the Olympic Village in principle, and each member pledged to support it when the matter came before his National Olympic Committee. This didn't amount to formal approval of the village, for in the end every nation would decide for itself whether to house its athletes there. To go forward with the village, Farmer would need to resurrect the plan in the spring of 1932 and gain firm commitments from all nations, individually. But he and Billy had planted a seed.

IOC minutes for this day relate that, after viewing the film about Los Angeles and hearing the detailed presentations by Zack Farmer and Billy Garland, "the President [Count de Baillet-Latour], in the name of his colleagues, spoke of the great progress that had been made in the last year and congratulated [Billy and Zack] on the very advantageous conditions of transport and housing which they had been able to guarantee." The IOC seemed persuaded to go forward. "The first two weeks in August," the minutes report, "were definitely fixed for the Summer Games."

Rather than celebrate, Billy, ever the hustler, at this moment chose to convey a cautionary message to authorities in Los Angeles. He'd left for Berlin openly frustrated over the county board and city council's failure to appropriate their respective shares of funds for the completion of the Coliseum expansion and upgrades. Now he saw a way to apply pressure. On Saturday, May 24, one day before the start of the Olympic Congress, he cabled the LA Board of Supervisors, intimating that Los Angeles might lose the 1932 games unless LA could confirm to apprehensive foreign countries that the Coliseum's reconstruction would be completed in ample time. Billy urged the board to reassure the foreign countries by the following Wednesday.

The next day, on the morning of Sunday, May 25, the Olympic Congress opened with a formal gathering at the University of Berlin. There Billy and Zack listened to the Cathedral Choir sing a hymn by Brahms and an ode by Pindarus, a series of speeches by German ministers and officials, and a welcome from Count de Baillet-Latour. The IOC president thanked their hosts, who, "in obtaining the permission of the authorities for the Great Hall of this University to be put at our disposal," had "respected the traditions of the Olympic movement."

Just what Zack Farmer—a salty cowboy in his youth—thought of all this can only be imagined. At the least, it's fair to say that shortly after noon the next day, he and Billy altered the ambiance of the gathering. For the first time at an Olympic Congress, delegates watched a movie, the one made by Louis B. Mayer's MGM Studios about Los Angeles' Olympic preparations. Later that afternoon, after the plenary session, the international delegates to the Congress called on Germany's President Von Hindenburg for tea. "The American delegation was the spiffiest of all," reported the *Los Angeles Times*. "They had silk hats and striped trousers . . . which gave the delegation an air of elegance so dear to the hearts of diplomats. The Americans were headed by William May Garland."

That same day, back in Los Angeles, the board of supervisors, swayed by Billy's cable, voted unanimously to appropriate $225,000 for upgrading and enlarging the Coliseum. At the same time, Mayor Porter added the city's share of the expense to the general budget he was then preparing. "Olympic Congress Fears Will Be Assuaged Thereby," declared a *Los Angeles Times* headline. With the fate of the 1932 LA games hanging in the balance, Billy and Zack had prevailed in Berlin.

Three days later, on Thursday, May 29, so did women athletes everywhere. For years, the IOC had been debating whether women should be allowed to participate in the games. Coubertin had seen no place for women at all, but female swimmers and divers did compete in 1912 (Stockholm) and 1920 (Antwerp). Fencing was added in 1924 (Paris). Not until 1928 (Amsterdam) did women compete in a limited number of track and field events (100- and 800-meter races, a 4 x 100-meter relay, high jump, discus). The women's 800-meter race that year created an uproar when some runners collapsed at the end, exhausted. In response, Count de Baillet-Latour in 1929 had proposed eliminating all women's events. Now, backing down a bit at the 1930 Berlin Congress, he proposed admitting women to the Olympic Games only in gymnastics, lawn-tennis, swimming and skating. After a heated debate, delegates voted by a large margin to reject Baillet-Latour's proposal and instead adopt one that added track and field and fencing to the women's events. Though they deferred final action until the 1931 IOC meeting in Barcelona, at least for now all looked promising for both Los Angeles and women athletes.

After nine weeks in Europe, Billy returned to Los Angeles on July 16 sounding well pleased and not the least modest. "Europe's enthusiasm for the 1932 Olympic Games is unbounded," he declared to a large welcoming crowd as he stepped from the train at the Santa Fe station in the late afternoon. "The completeness of the report which our committee gave to the Olympic Congress simply swept them off their feet. The special and remarkably low transportation costs[ ,] . . . the completeness of the training facilities[, and] . . . the plans for further enlargement of our Coliseum were a revelation to the Europeans." The films made in Los Angeles by MGM and brought to Berlin by Billy also had a "tremendous influence." European newspapers "are giving tremendous publicity to our preparations." The games in LA, Billy believed, would have the "largest ever" number of nations participating and unequalled attendance by royalty and high dignitaries from all corners of the globe.

The next morning, Billy was the guest of honor at the Breakfast Club, a peculiar Los Angeles group formed in the early 1920s by businessmen who wanted to get together for a meal after early morning horseback rides in Griffith Park. By 1930, it had coalesced into a club that featured guest speakers and entertainment, with quarters at a former dairy farm on Riverside Drive and members ranging from E.L. Doheny and Harry Chandler to Will Rogers, Louis B. Mayer, Jack Warner, Cecil B. DeMille, and Darryl Zanuck. Breakfast always consisted of ham and eggs, but the club added mountain trout to the menu on the day Billy spoke, served to the accompaniment of Gus Arnheim's Cocoanut Grove Orchestra. Before an array of government officials, Hollywood moguls, and prominent citizens, in a talk broadcast over the local KFWB radio station, Billy projected what a reporter called "quiet optimism." Again, he did not let modesty dilute his buoyancy.

"The report of work that we have already accomplished . . . ," he said, "was so startling that the Los Angeles committee completely captivated the Congress which met in Berlin in May. . . . Following the report, we were given the wholehearted assurance that the 1932 Olympic Games will be the best ever held in the modern era." Once

**FIGURE 8.** Harry Chandler, *left,* publisher of the *Los Angeles Times,* shaking hands with William Randolph Hearst, publisher of the *Los Angeles Examiner,* at the Breakfast Club in Los Angeles on October 16, 1930. Los Angeles Herald Examiner Photo Collection/Los Angeles Public Library.

more he applied pressure: "It is hoped that the completion of the Coliseum will be accomplished immediately. Without that the Games could not even be held here. . . . In fact, we permitted the congress to adjourn in Berlin with our pledged word that the Coliseum additions would be completed immediately." Before closing, Billy could not help but again predict a future population: "I have learned that Los Angeles inspires people in every part of the world . . . and I want to pause to ask you, my friends, if this city has been able to gain 700,000 souls within the last ten years, five of which were what we realtors call quiet years, what will the next ten years show?" Certainly, he thought "it is not too much to say that the 1940 census will show at least 2,250,000 people in Los Angeles."

The prophet didn't quite have that right—Los Angeles' population would hit 1,504,277 in 1940. Still, the day after this Breakfast Club talk, a *Los Angeles Times* editorial hailed his foresight: "Col. William M. Garland, consistent worker for the good of his city, has made many optimistic predictions at various periods of its growth about the future of Los Angeles, and—be it noted—his predictions have invariably been exceeded by the event. The reports, therefore, which he has brought back from Europe . . . will be received with extreme satisfaction by workers at this end of the line interested in making 1932 a red-letter year for Southern California."

That summer of 1930, young athletes across the country had good reason to hope Billy's "optimistic predictions" were true. In meet after meet, they were setting new records and aiming ever higher. At the National Collegiate Athletic Association's Track and Field Championships at Stagg Field in Chicago on June 6–7, a small group of athletes from the University of Southern California won the team championship, with the highlight of the meet being the 100-yard race, where twenty-year-old Frank Wykoff—who'd been aiming for the Olympics since the sixth grade in Des Moines—had to set a world's record to defeat what an AOC report called "the finest field of sprinters ever gathered," including Eddie Tolan out of Detroit. Tolan, by now known as the Midnight Express, came back on July 1 to defeat an all-star field in the 100-meter race at an international meet in Vancouver, BC, leading from start to finish and setting a new world record, a feat considered particularly extraordinary because the track was higher at the finish than the start by thirty inches—which meant Tolan was running slightly uphill all the way.

At the National Amateur Athletic Union Women's Track and Field Championships in Dallas on July 4, two thousand spectators watched nineteen-year-old Stella Walsh of Cleveland, the daughter of a Polish immigrant steel mill worker, take top individual honors while breaking the existing world's records in the 100-yard race, the 220-yard race, and the running broad jump. Not far behind her was nineteen-year-old Mildred "Babe" Didrikson out of Beaumont, Texas, the daughter of Norwegian immigrants, her father a sailor and carpenter, who set new records in the baseball and javelin throws. Two others also shone: Evelyne Hall, a twenty-year-old who'd survived a sickly, impoverished childhood in Minneapolis, won the 80-meter hurdles; Jean Shiley, an eighteen-year-old from rural Pennsylvania, came from nowhere to win the high jump.

At a major four-day meet held at Long Beach, California, July 3–6, athletes set ten world records as the men's and women's swimming teams of Billy Garland's Los Angeles Athletic Club each won national team championships—the first time any club had taken both titles. Buster Crabbe of the Los Angeles Athletic Club, still washing dishes at USC fraternities, had to break three world records in order to beat Maiola Kalili of Honolulu in the 880-yard, 1-mile, and 300-meter medley swims. Helene Madison, now seventeen, again was spectacular, winning all four races she entered, setting world records in each one, stymying Josephine McKim, the defending champion in the quarter-mile, half-mile, and mile events, who finished second to Helene in all three of these races. The backstroke ace Eleanor Holm, to no surprise, won the 220-yard backstroke and 300-meter medley. The diver Georgia Coleman won the ten-foot springboard and high platform dive. Fifteen-year-old Dorothy Poynton, who'd just turned thirteen when she won a silver medal at the 1928 games—the youngest Olympic medalist in history—took third off the springboard.

Every one of these athletes longed to compete at the 1932 Olympic Games in Los Angeles. For many, the games promised an escape, a path to the future. But with the Great Depression now spreading and deepening across the globe, a fundamental question still remained: Would there be a 1932 Olympic Games?

# A SACRED DUTY

In promoting his Olympic campaign, Billy Garland had long relied on the local newspaper publishers, but as the 1920s unfolded he grew keenly aware of how many Americans were now also listening to radio broadcasts. On Sunday, September 14, 1930, two months after returning from Berlin, he delivered a nationwide radio address over Los Angeles–based KFI and stations associated with the National Broadcasting Company. Though he would not have favored the comparison, his radio talk suggested the type of "fireside chat" that President Franklin Roosevelt would later employ so effectively.

"On this Sabbath day," he began, "when millions throughout our nation turn from their toil to worship, each according to his own particular religion, it is only fitting we give a thought to Youth. Specifically, I refer to the Youth which will assemble in the United States from all parts of the world in 1932, to participate in the Olympic Games." From there, Billy offered a brief history of the games, from ancient times in the Greek province of Ellis to the modern revival by Baron Pierre de Coubertin. He told of the "pleasure and honor" he had in carrying LA's invitation to the IOC meeting in Antwerp in 1920, and in having it finally accepted in 1923 in Rome. He spoke of "the pleasure, last May, of presenting at the meeting in Berlin . . . our report." Then to the pitch: "The entire nation certainly must realize the importance of the Olympic Games and have a deep pride in their success. We of California, and particularly Los Angeles, feel the responsibility of the trust that is ours.

To us falls the sacred duty of lighting the great Olympic torch." And so: Los Angeles "invokes and craves the cordial and interested support of all portions of our nation in helping to make these games such an event as will reflect honor and glory to the entire universe."

Billy sent a transcript of this radio address to Baron de Coubertin, who in retirement seemed to be growing ever crankier. He wrote Billy back on October 10, 1930, gratified for Billy's "friendly letter," particularly since "I had been grieved to find that whilst in Europe you had not even attempted to meet me or sent the slightest bit of a message." He did not intend to be present at the 1932 games, for he was "growing old" and busy with his own work. Though he appreciated receiving Billy's radio talk, he felt obliged to point out several errors in it, including the claim that the IOC in 1923 voted for the United States, then selected Los Angeles—"the IOC chooses a *city*, not a *nation*. . . . No such vote as you mention was given in Rome. The vote was in favor of Los Angeles, not of the U.S."

Coubertin wasn't just being cranky, though. He was also at that moment increasingly alarmed by the darkening threats of war in Europe. Just a month before, the Nazis under Adolf Hitler had emerged as a major political party, winning 107 seats in the Reichstag elections, an event that represented the start of severe political disorder in Germany, with Nazis battling Communists in the streets. In mid-October, one hundred thousand German socialists held an anti-Nazi rally in Berlin, followed a day later by three hundred Nazis storming through downtown Berlin, firing pistols and smashing windows of Jewish shops. In Italy at the same time, Benito Mussolini was calling for a revision of the Versailles Treaty, saying he could foresee "a Fascist Europe which seeks the inspiration for its doctrines and its practices from Fascism." In a speech that October in the hall of the Palazzo Venezia, he accused Europe of hypocrisy when it "babbled about peace at Geneva but prepared for war everywhere."

Near the end of his letter to Billy, Coubertin, pointing to the Olympic protocols, wrote, "It is impossible, whatever the adverse circumstances, to postpone the celebration of the Games. Therefore, you must be prepared in California to celebrate the Xth Olympiad even if war would be raging over Europe and the Eastern part of the world. You know of course that such was the spirit of antiquity, but many amongst your co-workers may ignore it or never have thought the question over. It is why I think it would be wise of you to let them understand this, strange as it may seem to them."

There is no evidence that Billy ever shared Coubertin's warning of "war raging over Europe" with any of his colleagues. Instead, in early February 1931, addressing the consequences of the Great Depression, he proposed a plan for the immediate relief of the unemployment situation in Los Angeles and Southern California generally—a plan that would at the same time help his Olympic cause. "There can be no doubt that concentration on the construction of public improvements will do much to relieve the present unemployment," he declared. "Not only does any kind of construction provide jobs for workers . . . but the purchase of materials with which to make such improvements creates additional employment." For instance, the improvements to the Coliseum that had been started less than a year before "immediately put several hundred men to work directly and helped create employment for many more indirectly." Another benefit: "Next year Southern California will play host to thousands of people who will come here to witness the Olympic Games. Every effort should be put forth to have adequate highways and wide streets for these visitors." Billy urged the "waiving of all red tape and the starting of immediate action, so that two most important ends will be served: the employment of labor and preparedness for the Olympic Games' visitors."

His campaign continued that April at the IOC annual session in Barcelona, where members formally and overwhelmingly confirmed participation of women athletes in track and field events at the 1932 games. Billy—now on his ninth trip to Europe in the interest of the LA Olympic Games—gave a final report about preparations being made in Los Angeles, for which he drew applause from members and congratulations from the IOC president, Count de Baillet-Latour. After surveying the members, Billy announced he so far had eight countries favorably inclined toward the Olympic Village—a nice start but not nearly enough to justify building the compound. Billy asked that every nation determine, at the earliest possible time, the number of athletes they'd be sending to Los Angeles, so he could avoid constructing lodgings that would be unused. In truth, it wasn't just the building of quarters that concerned him. At this stage he had no idea which countries would be participating, let alone how many athletes they'd be sending. None had formally responded to his invitation.

That didn't stop Billy from declaring publicly, upon his return to Los Angeles on the evening of July 2, that three thousand athletes from forty-eight countries would be crossing oceans and continents to compete next summer in the 1932 games. "Intense interest is growing in Europe over the coming Los Angeles meet," he said. "Everywhere the youth of each nation is getting ready. . . . The Los Angeles Games, and I say this without conceit for local things, will equal or surpass any in the past."

At least the youth of America were getting ready in that summer of 1931. In Lincoln, Nebraska, in late June, at the National Amateur Athletic Union Men's Track and Field Championships, Frank Wykoff (now being called the "Coast Comet" from LA) held off Ralph Metcalfe (now a Marquette University freshman) in equaling Eddie Tolan's world record in the first heat of the 100-yard dash. Then he held off Eddie Tolan himself in the final, again equaling the world record. At the same meet, Percy Beard of the New York Athletic Club set a new world's record in the 120-yard high hurdle as he, in the words of the *New York Times* sports writer Arthur Daley, "skimmed over the high hurdles with the grace and power of an eagle." In Palo Alto, Ben Eastman equaled a fifteen-year-old record for the quarter mile and led Stanford to a new world record in the 4 × 400-meter relay. In Honolulu, at the National Amateur Athletic Union Outdoor Swimming Championships, Buster Crabbe, representing the Los Angeles Athletic Club, retained his title as he easily trounced contenders in a blazing one-mile race.

For many of the female athletes, the National Amateur Athletic Union Women's Track and Field Championships in Jersey City, New Jersey, would be their path to the Olympics. On July 25, 235 women competed there at Pershing Field. Jean Shiley won the high jump, topping her previous year's championship mark by a full inch. Eleanor Egg upset Stella Walsh in the 100-yard dash, but Stella came back to win the 220-yard dash. To little effect, though: nineteen-year-old Mildred "Babe" Didrikson, still relatively unknown at the start of this meet, overshadowed everyone. Babe won three events before a crowd of fifteen thousand fans, who roared as she first bested Evelyne Hall, the defending champion, in the 80-meter hurdles, breaking the world's record by a full two-tenths of a second—even though the course turned out to be two feet four inches too long. Looking a bit appalled at her "slow" time in the hurdles, Babe then won the broad jump and broke another record in the baseball throw, this time by twenty feet. Pandemonium followed, with spectators rushing from the stands to get closer to this singular star. Wrote Arthur Daley of the *New York Times:* "A new feminine athletic marvel catapulted herself to the forefront as an American Olympic possibility yesterday."

The National Amateur Athletic Union Women's Outdoor Swimming and Diving Championships, held in mid-July at the Bronx Beach Baths in Long Beach, Long Island, also provided athletes a path to the Olympics. Once again Helene Madison sparkled, winning all four of her races, shattering three records. Georgia Coleman, by now rated the world's greatest woman diver, retained her title in the ten-foot springboard, executing faultlessly on all her dives. Lenore Kight took the 100-yard swim, Josephine McKim the 220-yard swim. Eleanor Holm broke the world record in the 50-meter backstroke.

Competing in fields and pools across the country, these athletes and others were more than ready: the Olympic trials, they well knew, would take place in one year, in July 1932—if all went as planned.

At this moment, not only the Olympic Games offered Billy Garland and his fellow boosters the chance to promote and advertise Los Angeles. In September 1931, in determined defiance of naysayers muttering about the Great Depression, the city staged a decidedly peculiar ten-day fiesta to celebrate the 150th anniversary of its founding. The *Los Angeles Times* thought this half-million-dollar party would, like the Olympics, "spread the fame of Los Angeles far and wide and bring in a harvest of tourists." The sight of so many Anglo-Saxon men dressed up as the city's Spanish founders, reenacting a mythic birth of the city, understandably gave some observers pause. There was Mayor Porter (who'd recently denied LA had soup kitchens, saying, "The situation is not at all alarming") outfitted as a ranchero. There was Douglas Fairbanks, riding a horse, looking very much the caballero. There was Mrs. Elizabeth Hicks Gross, the thirty-eight-year-old blonde granddaughter of a local banker, serving as the queen of La Fiesta (over objections from the city's old Spanish and Mexican families).

The party began on the morning of September 5, with ten thousand people gathered on the steps of city hall for an opening ceremony in which speakers narrated the city's history and the fiesta's director introduced "a slight, bewildered little girl," as the *LA Times* put it—eight-year-old Patti Young, ward of the Kiddie Coop Home orphanage, "who was to reign over all La Fiesta until the coronation of the Queen. A modern day Cinderella, she was to be wafted as if by fairy magic from the atmosphere of the orphanage to the regal splendor of throne rooms."

**FIGURE 9.** The fiesta at Plaza Church on September 5, 1931, during the celebration of the 150th anniversary of Los Angeles' founding. Security Pacific National Bank Collection/Los Angeles Public Library.

From city hall, the crowd moved to the Old Plaza, where a company of actors portrayed the city's founders. Then came a parade that wound its way down Figueroa to the Coliseum, where eighty-seven thousand people prepared to watch the coronation of the fiesta's queen.

First to enter for the ceremonies was "the Cinderella-like Princess of La Fiesta," the *Times* reported, riding in a royal coach, now shed of her Kiddie Koop Home garments, dressed instead in a "glinting gown of satin and silver and underneath, peeping out . . . silver slippers." Behind her came "the soldiers of Spain, and the heralds, the lackeys and all the rest," followed by a carriage bearing "her Majesty, the Queen of all La Fiesta," who alighted at a throne platform, where sat a bishop who rose and placed "a crown of brilliant jewels upon her blond head while she knelt before him." In more prosaic times, the *Times* revealed, this bishop "answers to the name of William May Garland."

On October 1, 1931, the official Olympic Campaign for Funds launched with a nationwide radio broadcast over the Columbia Broadcasting

System. Among others, Avery Brundage, president of the American Olympic Committee, spoke. Back in July, Billy Garland had claimed forty-eight nations would be participating at the 1932 games. Brundage now upped the total. "About fifty different nations are interested in the Olympic movement and most of them will be represented at Los Angeles," he told listeners across the country. "We can safely predict that the Games of the Tenth Olympiad . . . will be the greatest events of their kind ever held."

Ten days later, on October 10, President Hoover officially accepted an invitation, delivered personally by Louis B. Mayer, to formally open the Olympic Games in Los Angeles the following July 30th. They made a presentation ceremony out of it on the south grounds of the White House, where Mayer handed Hoover the invitation, encased in a red morocco-bound volume, with hand-illuminated text on sheepskin, bearing the signatures of Governor James Rolph, Chairman Henry W. Wright of the LA County Board of Supervisors, and Billy Garland. Taking the invitation, Hoover said, "Mr. Mayer, I wish you would inform the Governor of California that I accept his invitation." Hoover, planning to spend a full week in Los Angeles—his first return to California since being elected—also agreed to be the guest of honor at an international banquet to be held several days before the opening of the games.

Billy, ecstatic, described the president's announcement as "glad tidings." He believed "the entire worldwide Olympic organization will welcome the news that the President of the United States will open the games." Hoover's acceptance "will continue the Olympic tradition and follow the precedent," for in European countries, "the reigning head of the government has always performed this official function."

Mayor John Porter, saying, "This is the best news we have had in a long time," promptly announced plans for what Olympic organizers imagined to be the greatest banquet ever held in America. The largest available hall in Los Angeles would be engaged, with more than ten thousand persons expected to attend, surrounded by the colors of every nation in the world. Ambassadors, ministers, plenipotentiaries from the kingdoms and republics of the six continents—all would be at the president's table, flanked by military and naval officers in gold-braid-trimmed uniforms, with, as the *Los Angeles Times* put it, "the feminine beauty of the world appearing in a variety of costumes such as never has been seen in any one place." The guest list, the mayor said, would include the president's cabinet, ambassadors and other official representatives of foreign countries, United States senators, congressmen, army and navy officers of the United States, military attaches of foreign countries, and leaders of visiting athletic teams. They even had a date penciled in: the night of July 29—provided, of course, that this date suited the president's convenience. They needed only to find a banquet hall that could accommodate at least ten thousand people.

What were they all thinking? As the LA organizers planned a fabled banquet and predicted participation by fifty nations, talk across Europe was of postponing the 1932 games because of the Great Depression. In late September, that talk made it into news headlines. "Suggest Olympics Should Be Put Off" read a *New York Times* headline over an Associated Press story out of Stockholm on September 24. "An opinion that the 1932 Olympic Games should be postponed because of the financial depression has been expressed in Swedish sporting circles," the article began. "It is the opinion here that such a move would meet with almost unanimous support of European nations, where the depression is most keenly felt." Several European nations, the story added, "have experienced difficulty in raising the money for the expenses of their representatives at the Olympic Games."

Undeniably, Billy and LA's elite worked hard, always, to obscure whatever ran contrary to their boosterism. They were expert at fashioning myths and illusions about their city. Now the 1932 Olympic Games seemed to have become a part of that tradition, an extension of that world: another myth, another illusion, another glittering mirage shaped by an untouchable circle of shrewd visionaries. Billy certainly knew that the winter of 1931–32 was a terrible time in California. Many thousands were hungry, homeless, and jobless; soup kitchens and Hooverville encampments abounded; the suicide bridges kept drawing the hopeless; business failures multiplied. Against this backdrop, hunger marchers were demonstrating at the state capitol in Sacramento, brandishing placards that called for "Groceries not Games." In Los Angeles, activists seeking jobs marched through the streets one night, breaking windows in stores that displayed Olympic pennants. California's governor Jim Rolph thought it "impossible" to stage the games—"What do they want, riots?" he asked. Still, the governor, mindful of the power wielded by Billy's group, avoided asking for a cancellation.

For his part, Billy never entertained the notion. Although he harbored fears that news photos of the demonstrators in Sacramento would further convince nations to stay away, his public remarks even now remained positive: What the region needed, he kept explaining, was "a big, rousing, blues-chasing party" that would "show how stout the public's spirit remained."

# 14

# DESPERATE HOURS

The year 1932 in fact did begin with a big rousing party—the Tournament of Roses parade with Billy Garland acting as grand marshal. Yet such a party could not obscure the fact that the country was facing the depths of its harshest economic calamity: Between 1929 and 1932, new investments had plunged from ten billion dollars to one billion, and the nation's income had fallen by forty billion. Stocks had shriveled to 10 percent of their 1929 prices. Some eighty-five thousand businesses had folded. Automobile production, at 4.5 million cars in 1929, had dwindled to 1.1 million. Fifteen million men and women were unemployed in 1932.

Still, Billy tried to insist that the Depression was ending. "We are now emerging from a depression which was bound to follow the prosperous decade of ten years when population and realty values more than doubled," he told an interviewer in late February of 1932. "It was perhaps more acute because it came in the midst of a world depression, the aftermath of the World War. Yet we have lost nothing but faith. No real values have been destroyed. When faith is recovered, all will be recovered." Experience over forty years had taught him that "the first to lose courage . . . are the home folks right here in Los Angeles." Three times before he had seen "the people of Los Angeles lose faith . . . enough to make a depression more acute than this has been." Once again Billy ventured to make his not-quite-right prophecy about 1940:

"The 1940 census will give Los Angeles a population of 2,250,000. Realty values will increase in proportion, for realty values here always follow the census, and those who invest wisely now will double and quadruple their investment."

In a radio talk soon after, over local stations KKI and KGO, Billy urged "all Californians to return to habit" of normal living and spending, in order to speed up the resumption of good times. "It is a historical fact," he declared, "that every depression has been followed by good times. As individuals, we either hasten or retard, but we can't prevent the ultimate return to good times." All over California, "thoughtful people are returning to normal buying habits—and they are getting some of the greatest bargains of their lives."

Billy himself seemed never to have left the good times. On the evening of March 31, the day he turned sixty-six, he was toasted and feted by a crowd of two hundred at a birthday banquet in the main dining room of the Los Angeles Athletic Club. High-level state, county and municipal officials—among them Governor James Rolph and Mayor Porter—competed with representatives of realty boards, chambers of commerce, the Community Development Association, and the Los Angeles Athletic Club in paying him tribute. Some speakers traced Billy's history since he arrived from Maine in 1890 "and embarked in the then somewhat dubious vocation of real estate—when he began boosting for Los Angeles and for all California." Others talked about his "manifold activities" in the service of the community, the state and the nation. "Few Californians," the *Los Angeles Times* observed the next day, "have received in their lifetime tributes for so many activities from such high sources and so lavishly bestowed."

The evening's serious mood at times gave way to jest. The noted artist Arthur Cahill had been commissioned to paint a portrait of Billy, to be unveiled at this party and presented to the people of Los Angeles. The crowd, expecting the portrait to depict Billy in his familiar tuxedo or formal morning attire, was for a moment taken aback when the painting brought out, titled *Our Champ*, offered Billy clad only in tortoise-rimmed glasses and a two-piece Olympic running suit, his fists clenched, ready for the starter's gun to explode. "For a moment there was silence," reported the *Los Angeles Times*. "We were too shocked either to cheer or boo. The laughter was slow in starting. . . . But the news spread quickly from table to table that this was only a preliminary to the unveiling of the canvas that is to be presented to the city." It turned out *The Champ* was meant for Billy himself. He hung it on a wall in the offices of W. M. Garland & Co.

Nothing Billy might do, though, could ease the mounting misery. Conditions in America stirred anger and sorrow now, not celebration. In the spring of 1932, simmering bitterness began to spur wrathful hunger marches across the country. Rioting roiled a few cities. As athletes such as Helene Madison and Eddie Tolan were training and aiming for the Olympic Games, a riled group of World War I veterans advanced on Washington, DC, marching, for days on end, from states all across the country. For more than eight weeks, starting in early June, some twenty thousand men occupied a giant Hooverville shanty town along the Potomac, demanding early payment of promised bonuses for their service in the Great War. The "Bonus Army" became an unceasing font of angst, confusion, confrontation and distress in the summer of 1932. Its leaders lobbied Congress while thousands of veterans marched up and down Pennsylvania Avenue. Capitol police talked of a "desperate situation" and sought funds to feed the grim, starving men. Doctors called conditions in the camp "frightful" and warned of an epidemic. District officials vainly pled for the protesters to disband. One night, scores of policemen threw a barricade around the White House, shutting off automobile and pedestrian traffic, to prevent veterans from establishing a picket line. Through it all, the Bonus Army ranks kept growing as more veterans streamed into the country's capital. In mid-June, with tensions high, thousands from the camp jammed the Capitol steps to demonstrate in favor of a bill that would fund payment of their bonuses. Others, including 450 from California, began an all-night siege, sleeping on the Capitol grounds. Talk grew in the Hoover administration about calling in the marines to relieve the police guard.

Unrest in foreign countries made matters all the worse. The disorder triggered by the world war became ever more evident as the international depression intensified. People everywhere suffered from poverty, hunger and despair. Hitler and the Nazis continued their ascent in a rearming Germany; Mussolini ruled in Italy, Stalin in Russia; Japan had invaded Manchuria.

Billy Garland, and Harry Chandler too, with their close ties to Hoover's White House, watched with a mounting sense of trepidation. But there was little they could do. Billy's focus necessarily remained local: By then, despite the parties and optimistic interviews, he was desperately struggling to salvage the LA Olympics. In early 1932, five months before the games, not a single country had officially accepted the invitation to participate. The silence was alarming. Fear and anxiety abounded. By mid-April of 1932, ticket sales and guarantees of participation were still near zero, with only twelve countries fully committed (though the LA Olympic Organizing Committee, in its May *Olympic* bulletin, claimed fifty countries were sending teams). People were openly speculating that the games would not be held or would be a sham if held. By late April, less than $40,000 of the needed $350,000 had been raised to bring the United States' own athletes to the games. Wrote Avery Brundage, "We may as well face the music now and consider drastic measures. . . . If we cannot raise enough money to send more than a half dozen athletes to LA, why we will not send more than half a dozen."

Soon after, the IOC announced the suspension of an Olympic superstar—Paavo Nurmi, the "Phantom Finn" distance runner and most famous track athlete of his day, the holder of twelve Olympic medals, including nine gold, and sixteen world records. If anyone could draw an impoverished public to the LA games, it was Nurmi. But the IOC had found him guilty of taking appearance fees hidden as expense reimbursements, invalidating his amateur status. "How could you do this?" Billy asked the IOC president in anguish, but there would be no reversal (Nurmi was officially banned on July 29 after an appeal). Yet another blow landed when Japan—expected to field one of the largest and best teams—threatened a boycott of the games because the IOC wouldn't grant credentials to its recently invaded puppet state of Manchuria. Avery Brundage, as always blunt and abrupt, began openly predicting a "calamity." The Tenth Olympiad promised to be a horrifying embarrassment for Southern California, just as the region was seeking to forever establish itself.

Then came Billy's loss of support from a sizable majority of his own committee members. Speculation about abandoning the games was no longer just talk on the street or in newspapers: The California Tenth Olympiad Association itself began to consider withdrawing LA's invitation to host the games. Many directors called for a last-minute cancellation. So did half the sponsors.

This retreat dismayed Billy. When he summoned everyone to a Los Angeles Athletic Club conference room for a noon faceoff, he was in no mood to cajole or negotiate. We have given the IOC our word, he said, his face ashen. Would you forget honor and walk away? Harry Chandler, in the room that day, rallied to Billy's assistance. So did his good friend Frank Garbutt, vice president and cofounder of the Los Angeles Athletic Club. Together, they denounced the "cold feeters." Arguments broke out. Billy called a recess, during which Chandler summoned Bill Henry, a veteran Los Angeles newspaperman slated to serve as sports technical director for the 1932 games. Henry also provided backing, speaking with emotion about "keeping our sacred word." From around the conference room table, more than two dozen of the most powerful men in the city listened as Billy Garland and his allies argued on. Their words, in time, began to take hold. The recalcitrant directors finally backed down. OK, they agreed. They would hang on, they would keep going. "I guess you know how d——— near that was," Billy later wrote, in a letter to Bill Henry, "when Harry Chandler, you and Frank Garbutt rallied to my assistance one noon in the LAAC! As a matter of fact, Bill, 75% of the Committee were against the Games coming to LA."

The next day, Billy, besides ordering the printing of two million tickets for the Olympic Games, also began hiring, reserving, planning and preparing facilities—and issuing bulletins that predicted "droves." Most important, he encouraged the press to publicize news of foreign teams preparing to travel to LA—and Harry Chandler, of course, accommodated him, skillfully spinning the news. The result could be seen beyond Harry's own newspaper—a number of *New York Times* articles around this time breathlessly (and wrongly) reported on the mushrooming number of spectators and athletes coming to the games. These stories read like press releases, and in fact most ended by inviting readers to write Harry Chandler's All-Year Club (the obvious source) for more information "free of charge." At some point in all this, the woeful 1904 Olympics in St. Louis were entirely forgotten. The LA games were now being described as the "first ever" in the United States.

# COMPETING NARRATIVES

Even before he prevailed at the showdown meeting in an LA Athletic Club conference room, Billy had already rolled the dice: on April 1, at a cost of five hundred thousand dollars, construction had begun on an elaborate 550-cottage Olympic Village. At this critical moment, just four months before the games, Zack Farmer's unprecedented idea was finally rising on 250 acres of private land in the Baldwin Hills section of Los Angeles, part of the vast estate of E. J. "Lucky" Baldwin, who a generation before had made a momentous oil strike in these hills. Persuaded by Billy, his heirs had agreed to lend the acreage to the city free of charge for use during the Olympic Games.

To supervise construction and arrangements at the village, Billy had picked H. O. Davis, the swashbuckling publisher of the *Ventura Free Press,* who just then was also ferociously fighting against the country's new commercial radio broadcasting system. Davis faced a challenging task. The site was undeveloped, with no water, gas, electricity, sewerage, or telephones—nothing but bare brown hills. And yet, Davis could not in any way grade or disfigure the land, which had to be returned to Lucky Baldwin's estate as received. That meant laying out the village to fit the land's contours. That also meant sprinkling five miles of paths with water nightly, rather than oiling them—oil would have left a permanent mark. Still, Davis decided the village, to be a home, needed beauty, so he ordered the planting of twenty-five thousand geraniums, five thousand shrubs, eight hundred six-foot-tall Phoenix palms and

**FIGURE 10.** Cottages at the Olympic Village in Baldwin Hills, June 6, 1932. Downtown Los Angeles is visible just left of center. Los Angeles Herald Examiner Photo Collection / Los Angeles Public Library.

seven acres of new green grass, thereby converting sixty barren acres into lush parkland that would astonish athletes once they began to arrive.

But how many athletes? Davis had no idea; at this late date it was still impossible to determine or even estimate. "One nation might figure on sending 100 men, then arrive with ten," Davis later recalled. "About all we could do was guess." So they had to build quarters they could extend to meet the demand. They ended up erecting fifty bungalows a day, each able to accommodate four men, and were prepared to set up forty more daily if needed. All told, construction crews took exactly two months to raise this temporary city—they finished their work on June 1.

Since many countries still doubted that multiple temperaments and dietary preferences could reside together in one community, H. O. Davis responded with a village that contained distinct national sections, dining rooms, and almost fifty kitchens; countries were invited to bring their own chefs. As nearly as possible, the *New York Times* reported in mid-June, the various teams would "be given neighbors in accordance with their known national sympathies." The Latin Americans would be together except for the Portuguese-speaking Brazilians, who would align with the southern Europeans; France would be next to its Little Entente allies; Germany and the former Central Powers would line up with the Scandinavian nations; the British would dwell with other countries of the Commonwealth.

Yet in the end, the world's athletes would be part of a single village. For the first time since the competitors of ancient Greece pitched their tents on the plains of Elis, the LA Olympic Organizing Committee proudly declared, "men from all lands, speaking many tongues, were to live together in one communal establishment." More than two thousand athletes and support personnel (if they all came to Los Angeles) could be housed in the 550 cottages, each fourteen by twenty-four feet, spaced ten feet apart, spread over three miles. Every bungalow contained a wash basin, a cold-water shower and two ten by ten bedrooms, both with an entrance from the outside. Bath houses manned by attendants were spaced throughout the grounds, featuring hot showers, steam rooms, and rubbing tables. For security, besides an encompassing wall, there would be fifty-four guards, watchmen and gatemen, including eight patrolling the grounds on horseback, four by day, four by night. The village would have its own firehouse, emergency hospital, barbershop, post office, laundry, radio-telegraph station, amphitheater, saunas, recreation rooms, physiotherapy centers and a lounge furnished in chic Spanish mission style. All this would come with a splendid view and temperatures ten degrees cooler than on the flatlands of LA: the Baldwin Hills tract, just ten minutes from the Coliseum, overlooked not only Los Angeles but also the Pacific Ocean, the Santa Monica Mountains and the distant Sierra Madre range.

And—the whole point—the rent would be as Billy had promised at the Berlin IOC Congress in 1930: two dollars per day per athlete for room and board—well below actual cost. In the spring and summer of 1932, in the depths of the Depression, that was an exceedingly persuasive offer. With that figure now confirmed, not just promised, the cost of participating in the Olympics began to look a lot more possible to a number of countries.

Those countries found additional encouragement in the reduced steamship and railroad fares that Billy also could now confirm. With a cost per athlete of under five hundred dollars, late interest began to develop among countries that had been hesitating. Britain, Denmark and Sweden thought that, yes, they could attend. So did Austria. France and Italy soon after dispatched entry forms for nearly 200 participants. Germany promised 125. They still had just twenty-seven countries certified, but it seemed matters were beginning to improve.

That women athletes were going to be fully included in the Olympics also fanned interest. The IOC had been ambivalent about the matter, even after the vote in Barcelona, but an influential American voice, Gustavus Kirby (a former president of the American Olympic Committee), had campaigned vigorously for women's participation. He had a personal reason—his daughter was a talented equestrian—and enough clout to threaten a boycott by America's male track and field athletes. He also, it turned out, had support from an improbable source—Avery Brundage. Both men had been impressed by the exhibitions women athletes put on for delegates at the Berlin Congress in 1930. Kirby later appreciatively wrote of seeing "groups of young girls in the scantiest kind of clothing trotting around the fields or running tracks, engaging in 100 metre runs, taking part in the broad jump, and hopping about in all kinds of athletic and gymnastic movements." Brundage added, "Anyone who observed the exhibitions put on by girl athletes in connection with the Olympic Congress in Berlin would be a strong advocate for sports of all kinds for girls." As a result, it was finally settled: The "fair damsels," as newspaper headlines put it, would be fully competing at the 1932 games. They'd be housed apart from the men, at the upscale Chapman Park Hotel on Wilshire Boulevard, near the Brown Derby. The Chapman would give the women exclusive use of the hotel and collect just two dollars per day from each guest; the LA Olympic Organizing Committee agreed to pay the difference out of its own funds.

Now, entering the summer of 1932, the newspapers, led by Harry Chandler's *Los Angeles Times,* stepped up the Olympic Games boosterism, banging the drums ever louder. Contributions to support the American team started rolling in from public schools, police stations, United States military bases, even ships at sea. Olympic hostesses in LA held a luncheon rally where speakers cited all the games' benefits. Citizens across California began mailing out special Olympic postcards and letters printed up and supplied for free by the *LA Times*—the state's invitation to the world to attend the games. Headlines reported Olympic construction progress: "Work Speeded as Games Near" . . . "Olympic Plans Complete" . . . "Nations' Parade to be Greatest" . . . "Games' Closing to be Colorful." The LA Olympic Organizing Committee's *Olympic,* claiming fifty countries would be sending two thousand athletes, declared, "Los Angeles is Ready for Games of Xth Olympiad."

This was, however, a summer of competing narratives. Contrary to the *Olympic* report, the organizing committee did not have anywhere close to fifty countries committed to participating. Ticket sales, despite all the hoopla, despite the printing of two million ducats, were still disastrously slow—so slow that in May the Olympics ticket sales force went on half-time shifts. For once Billy and Harry's spin didn't work: The *New York Times* reported an unenthusiastic "calm" in LA about the coming Olympics, with citizens "sitting on their hands." June saw no improvement. In a July 7 letter to Zack Farmer, Avery Brundage reported he still hadn't been able to raise the $350,000 needed to finance the American teams—"We are short a considerable sum"—and so thought full American participation unlikely. This letter, Brundage emphasized to Farmer, was for his eyes only, as "the wrong kind of publicity at this time would be most harmful to our campaign." To others, Brundage wondered "if this would be the first Games to play mostly to a crowd of newspapermen."

As the Olympics organizers struggled to raise funds and sell tickets, tensions across the country at the Bonus Army encampment continued to mount. On the evening of June 17 in Washington, the US Senate voted overwhelmingly—sixty-two to eighteen—against issuing $2.4 billion (more than $40.5 billion in 2018 dollars) in new currency to pay World War I veterans their certificates in cash. Those attending the Senate session that night feared the ten thousand bitter protestors outside might try to charge the building. "City at High Tension as Hundreds Camp in Plaza," read a *New York Times* headline the next day. "Metropolitan Police and Marines are Held in Readiness for an Emergency." It never came, at least not at this time. The crowd scattered as a band started playing "America," with some leaving the Hooverville for home. Responding to the retreat and discouraging vote, leaders of the Bonus Army issued a call for recruits, aiming to swell their numbers from 20,000 to 150,000, while the *New York Times,* under the headline "Reds Urge Mutiny in the Bonus Army," reported that "organizations reputed to have the backing of Communists" had opened "a determined campaign to enlist the disappointed veterans under their own banner."

That same day—June 18—President Hoover announced he was canceling his trip to California to open the Olympic Games. He would not attend the LA Olympics, despite his close friendship with Harry Chandler, a personal invitation from Billy, fixed Olympic protocol, and the planned ten-thousand-person banquet in his honor. "The press of duties" was the official reason given. "At the moment my paramount duty is here," Hoover said in Washington. Privately, he expressed other reasons as well, knowing that California's "athletic carnival," at a cost of $2 million, would be considered frivolous by many. "It's a crazy thing," he reportedly told friends. "And it takes some gall to expect me to be part of it." Soon after, to add to the sting, Hoover's predecessor, Calvin Coolidge, turned down an invitation to open the Olympic Games as the president's representative.

Looking at the front page of the *Los Angeles Times* on Sunday morning, June 19, Billy had good reason to feel dismayed. There at the top left, the headline read, "Bonus Recruit Pleas Begun: Call Issued for 150,000 in Capital: Reds Renew Activities." At the top right, the headline read "President's Trip Off: Hoover Cannot Open Olympics." Despite all of Billy's efforts, despite the uptick in interest from other countries, the games still seemed primed for disaster. Behind closed doors, beyond the parades and promises, in the rooms of his home at 815 West Adams, Billy was now enduring haunted nights. In later years, he spoke of a recurring nightmare he'd had about Vice President Charles Curtis—Hoover's replacement, after Calvin Coolidge had declined the role—opening the games to ten thousand kids, pensioners and his organizing committee's creditors. Billy's indelible faith had started to waver. What to do? How to save this? Then it came to him: time now to play the Hollywood card.

# PLAYING HIS CARDS

In late June 1932, Billy Garland approached the celebrated movie stars Mary Pickford and Douglas Fairbanks—the queen and king of Hollywood—with a request: Would they help promote the Olympic Games, would they take to the radio to urge everyone to come to Los Angeles and participate in the games? Pickford and Fairbanks readily agreed. Their involvement wasn't by chance—Fairbanks had long been an active member of Billy's Los Angeles Athletic Club. In fact, ever since his childhood in Denver, he'd been fascinated by sports, athletes and physical activity. When he first came to New York to pursue an acting career, he'd taken formal gymnastic and fencing lessons, displaying a lively athleticism. He appreciated athletes as much as his fans revered him. He'd attended not just the Olympic Games of the 1920s but also a range of less celebrated track meets held at the LA Coliseum. He particularly liked to hang out with Olympic athletes, and he often invited them over to train at Pickfair, his and Mary's legendary Beverly Hills hilltop estate, which he'd outfitted with a world-class cinder track and well-furnished gym.

Billy's decision to involve the two in promoting the Olympic Games was more than shrewd. Fairbanks and Pickford were then considered not just big movie stars but the "most popular couple in the world," enjoying an intimate bond with their millions of fans. Mary and Douglas at Pickfair somehow managed to present the world with a style at once glamorous and approachable, projecting an indelible Southern

Californian way of life. As Billy well knew, no couple could be more influential boosters for the Olympic Games—and Los Angeles.

On June 26, Billy publicly announced his plan: Mary Pickford and Douglas Fairbanks would be the featured speakers the following Thursday, June 30, on a one-hour worldwide radio program to be broadcast across the country by the National Broadcasting Company network and by shortwave to foreign stations. The broadcast would originate in two places, with Pickford leading a group at the Hollywood Bowl, Fairbanks at the Coliseum, both accompanied by musical programs. Pickford would invite the women of the world to attend the Olympic Games, Fairbanks the men. They'd also introduce a small sampling of Olympic athletes—the highlight, Billy revealed, would be Pickford presenting the spectacular Seattle swimming star Helene Madison.

As late as the morning of June 30, this remained the plan, with the broadcast scheduled to run from 8 p.m. to 9 p.m. At the last moment, though, Billy realized they had a conflict with another major event—the Democratic National Convention, underway in Chicago, was about to start casting ballots that night for the party's presidential nominee. It must have galled Billy, a staunch Republican who over his lifetime served as a delegate to five Republican National Conventions, but he decided to postpone their radio broadcast. (The next day, after four ballots, the Democrats chose Franklin Delano Roosevelt, who on July 2, in his acceptance speech, implored delegates to join him as "prophets of a new order" in a country trapped in a "crisis of the old order.") Douglas and Mary instead broadcast their show on the evening of July 7. Introduced by Billy Garland and supported by a special band of two thousand musical instruments and a chorus of one thousand voices—the largest band ever heard over the air—Fairbanks addressed the men at the Coliseum. At the Hollywood Bowl, after extending an invitation to women—"The important thing is to be there"—Pickford spoke generally about women's participation in athletics: "While their records have not yet equaled the men's—notice I say 'not yet'—they have accomplished wonders in the short time in which they have been competing." Then she introduced Helene Madison, now eighteen, who would soon shine brighter than ever. Billy couldn't be happier: the whole world was listening.

There was a final card to play. It can't be said that Billy put this one on the table himself, at least not directly. But what unfolded in mid-July 1932 can only be seen as the result of all his endeavors. Across the country (in Evanston, Illinois; Jones Beach, New York; Palo Alto, California; and Cincinnati, Ohio) the American Olympic trials in swimming and in track and field began for both men and women athletes. Whether intended or not, Billy here created opportunities for many American children of the Depression, a range of penniless young athletes who—even while pessimistic LA business leaders wavered—had been training, yearning, and searching for ways to finance their journey to LA.

Among them were the African American sprinters Eddie Tolan and Ralph Metcalfe, who by now had vaulted to the top of the racing world; the miler Glenn Cunningham, who'd climbed out of an invalid's bed after nearly losing his legs in a devastating childhood accident; the quarter-milers Bill Carr and Ben Eastman, never ceding an inch to each other; the brash Babe Didrikson, basking in ever-more clamorous attention; the power swimmer Helene Madison, a seemingly unbeatable superstar; the vibrantly appealing backstroke champion Eleanor Holm (described by the *LA Times* as "the beautiful little New Yorker who turned down a job in the Ziegfeld Follies to train for an Olympic place"); the hurdler Evelyne Hall, a 1930 national champion who, for want of fifteen dollars, hadn't been able to travel to the East Coast to defend her title in 1931; and the high jumper Jean Shiley, who'd come out of nowhere to compete in the 1928 Olympics but now, leaving home for the Evanston tryouts with just five dollars in her pocket, had to cash in her train ticket and hitch a ride with a reporter driving to the trials.

In mid-July at the assorted Olympic meets, these and many other athletes would amaze and arouse the country with their great spirit, fierce competitiveness, and record-breaking accomplishments. They would, in the end, do as much as the boosters and Hollywood stars to ignite American interest in the LA 1932 Olympics. And some of them would have to do it on their own, with little or no support—even if they had Billy Garland as their sponsor.

In early July, the Los Angeles Athletic Club announced it would, for budgetary reasons, send only two of its women athletes to the Olympic swimming and diving trials in Jones Beach, New York. The club would fund diver Georgia Coleman and swimmer Josephine McKim, both national champions, but not the other three members of its national champion relay team (Jennie Cramer, Marjorie Lowe and Norene Forbes). The exuberant, always smiling Georgia Coleman had, at age sixteen, taken silver in both platform and springboard diving at the 1928 Olympics, then won the Amateur Athletic Union (AAU) national titles in both events for the next three years. Josephine McKim, from Oil City, Pennsylvania, now a student at USC, had taken bronze in the 1928 Olympics four-hundred-meter freestyle, then in 1929 had won three AAU championships, in the four-hundred-, eight-hundred-, and fifteen-hundred-meter freestyle competitions. Jo and Georgia's response to the LA Athletic Club: "Either we all go or we quit the team."

The club held firm so the five said they'd compete at Jones Beach "unattached," even if they had to hitchhike there. That drew plenty of press attention—including playfully posed photos of the girls in bathing suits, carrying hobo bundles over their shoulders—and an offer from a nascent American Airways to fly them to Newark at no charge. When they arrived there, Georgia Coleman told reporters, "All five of us qualified in our sectional tryouts. . . . Our club was willing to stand the expenses of Josephine and myself only. The other girls had been faithful to the club. We are all good friends and we were all angry, so we walked out together." On the East Coast, the AAU would be paying travel expenses, but again only for Coleman and McKim, so "we are splitting that up five ways," Georgia explained. "It will keep us while we're here."

So began the Olympic trials. The men's swimming and diving events were held in Cincinnati, where Buster Crabbe's narrow victory in the fifteen-hundred-meter freestyle over Ralph Flanagan, a freckle-faced fourteen-year-old from Florida, was nearly overshadowed by the presence among the spectators of Johnny Weissmuller, the former Olympic swimming king turned movie hero (a path Crabbe himself would soon follow). The women's swimming and diving trials, covered by a national radio broadcast, were held before thirty-five thousand spectators in Jones Beach, where two world records fell when Eleanor Holm broke the hundred-meter-backstroke benchmark and Helene Madison cracked the four-hundred-meter-freestyle standard—in a torrid race that saw second-place Lenore Kight, of Homestead, Pennsylvania, also better the world record. In diving, Georgia Coleman, to everyone's shock, was dethroned on the springboard by the flawless performance of tiny fourteen-year-old Katherine Rawls and on the platform dive by fellow Californian Dorothy Poynton.

At the equally spectacular men's track and field trial, held in Palo Alto, six-foot-tall Bill Graber set a new world's record in the pole vault—besting a world standard that had just been established moments before by five-foot-tall Bill Miller. Bill Carr upset Ben Eastman (who was fighting a sinus infection) in a ferocious four-hundred-meter race that foreshadowed their epic competition at the Olympics. Ralph Metcalfe twice edged out Eddie Tolan in the one-hundred-meter and two-hundred-meter races, leaving them poised for a blockbuster rematch in Los Angeles (Frank Wykoff, dominant in past months, could not match them and qualified only for the relay team). Most stirring of all, Glenn Cunningham, capping his storied comeback from tragedy, placed third in the fifteen-hundred-meter race, making the Olympic team.

Cunningham, considered by many to be the greatest American miler of all time, would go on to receive the James E. Sullivan Award as the top amateur athlete in the United States in 1933. Other athletes were in his thrall. They admired him for his talent but even more for his character. They all knew his story, what had happened to him when he was eight years old, and retold it often. Living in Kansas on a farm, he and his brother hiked daily to a small country school. One winter morning, they were the first to arrive there, so they had a job to do—get the old stove going to warm up the place. Glenn's brother, Floyd, poured what they thought was kerosene on the coals from the night before, but inadvertently somebody had filled the can with gasoline instead. The building exploded, leaving Glenn and his brother pinned against a wall, burned horribly. Floyd lived only three days. The doctors recommended amputating Glenn's badly damaged legs, saying he would never walk again. But he wouldn't buy that, so neither would his parents. He remained a bedridden invalid for two years. When he first tried to walk, in the summer of 1919, at age ten, he fell on his face. Eventually, he got himself up and outside, where he'd hang on to the plow while his dad tilled. Gradually, his legs reacted to that and he started walking. Then, in high school, he began to race. Now here he was, ready to run in the Olympics and destined in coming years to set world records for the mile.

The women's track and field trials, held at Northwestern University in Evanston, Illinois, drew the most attention of all. In legendary fashion, Babe Didrikson, twenty-one then, entered eight of the ten events, won five outright, and tied for first in a sixth, the high jump—piling up enough total points by herself in one day to win the national team championship and the enmity of some fellow athletes, who came to resent what they considered Babe's "swaggering, me-first" attitude. The AAU rule, at the time, said each woman could enter only three events, so Babe's competitors were both puzzled and shocked that officials allowed Babe, for some unknown reason, to enter eight. She had a press agent and photographers following her around. Like a three-ring circus, some of the young women thought.

There was no disputing that Babe could be abrasive. With determination, she had pulled herself up from a hardscrabble background. Five feet five and a half inches tall, she was physically strong and made no attempt to hide her abilities. Born in Port Arthur, in southeastern Texas, she at age four moved with her parents and six siblings to Beaumont. The family was not well off, but her father built a makeshift gymnasium in their backyard, and before her teens Babe already knew she wanted to be the greatest athlete that ever lived. She claimed to have acquired the nickname "Babe" after hitting five home runs in a childhood baseball game, but in truth her family always called her "Baby," and that eventually evolved to "Babe." In high school she starred on the girls' basketball team, making all-state, then landed a position as secretary for the Employers Casualty Insurance Company of Dallas, where her real job from the start was to play basketball on the company's amateur team, the Golden Cyclones, which she led to an AAU basketball championship in 1931. By then, she was already drawing even wider attention for her feats in track and field.

In fact, the commotion over her had started with her first track titles in 1930 and seemed to affect her. At the 1931 nationals in Jersey City, she arrived with a retinue and a cocky, unfriendly manner. By the time of the 1932 AAU national meet, she had become crabby and demanding, close to unbearable, alienating other athletes. All the same, newspapermen lionized her, giving her more and more coverage.

The hurdler Evelyne Hall first encountered Babe at the women's 1930 outdoor national championships in Dallas. It was a broiling hot Fourth of July. Evelyne won the hurdles there, placed in the broad jump, and started on the winning relay team. She thought Babe, at the time, was a good-natured if boastful girl. She did not imagine competing against her or anyone else in the Olympics, because the hurdles was not yet an Olympic event for women.

Still, Evelyne stuck with it, scraping together gas money to drive through blizzards to the 1930 indoor championships in New Jersey, where she won again, setting a new record in the fifty-meter hurdles. It was the custom then for the Amateur Athletic Union to pay each champion athlete's way to the next year's game, but that didn't happen in Evelyne's case. She tried every means she could to save enough money to drive once more to the East Coast for the 1931 indoor championships but, in the end, had to forfeit her title.

Now here she was in Evanston, at the Olympic trials. From her earliest years, it had been a struggle for Evelyne to get to this moment, and not just for want of gas money. Born prematurely in Minneapolis on September 10, 1909, she'd endured double pneumonia and scarlet fever as a child. After her parents divorced, she spent a few years in a Chicago orphanage, though she'd later say, "I think that kind of helped me grow a little stronger." Then when she was twelve, after she'd rejoined her now remarried mother, she developed double scoliosis. She should have been in a body cast for more than a year, but her parents were too poor even to take her to a clinic. Living with double scoliosis in its way encouraged her to develop as an athlete. That and where she lived: "As an only child I grew up in a neighborhood where they had large families. In order to survive . . . I had to develop some skills of my own. . . . I was quick and wiry and I learned to run."

Beyond being a runner, Evelyne was a daredevil. In 1929, at age nineteen, just as she started competing in national meets, someone offered her twenty-five dollars to make an exhibition parachute jump. "Of course, twenty-five dollars in those days was a lot of money," she recalled. "I was one of those who would take chances without giving it a thought." So off they went: "The pilot was a captain, but he still overshot the field. . . . I had to hang on the struts while he circled the field before it was time for me to let go. . . . There was a river right alongside of the field and I almost landed in the river. I was pulling on the strings to see if I could drop quicker so I wouldn't float over into this river. Then, when I did land, people said I landed like a rabbit—I just hopped along. I would have kept doing this because twenty-five dollars was really something sixty years ago, but members of my team said they were afraid that I would hurt my ankles. So that was the end of my jumping career."

On the day of the Olympic trials in Evanston, Evelyne, suffering from a nervous stomach, followed her usual routine, just drinking hot tea and eating unbuttered toast. After breezing through her preliminary heats, she found herself facing Babe Didrikson in the finals. Babe had beaten her the year before at the 1931 women's outdoor national championships in Jersey City, New Jersey, breaking the world's record. Now they took off again, Evelyne running alongside the taller Babe, fighting to match her stride by stride, trying to take three steps to Babe's three steps so she could, like Babe, bring the same foot over each hurdle— much easier than alternating. With a burst at the end, she gained on Babe. It looked like a dead tie across the finish line. Evelyne waited for the officials to announce the time and winner. As she recalled, "The clerk asked the two judges that were judging first place, 'Who was first?' They both said, 'Hall.' Then he asked the second-place judges, 'Who was second?' And they both said, 'Hall.' So he queried, 'Where was the Babe?' And then he said, 'Well, she must have been first.' And so that's the way the Olympics started for me." Babe had won, but they would face each other again three weeks later in the Coliseum in an even more hotly disputed race.

The high jumper Jean Shiley, also destined to compete against Babe in the Olympics, first met her at these tryouts in Evanston. Jean's family had lost everything in the Depression, which was one reason she'd cashed in her train ticket and hitched a ride to the trials. The day of the meet, so terribly hot in mid-July, Babe took to the field early, already being trailed by photographers, already the star of the show. But Jean, at twenty the reigning high jump champion, was prepared to take her on.

She'd come a long way to reach this spot. A blue baby at birth, she'd gained strength growing up in the Pennsylvania countryside, roaming freely, far from home, catching polliwogs in the creek, climbing trees, and baiting the bull on the big farm across the street by waving a red sweater. She ran with her three brothers, being the only girl in the family, and never wanted to play dolls. She wanted to play football, baseball, marbles, or whatever the boys were doing. In high school, that's just what Shiley did. One afternoon in 1927, a reporter from the *Philadelphia Enquirer* saw her jumping so high in a basketball game that she called Jean the next day to ask, would you like to compete in the Olympics? Jean said, "What is it?" for she had no idea. After the reporter explained, Jean thought, "Well, it's just another track meet."

Everything happened fast after that. The reporter arranged an appointment with Lawson Robertson, the legendary head coach at the University of Pennsylvania (and future head coach of the US Olympic teams in 1928 and 1932). Jean was petrified while talking to him—he had a gruff Scottish burr and he didn't smile. But after she showed him her routine in the high jump, he agreed to take her on, though she'd still be without a club or school sponsor—or the support of her father, who disapproved of his daughter competing in sports. She had to pay all her own expenses to the 1928 Olympic tryouts in Newark, New Jersey, where, as a complete unknown, she came in second. A week later, at age sixteen, she was aboard a ship—her first—carrying the US Olympic team to Amsterdam. Reaching the coast of Holland, they came into the canal at Rotterdam just as an American warship was departing, with a band out on the foredeck playing "The Star-Spangled Banner," the sailors giving the athletes a big salute. Watching that, Jean cried.

Once in Amsterdam, the team lived aboard their ship, taking water taxis back and forth. One day, Jean found a boxer from their team standing by the ship's rail, tears rolling down his cheeks. "I'm homesick," he told her. Jean said, "Oh, for goodness sakes, let's go do something." So they took the water taxi to shore and encountered a little man with a horse and buggy who looked to be about ninety-seven years old. He kept saying, "Show you. Show you. Show you." So they climbed into his buggy and he took them for a ride through the city, stopping finally at what Jean, getting out, realized was a museum. The little old man, still saying, "Show you; show you," took them into the museum and led them to a big picture that Jean thought had to be fifteen feet by fifteen feet (in fact, it was eleven feet eleven inches by fourteen feet four inches). Looking at it, she said, "Oh, my goodness, we have that on the wall in our living room." No one in her family knew it was a reproduction of the *Night Watch* by Rembrandt. "That was my first indication that there is a lot to see in this world, a lot to know that I didn't know," Jean recalled years later. "From then on I was just so curious about everything."

Happy to place fourth in Amsterdam, she came home changed forever. Her father realized it, but didn't like it much—and never did watch her compete. Jean finally gained support from a men's club sponsored by Wanamaker's, a department store in Philadelphia, but for two years still could practice only in the cornfield across the street from her home, jumping over a makeshift bar constructed from clothes props and nails. On her mind always: the 1932 Olympics, her abiding goal.

Now here she was at the Olympic trials in Evanston, on the same field as Babe Didrikson. Standing 5 feet 10 ½ inches tall, Jean towered over Babe. She found her opponent to be loud and obnoxious, but she had to allow that Babe certainly did everything well. The pressure built all afternoon as high jumpers, one by one, fell out of the competition. One of them protested Babe's technique, saying it amounted to illegal diving. Babe had been using the same "Western roll" style ever since she'd begun high-jumping, rotating horizontally across the bar instead of sitting up, which gave her greater elevation but also a greater chance of illegally crossing the bar head first. The judges, though, saw no foul this afternoon. In the final minutes of the meet, Jean Shiley had the lead. Then Babe, once again using the Western roll, matched Jean at 5 feet 3 ³⁄₁₆ inches. They had tied for first place—and they both had broken the world record. Their high-jump showdown was only starting: they would meet again three weeks later in Los Angeles and ignite one of Olympic history's more enduring controversies.

"We will win the women's Olympics all right," Babe said as the meet closed in Chicago. "I don't know how good the foreign girls are, but I don't think it will be good enough to beat us." Her words reverberated across the country. And other words as well: in July 1932, the athletes who'd made the US Olympic team—among them Eddie Tolan and Ralph Metcalfe, Bill Carr and Ben Eastman, Evelyne Hall and Jean Shiley, Helene Madison and Josephine McKim, Eleanor Holm and Georgia Coleman—began claiming headline after headline in the nation's newspapers.

# 17

# A LUSH NEW WORLD

Finally, it happened: the boosters' promotions, the Hollywood stars' pleas, the young American athletes' great achievements at the Olympic trials—somehow, combined, they began to take hold everywhere. A frenzy of ticket buying started in early July, and then, during the week of the Olympic trials, ticket sales skyrocketed, with thirty-five thousand seats scooped up in seventy-two hours. It now appeared that everyone wanted to come to Los Angeles—that everyone *was* coming. Despite the Depression—or, perhaps, because of it—spectators were flocking to LA by car, rail, ship, and even air, a few pioneering souls landing at Mines Field, a small municipal airport west of Inglewood that, years later, would become Los Angeles International Airport. US border control officers found it necessary to keep gates open late into the evenings, well past normal hours, to accommodate the influx from Mexico (the City of Los Angeles vainly objected, even wiring President Hoover, since this also meant Olympiad visitors could visit the Tijuana saloons and gambling halls that LA lacked). The California Department of Highways had to set up additional automobile routes from San Francisco and the Pacific Northwest—many people were coming from Seattle to cheer on their great swimmer, Helene Madison. Special trains designated as Olympic runs were heading toward Los Angeles; on one, Al Jolson had bought two hundred seats for his friends. More than seven hundred Texans, traveling as a group, had leased an entire hotel in the city. Franklin Delano Roosevelt was said to be on his way—though he later dropped his plans to avoid a political battle then brewing in California over a Senate seat. Amelia Earhart for sure would be flying in. Movie stars of all sorts were volunteering to entertain visitors. Merchants were stringing streets with five thousand flags and banners, turning downtown LA into an undulating sea of bright colors. Seemingly overnight, the number of worldwide press representatives had doubled, to seven hundred.

What's more, LA was now drawing more than spectators. A cascade of countries had belatedly signed up to participate in the games, including Japan, which dropped its boycott threat. The early core of twenty-seven nations had mushroomed at the last minute to thirty-seven, still well below the number that competed in the 1928 Olympiad (and below Billy Garland's claimed number), but a strong showing for the depths of the Depression. Even China would be sending one athlete, in response to Japan's participation—the first appearance by China at any Olympics.

Extreme poverty did not seem to be stopping many countries, either: Brazil, for instance, had little money but lots of coffee, so when its sixty-nine athletes left Rio de Janeiro (headed for the country's first-ever Olympics appearance), they sailed on a steamship carrying fifty thousand bags of donated beans, which they meant to sell off as they traveled, raising the dollars needed for the team to compete. When they reached LA on July 22, however, they had disposed of only enough beans to permit twenty-four athletes to disembark; the rest did not even have sufficient funds to pay the one-dollar poll tax required to get off the ship. They were obliged to leave LA and sail north, selling coffee during stops at San Francisco, Portland and other coastal ports. Only after days at sea—with the athletes employed on board in nearly every capacity, including serving as crew—did the Brazilian team make it to the Olympics.

As late as April 1932, the Union of South Africa had thought it couldn't afford to send anyone to the games, but the country rallied over the next few weeks, raising enough money for eleven of the twelve athletes on their team. That left only swimmer Jennie Maakal unfunded—her swimming club had failed to raise its share, and her mother, a widow with three young children, couldn't contribute. Jennie's mom wouldn't give up, though: at the last moment, she put up her own house as collateral for a loan. Jennie boarded the ship to LA—where she would end up winning the bronze medal in the four-hundred-meter freestyle.

In Australia, the nation's Olympic Federation, nearly broke, figured out that the cost of holding their next meeting matched the expense of sending one athlete to LA—so the federation canceled its meeting and instead funded an athlete. Then, not finished, the federation decided to ask every amateur athlete in the country to contribute sixpence. The change flowed in, and Australia ended up able to send twelve athletes to LA. (The best of the best from that country, they would win three gold medals, one silver and a bronze.)

And in Wisconsin, Governor Philip F. La Follette intervened personally to assure Olympic financing for the star sprinter Ralph Metcalfe. On a temporary basis, he announced, Metcalfe would replace the governor's longtime, seventy-two-year-old messenger, allowing Metcalfe to earn what amounted to $115 a month.

By the third week of July, visitors were thronging LA's hotels, and athletic teams from all over the world were arriving by ship and train. On July 17, ten thousand members of LA's Italian colony hailed Italy's team as it arrived at the Union Pacific station. On July 18, another huge crowd, many of them residents of downtown LA's Little Tokyo, greeted the Japanese team as its ship docked in San Pedro. On July 19, LA's French community sang "La Marseillaise" as the team from France stepped off its train. Two days later, the city's German community swarmed the Santa Fe station to welcome its team with two bands and much exuberant singing of "Deutschland Uber Alles."

Los Angeles—in fact, the entire country—greeted the American athletes as well, with some of the warmest welcomes saved for the extraordinary group of pioneering women. On July 18, the women's swim team and more than one hundred other Olympians left New York's Penn Station for LA in a seventeen-car "Olympic Special" train that featured air-conditioned dining and lounge cars, two chefs, a nurse, and a gymnasium equipped with showers, weights, pulleys and rubbing tables. To the athletes' amazement, cheering crowds greeted them at stops all along their thirty-six-hundred-mile journey. Also on July 18, the women's track and field team (including Babe Didrikson, Jean Shiley and Evelyne Hall) left Chicago's Union Station in its own Pullman sleeper car adorned with a banner announcing "the US Olympic Team." They too encountered a string of cheering crowds. Pillow fights, ice showers, hanging out in the observation car, talking to everyone, basking in the unaccustomed limelight—the young athletes were having a blast. In Denver the track and field team stopped overnight at the upscale Brown Palace Hotel, with each girl assigned a car and driver. They drove up to Pike's Peak, they met Buffalo Bill, they worked out at Denver University, and they answered interviewers' questions on a radio broadcast. When one reporter chose to question girls other than Didrikson, Babe started playing her harmonica to get attention—"and she was very good at it," recalled Jean Shiley, later elected team captain over Babe.

The Brown Palace honored the athletes with a banquet, but overt racism marred this event and the team's stay at Denver's premier hotel. The relay-team runners Tidye Pickett and Louise Stokes, the first black women to be selected for a US Olympic squad, had to share an upstairs room near a service area, far from their teammates, and could not attend the banquet—the hotel dining room refused to serve blacks. They ate dinner in their room instead, on trays. American Olympic Committee officials traveling with the team let this pass without protest.

Evelyne Hall, who knew Tidye from Chicago, later said she wasn't aware of this discrimination at the time. What she remembered more clearly was the train heading west after leaving Denver, past more cheering crowds at every stop, then crossing into California and reaching San Bernardino, with its abundance of orange trees, the image so glorious, a lush new world for her and many other Midwesterners. "In 1932," Evelyne recalled, "we were in the throes of the Depression. Under President Hoover we had long soup lines because money was very, very scarce. No one today can fully realize how hard these times were and how they affected the athletes. I had five dollars in my purse and that was a real sacrifice."

Early on the morning of July 22, the women's swim team, aboard the "Olympic Special," pulled into LA's Union Station, where an exuberant crowd hailed the young athletes. The women's track and field team drew the same welcome when it arrived the following morning, the squad members singing "Hail, Hail, the Gang's All Here" as they exited the train. Asked by reporters how many events she would enter, Babe said, "As many as they'll let me." There were now nine hundred journalists in town from all over the world, including seventy-seven from Japan alone, all provided sightseeing trips and special entertainment by the LA Chamber of Commerce. Given that newspapers were the primary news source of the era, the molders of opinion, Avery Brundage and Billy Garland had shrewdly solicited the cooperation of sports reporters, forming an AOC Press Committee chaired by none other than the celebrated sportswriter Grantland Rice. "Depression or no depression, slump or what not," Rice wrote in an early dispatch, "this is going to be the greatest sporting show ever held upon the crust of this spinning globe."

A Lush New World | 145

Despite the purple prose, that indeed seemed possible. "Olympic Games Visitors to Leave Fortune Here," screamed one *Los Angeles Times* headline. "In almost every part of the world, Los Angeles has been advertised," Billy Garland cheered. By July 21, with the numbers doubling and redoubling in just a few days, ticket sales had gone over 1,300,000, shattering all previous Olympic attendance records. The White House on this day announced that Vice President Charles Curtis, in place of Herbert Hoover, was en route to Los Angeles to open the games. A telegram from Curtis on July 23 advised that he would arrive in LA on the Los Angeles Limited Union Pacific at 8:30 a.m. Friday morning, July 29: "Have no official party. Will be alone except one secret service man." Against all odds, the LA 1932 Olympic Games' raucous two weeks on the world stage were about to begin.

Harry Chandler's *Los Angeles Times* exulted in an emotional editorial: "Louder, clearer, more arrestive, the call of the Tenth Olympiad, with every passing day, swells from its home city of Los Angeles into a universal summons that is reaching the farthest outposts of the world. . . . Never before was the name of Los Angeles in such favorable prominence in the press dispatches of the world. . . . The Games are just the antidote all nations required for the too long dwelling on difficulties and setbacks. . . . A rousing vote of thanks is due the Tenth Olympiad Committee and its presiding spirit, Mr. W.M. Garland. . . . Instead of the Depression discouraging the Tenth Olympiad, the Tenth Olympiad is discounting the Depression."

# A PARALLEL UNIVERSE

What sort of city did spectators, athletes and journalists see when they arrived in Los Angeles in the summer of 1932? It was, to be sure, not the same shambling village that had bid for and won the Olympics nine years before. LA's population had doubled, to 1,470,516, during the decade. The dusty pueblo had burgeoned into a world center for moviemaking, oil drilling and citrus production. No fewer than six daily newspapers covered the region, all now boisterously heralding the Olympic Games. Olympic athletes still saw plenty of open space—there were no freeways—but downtown Los Angeles looked like a bustling metropolis, jammed with noisy automobiles, streetcars and pedestrians.

The city's movie stars, including Douglas Fairbanks and Mary Pickford, lived mainly on the elevated slopes of Hollywood and Beverly Hills. The corner of Sunset and Vine was a magnet for tourists, who could dine at the nearby Brown Derby while scouting the room for celebrities. LA's civic center boasted a lustrous new thirty-two-floor city hall, designed in part by John Parkinson, architect of the Coliseum. In Pershing Square, careworn vagabonds listened as roving evangelists shared their visions. West from there on Wilshire Boulevard, at the east end of the newly widened, art-deco-style Miracle Mile, the lush and expansive Ambassador Hotel, with its famed Cocoanut Grove nightclub, had become the hottest place in town, drawing everyone from the civic elite to Hollywood stars and—in August 1932—Olympic athletes, who didn't mind dancing to the Grove's big bands. (It helped that the

FIGURE 11. Spring Street in full Olympic regalia, as seen looking north from Fifth Street, downtown Los Angeles, in late July, days before the start of the 1932 Olympic Games. Security Pacific National Bank Collection/Los Angeles Public Library.

women athletes' Chapman Park Hotel was just a couple blocks away.) Thanks to deals cut by Billy Garland's committee, visitors could get a good hotel room for two to three dollars a night, though an outside room with private bath at the Biltmore would set them back five to eight dollars, and one at the Ambassador would cost five to fourteen dollars.

Los Angeles was vibrant, nearly boiling with Olympic excitement. Thousands were crowding into the city. All day long, hordes swarmed the Olympic ticket counters—more than 1,500,000 tickets had now been sold, easily eclipsing sales at all previous games. Far and wide, flags of some fifty nations brightly adorned the streets. The central boulevards, with bunting hanging from every building, projected the feel of a carnival. People throughout the city were talking of nothing but the games. With so many athletes in town, it was hard not to spot some of them on the streets of LA, obvious in their dress uniforms.

They and all the visitors to Southern California kept marveling at the organization and attention to detail provided by Los Angeles. They marveled also at the Olympic facilities, a seven-million-dollar plant, including nine stadiums and multiple venues for track, field, swimming, diving, fencing, rowing, cycling, riding, yachting, water polo, wrestling

**FIGURE 12.** A woman surrounded by musicians hangs a sign provided by the Automobile Club of Southern California identifying the location of the nearby Olympic marathon course, part of Los Angeles' enthusiastic promotion for the 1932 games. Eyre Powell Chamber of Commerce Photo Collection/Los Angeles Public Library.

and boxing—all highlighted by the unprecedented Olympic Village ("the crowning touch . . . a stirring spectacle," reported the *New York Times*) and the newly expanded 105,000-seat Coliseum. Every one of those seats promised to be occupied on the day of the Opening Ceremony. For that matter, it looked as if the entire games might sell out. Billy rejoiced, and for good reason. This stampede for tickets in the awful depths of the Depression was nothing less than phenomenal.

The scene in Los Angeles, at least before the games began, involved Hollywood's luminaries as much as it did the Olympians. The athletes, great motion picture fans, were mesmerized by the actors. Autograph hounds, they pursued such stars as Joan Crawford, Norma Shearer,

Douglas Fairbanks, Charles Chaplin, Gary Cooper and Clara Bow (and vainly asked for Garbo). The Argentine athletes caused a tumult one day at Paramount when four of them spotted—and started chasing—Marlene Dietrich. (She had a bodyguard; they were rounded up and escorted back to the main group.) Returning the interest, movie stars often visited the Olympic Village, and Joel McCrea regularly dropped by the Chapman Park Hotel for dates with the swimmer Josephine McKim. When the American javelin thrower Malcolm Metcalf arrived at the Olympic Village and discovered his luggage was missing, none other than Will Rogers straightened it out for him. They'd "bumped into each other" as Metcalf was walking to the main office, so Metcalf told him his problem, thinking Rogers was "one of the numerous Village officials."

A good number, usually women, tried to crash the Olympic Village. One of them, Marjorie Clark, a petite Olympic hurdler from South Africa, almost made it: clad in her sweat suit and South African blazer, a green beret pulled down over her eyes, coolly cradling a sixteen-pound shot, she slipped by the doorkeeper at the village entrance gate ("just for the fun of it") and probably could have reached the cottages if she hadn't then pulled off her hat, giggled, and whooped triumphantly. Male athletes emerged from everywhere and nearly mobbed her before a guard arrived to escort her back through the gate. Other women (many young and attractive) just hung around outside that gate, among the thousands of visitors who daily gathered there, pencils and autograph books in hand, eager to glimpse the athletes. One morning, a man tried to gain entry—a heckled, harassed-looking husband who sidled up to the guard at the main gate and asked, "Is it a fact that no women can get in here?" Told that was right, he said, "Brother, I just gotta get in there and stay—I've been looking for a place like that for forty years!"

Matters were a bit calmer for the female athletes at the Chapman Park Hotel, where the Japanese swimmers liked to gift the Americans with their kimonos. One night they did get to invite boys to a garden party, but it didn't heat up much, given the 10 p.m. curfew. More than a few of the girl athletes were restless in their isolation at Chapman. "Our nickname for it was the Happy Jesus Hotel," Jean Shiley recalled. Added the diver Jane Fauntz, "I really missed the boys."

The parties and mingling with Hollywood would continue even after the games started. One day, the American relay runner Hector Dyer found himself having lunch with William Randolph Hearst in the MGM commissary, the result of Dyer's frat buddy being good friends with

Marion Davies. Jane Fauntz ended up at a swimming party where she met Groucho Marx. "Do you know what I'm going to do next year?" he joked to her. "I'm going to build a house without a pool and teach my kids not to swim." Another day, at a Paramount Studios lunch, Fauntz marveled at Marlene Dietrich's eyebrows, which had been shaved off and penciled on. On August 4, Billy Garland hosted a traditional dinner for IOC members at the exclusive Bolsa Chica Gun Club in Huntington Beach, a group formed by Billy and other wealthy businessmen in 1899 as a base for their duck and fowl hunting. On August 6, Louis B. Mayer (the only Jew on the California Olympiad Commission) hosted a luncheon at MGM Studios and afterward opened his studio to International Olympic Committee guests, allowing them to watch movies being made. On August 9, Douglas Fairbanks and Mary Pickford hosted a dinner for two hundred Olympic officials and foreign visitors at Pickfair, where the party included Charlie Chaplin, Clark Gable, Constance Bennett and Marie Dressler. Chinese girls in native costumes served the meal in a large tent on the lawn that featured Oriental rugs and Chinese bunting. After dinner, the hosts screened a preview of Fairbanks's latest movie, *Mr. Robinson Crusoe,* which the actor had just completed filming in the Polynesian islands.

In an almost surreal way, those experiencing the Olympic gala were dwelling in a parallel universe, sealed off from a country wracked by angry riots; smoky, damp Hoovervilles; and the Bonus Army band of twenty thousand starving veterans still encamped on the Capitol grounds in ever more desperate conditions. Many of the American athletes in LA were themselves familiar with breadlines: the Olympic Village and Chapman Park Hotel were sumptuous resorts compared to their families' homes, and the extravagant entertainment provided by LA's celebrities something close to unimaginable. So too was the camaraderie—the village amounted to an unexpected, if temporary, equalizer in a city where restrictive covenants had long segregated classes and races. For the first time, Billy Garland proudly pointed out, athletes from the poorest nations lived as well at the games as those from wealthy countries. "Ah, it has been lovely," a Mexican fencer remarked, "we have all been on the same plane." A *New York Times* headline read, "Prince and Butcher Live Side by Side: In Strange Olympic Village Class Lines and Distinctions Are Obliterated."

On July 27, during the very heart of pre–Olympic Games festivities, President Hoover ordered federal troops, under the command of

General Douglas MacArthur, to disperse ten thousand destitute men in the Bonus Army camps, who five days before had defied an order to evacuate. The next morning, evictions began in a scattering of the smaller camps and continued all through a sweltering hot day, marked by street fighting between veterans and the police and the death of a thirty-seven-year-old protestor, William Hushka. The tanks started arriving in the late afternoon, accompanied by saber-waving cavalry and five hundred infantry with revolvers drawn. That evening, at 9:22 p.m., some fifteen hundred federal troops led by General MacArthur (and supported by Dwight D. Eisenhower and George S. Patton) encircled the Bonus Army's main camp in the Anacostia neighborhood of Washington, DC, positioned their tanks, and began to attack with tear gas, torches and bayonets, scattering and fighting the protestors in hand-to-hand combat before setting fire to their tents. At midnight, tear gas filled the air and flames soared over Anacostia as desolate veterans, hauling boxes and suitcases, walked aimlessly away from their make-shift home. The newsreel images were devastating, but in the White House, which stood under tight guard, President Hoover announced with satisfaction that the riotous challenge to government authority had been "met swiftly and firmly." Those driven out of the camps were not veterans, he maintained, but rather "Communists and persons with criminal records."

On the same day that Hoover ordered this assault, more than one hundred of the Olympic women athletes were honored at a star-filled luncheon hosted by Will Rogers at the Fox Hills studios, located in what is now Century City. Introduced to the diving star Georgia Coleman, Rogers (with his smile, wink and wad of gum) asked, "What's your racket?" She replied, "I'm wet." Babe Didrikson offered to meet Rogers at golf, tennis, horseback riding, boxing, wrestling or any other sport he chose. "Not me," Rogers said. "I've heard about you and you're too tough. I'll take somebody easier."

At 10 a.m. the next morning, the day of the Bonus Army assault, in the observation room of the new city hall tower, Los Angeles extended its official welcome to members of the International Olympic Committee, including the IOC president, Count de Baillet-Latour. Billy had chosen the location wisely, with full intent: The glass-enclosed room, near the top of the city's tallest structure, offered a stunning view of the many Olympic sites, stretching from mountain to sea. Flags and flowers filled the chamber, an orchestra played, speeches reverberated. Billy glowed.

Early the following morning, July 29, the day after the Bonus Army assault, Vice President Charles Curtis stopped briefly in Las Vegas on the last leg of his train ride to Los Angeles. Anticipating a demonstration connected to the Bonus Army confrontation, authorities there had surrounded the railroad station with mounted machine guns and a platoon of special police with gas grenades. The vice president, still traveling alone but for one secret service man, nonetheless chose to address the crowd. Hecklers interrupted him: "Why didn't you feed some of those ex-soldiers?" a man cried out. Curtis pounded the rail of the train's observation platform in response, yelling back, "I've fed more than you, you dirty coward. Come up here and talk like that. I have worked for the bonus during President Coolidge's administration." Police quickly swarmed the demonstrators and arrested six suspected leaders.

At 8:30 that morning, Curtis arrived at LA's Central Station, where he was greeted by Billy Garland, Louis B. Mayer, Mayor John Porter and a cheering throng of citizens. A parade followed, carrying the vice president through jammed, noisy streets to his quarters at the Biltmore Hotel. Later that day, he attended the dedication of the new State Building in downtown LA's Civic Center, where—after being accorded a seventeen-gun salute by a howitzer detachment of National Guard troops—he awarded the Distinguished Flying Cross to Amelia Earhart, in town for the Olympics. Accepting, she said, "I feel as though I'm an old story to California. I can say only one thing: I started my flying career in California—and I am proud of it."

That evening, Vice President Curtis and IOC president Count de Baillet-Latour were the honored guests at the LA Olympic Organizing Committee's highly exclusive ceremonial dinner in the ballroom of the Biltmore Hotel, followed by the grand reception and ball for two thousand leading citizens in the hotel's Sala de Oro. Among the half dozen speeches delivered at the banquet, Billy Garland's stood out: "There comes frequently to every man times in his life when he experiences genuine contentment and happiness. I feel, for me, that one of those moments is at hand. To have had a part in bringing together this distinguished body of men and women gathered here from every land, fills me with supreme joy. To reflect that we are gathered here on the eve of a great world event, the effects of which will be felt by generations to come, causes one to meditate on the solemnity of the occasion."

Savory food followed for a crowd that by then must have been hungry: California melon and alligator pear supreme, clear green turtle

**FIGURE 13.** Billy and Blanche Garland arrive for the Los Angeles Olympic Organizing Committee's ceremonial dinner and grand reception at the Biltmore Hotel on July 29, 1932, the evening before the start of the games. Los Angeles Herald Examiner Photo Collection / Los Angeles Public Library.

**FIGURE 14.** The head table at the Los Angeles Olympic Organizing Committee's ceremonial dinner and grand reception at the Biltmore Hotel on July 29, 1932. *Left to right:* Count Baillet-Latour, president of the IOC; Blanche Garland; Vice President Charles Curtis; Mrs. Angelo Bolanchi of Egypt; and Billy Garland. Los Angeles Herald Examiner Photo Collection / Los Angeles Public Library.

soup, brook trout sauté Doria, breast of chicken with Virginia ham and fresh mushrooms, new asparagus polonaise, potatoes Parisienne, salad Los Angeles, bombe Olympic, and petits fours, capped off with coffee, cigars and cigarettes. Billy, wearing white tie and a broad smile, personally escorted Charles Curtis and Count de Baillet-Latour from the banquet to the reception, even as federal troops in Washington, with one final gas and fire attack, swept through the Bonus Army encampment, mopping up and ousting the last protestors.

# THE GAMES

Billy Garland awoke the next morning to a complex world. There, at his breakfast table, on the front page of the *Los Angeles Times,* he could see the headline he'd pursued for twelve long years: "Seventeen Words Today To Open Tenth Olympiad: Vice-President Curtis Ready for Ceremony Starting World's Greatest Athletic Drama." Yet that wasn't the lead story of the day. Another headline, at the far right top of the page, claimed even more attention: "Last Bonus Band Ousted: Hoover Praises Troops; Veterans Quit City as Camps Burn; Quiz Ordered and Reds Seized; White House Under Guard." And just below it, yet another headline, foretelling an ominous future: "Paris Defied by Berlin: Threat to Arm Reaffirmed; Germany Notifies France It Will Gird Self Unless Others Disarm; Hitler Troops Mass."

If the Olympic Games were a mirage, they were a welcome one. By 9 a.m. on July 30, Los Angeles had already begun to stir and prepare for what the *New York Times* called "the greatest day in its history." Milling crowds filled the downtown hotel lobbies, cars and pedestrians the congested streets. Near the Coliseum, sidewalks for blocks on end were thick with vendors and street traders. Restaurants were packed, as were the parking lots. The merriment seemed even to color the harried policemen, who treated everyone with courtesy.

Never had there been an Olympic festival like this one. With tens of thousands on their way to a sold-out opening pageant in the Coliseum, the LA Olympics' estimated attendance figures wildly dwarfed all previous games. Though the number of participating athletes was well down from past games—the boosters' inflated reports at the time claimed two thousand but it was closer to fourteen hundred—those who did come had traveled up to ten thousand miles under trying conditions to get there. Given that and the superb facilities in Los Angeles—the training fields, the stadiums, and above all the Olympic Village—Billy Garland had reason to assert that the LA games might prove to be the grandest in history.

Besides the village, the 1932 games would be introducing other lasting innovations, among them the elevated victory stand, the photo-finish camera, and the high-tech media press box. Billy had paid particular attention to that press box, which offered seats for 706 correspondents and space for 198 Dow Jones electric printing machines, capable of instantly delivering the result of each event. Directly behind the press box, commercial operators in a telegraph section stood ready to transmit stories worldwide. Los Angeles would undoubtedly be the center of global attention.

At 1 p.m. that day, anxious officials assembled the athletes at the village and marched them from their bungalows down to the long line of waiting buses. Motorcycle police, with sirens blaring, led the vans through the village gates. The ten-minute journey to the Coliseum took the athletes past miles of cheering spectators. Once at the stadium, they joined with the 127 female athletes bused in from the Chapman Park Hotel. Together they began an extended wait in the underground tunnel leading out to the Coliseum's field.

Finally, at 2:30 p.m. came the Opening Ceremony, staged before a record-setting crowd of 105,000 spectators—and 20,000 more standing outside the Coliseum, hoping vainly for tickets. Prolonged cheers greeted Vice President Curtis as he entered the stadium, to be joined at the Olympic peristyle by Billy Garland and Count de Baillet-Latour. Waves of ovations followed the three men as they moved to the elevated Tribune of Honor while a band played "The Star-Spangled Banner" backed by a choir of a thousand voices. Billy, anticipating, turned his eyes to the tunnel at the west end of the Coliseum. From there the Parade of Nations began—Olympic athletes from thirty-seven countries marching onto the field, led (per tradition) by those from Greece. Argentina followed, then Australia and Belgium. The Brazilians wore white uniforms trimmed with blue. Canada, Chile, China, Columbia, Czechoslovakia, Denmark, the one-man team from Egypt wearing a red fez—on they came. Haiti, Holland, Hungary, Ireland, Italy (the "men of Mussolini"—as the *LA Times* put it—offering the Fascist salute), Japan, Latvia, Mexico, New

Zealand, Norway, Yugoslavia. As hosts, the American team, four hundred strong, appeared last. The men wore white flannels, blue berets, and white sleeveless sweaters with red, white, and blue piping. The women wore white skirts and blouses, red vests and uncomfortably stiff new white buckskin shoes. Marching in, they couldn't help notice all the excited movie stars in the nearby stands, just off the field, leaning over a low fence, cheering and waving. As the team passed by, a thrilled Norma Shearer leaned out so far she fell over the fence.

It was a hot steamy day. Lined up on the field, the American athletes were at once playful, uncomfortable and awed. There was Buster Crabbe with Georgia Coleman, goofing around with pieces of Kleenex, sniffing and laughing, then dropping the tissues here and there. There was Eddie Tolan with Ralph Metcalfe, Mutt-and-Jeff-like roommates at the village, ready to sprint past each other. There was Bill Carr with Ben Eastman, gearing up for another colossal confrontation. There was Helene Madison, off by herself, an aloof loner with bright red fingernails and toenails. There was Eleanor Holm, flashing her appealing, vivacious smile. There was Evelyne Hall with Jean Shiley, eying a noisy Babe Didrikson—the press had labeled Babe unbeatable, but Jean and Evelyne, preparing to face her in the high jump and eighty-meter hurdles, had other ideas. The steamy heat, the long wait in the tunnel, the new tight buckskin shoes—by now Evelyne had blisters on her feet. She and Jean kicked off their shoes and tilted their little hats to the back of their heads. So did many of the other girls, their feet aching. The American women athletes stood barefoot in the Coliseum's green grass, watching as the opening ceremonies began.

Members of the International Olympic Committee and the Los Angeles Olympic Organizing Committee formed in a semicircle facing the athletes. Billy—sporting striped pants, a formal cutaway coat, top hat and a Malacca walking stick—drew a roar of welcome when he stepped up to speak, though not all in the crowd knew who he was or what he had done. He couldn't help but promote. "The United States of America," he began, "appreciating most highly the honor conferred upon her by the selection of one of her cities in which to celebrate the Games of the Tenth Olympiad, bids you a hearty and sincere welcome. This welcome is doubly emphasized by the State of California, whose traditional hospitality is known the world over. . . . The citizens of Los Angeles are thrilled by your presence and are happy because you are their guests. . . . It is our earnest hope that . . . the International Olympic Committee will feel itself vindicated in its choice of Los Angeles as the setting for the world's supreme congress of sport."

**FIGURE 15.** Vice President Charles Curtis presides over the opening ceremony of the 1932 Olympic Games at the Coliseum, July 30, 1932. George Watson, George R. Watson Olympic Photograph Collection.

A moment later, Vice President Curtis approached the microphone and doffed his familiar silk topper. The Olympic Games' sacred protocol limited him to seventeen specific words, but he added a preface: "In the name of the President of the United States, I proclaim open the Olympic Games of Los Angeles celebrating the Tenth Olympiad of the modern era." Then he pushed a silver button near his chair.

High atop the peristyle at the east end of the Coliseum, the Olympic flame burst into being, underscored by a ten-gun salute. A vast cloud of two thousand pigeons (replacements for doves) wheeled and circled above the crowd as some of the American athletes playfully covered their heads and ducked. A two-thousand-person choir rose to sing the Olympic hymn (Bradley Keeler's "Hymne Olympique"). A single Olympic athlete, Lieutenant George C. Calnan, USN, stepped to the microphone to deliver the Olympic oath. Again the choir rose to sing as the athletes marched out of the stadium. Evelyne Hall felt filled to the brim.

**FIGURE 16.** The Los Angeles Memorial Coliseum (then known as the Olympic Stadium), with the Los Angeles Swimming Stadium in the upper left, during the 1932 games. Security Pacific National Bank Collection / Los Angeles Public Library.

"It was really something to swell inside of you," she'd say many years later. "It was really electrifying."

No one in the stands moved from their seats—the announcer, in fine Los Angeles style, had asked the crowd to give the athletes the opportunity to drive away without a traffic jam. Thus ended what the *New York Times* called "the greatest spectacle in California history."

The games were about to begin, but of course, the 1932 LA Olympics involved more than the sporting events. The elite of Los Angeles did not all immediately rush to fill the Coliseum. On Saturday afternoon, after the Opening Ceremony, a number of them attended an informal tea at Billy's home in honor of Vice President Curtis. That evening, Curtis dined at Louis B. Mayer's beach house on the Pacific Coast Highway in Santa Monica, where he stayed overnight (Mayer, not just a friend, was vice chairman of the State Republican Committee). On Sunday morning, Curtis and Mayer made social calls to the homes of Billy Garland and

Harry Chandler. Then they toured the Olympic Village, with H. O. Davis as guide and athletes as waving greeters. A lunch and three-hour reception for Curtis followed at Mayer's home, even as the first events got underway at the Coliseum. It seems everyone of importance was present at this reception: Governor Rolph, Mayor Porter, and, as the *Los Angeles Times* put it, "virtually every well-known political figure in this section, a number of judges and other public officials, a group of the prominent social leaders of Los Angeles, and a number of motion-picture notables, including producers, directors, writers and actors."

What a bash it must have been. Louis B. Mayer's beach house, a twenty-room, 6,416-square-foot Spanish-style dwelling—commissioned by him in 1926, designed by the MGM art director Cedric Gibbons, constructed by MGM carpenters and electricians—sat on an oceanfront tract in Santa Monica known as Rancho San Vicente. Besides the sand and sea, partygoers wandering through the house could admire a gate-keeper's apartment, thirteen onyx bathrooms, wood-beam ceilings, wrought-iron balconies, foot-thick exterior walls, a swimming pool, and a projection room. Billy Garland certainly was there—this was not the type of event he'd miss—so he would have heard Louis B. Mayer at one point reveal "a little incident of the morning" that he thought "shouldn't go untold."

It seemed that Vice President Curtis had spotted a story in that day's *Los Angeles Times* headlined "Jim Thorpe Denied One Little Ticket; Weeps as Huge Parade Passes." Curtis had read on. The story described how Thorpe, the Native American champion who in the 1912 Olympics had resoundingly won gold medals in the pentathlon and decathlon, only to be stripped of them because he'd played two years of semi-pro baseball, wept in the press box the day before as he watched the opening day parade of athletes in the Coliseum. He was present only because he'd managed at the last moment to borrow a pass, after being rebuffed by Olympic officials when he sought a season ticket to the games. "They forgot that Jim was a great hero for the United States twenty years ago," the article concluded. "Fame is fleeting and the years dim the luster of the past. Not even a ticket for Jim, the Indian."

As it happened, Curtis, like Thorpe, was part Native American. The news story astounded him. Please, he told Mayer, obtain a season pass in my name and present it to the great Indian athlete. Mayer had done just that. When the movie mogul finished sharing this account with his illustrious guests, Curtis offered his own thoughts: "I was not only surprised. I actually felt almost tearful when I read that story. If I had known Jim Thorpe was here and had not been made an honored guest at the Games, I'd have invited him to ride to the stadium with me yesterday and sit right next to me throughout the opening ceremony." He added, "I'd have felt honored too, because Jim Thorpe is the greatest athlete the world ever has seen, and I'm proud to think that he and I are descended from the American Indian race."

No record exists of what Billy said or thought about this incident. It's known only that the vice president later that evening paid him tribute as he was boarding the Santa Fe Chief with his sole secret service agent, bound for his home in Topeka: "I can't think of the Olympic Games without realizing what a debt the citizens of Los Angeles and all of America owe to William May Garland as the man whose untiring efforts made this splendid culmination possible. Mr. Garland has every right to feel happy and proud today."

To no surprise, Babe Didrikson claimed the most attention in the early hours of the meet. Even before the games began, she had been on center stage, as much for her boastful personality as for her spectacular athletic achievements. In Los Angeles in the dark depths of the Depression, here was a bright light with attitude. She was the first woman superstar to compete at the Olympic Games.

She was also a clever master at sometimes deceptive self-promotion. She would forever lament that Olympic rules didn't allow her to compete in more than three events, but this wasn't true—there was no such rule. Despite her five titles at the Evanston trials, Babe chose to compete in just three events in LA: the javelin throw, the high jump, and the eighty-meter hurdles. She set her own limits, probably selecting the contests where she thought she had the best chance to win.

Her first event—the javelin throw, making its debut as an Olympic competition for women—came at 5:30 p.m. Sunday, not long after the reception for Vice President Curtis concluded at Louis B. Mayer's beach home. Babe threw first, and her initial toss will forever be part of Olympic lore: As she released the throw, her hand slipped. Instead of rising into a customary arc, the javelin sailed in a straight line, "much after the manner of a catcher pegging to second base," *LA Times* sportswriter Braven Dyer reported. Yet incredibly, even without elevation the javelin kept flying, traveling 143 feet 4 inches, more than eleven feet beyond what the LA Olympics official program listed as the world's record.

Some fifty thousand spectators, many just realizing the event was under-way, burst into a wild cheer. Babe didn't come close to matching that throw on her next two tries, but neither did any of the other contenders. With one toss in the early moments on the beginning day of competi-tion, Babe had her first gold medal.

But she did not have a world record. Despite the official program, despite multiple *New York Times* reports, and despite the next day's *Los Angeles Times* headline—"Babe Didrikson Cracks World Javelin Record"—that title still belonged to Nan Gindele, who four weeks before, in Chicago, had thrown a javelin 153 feet 4 1/2 inches. No mat-ter. When Babe arrived back at the Chapman Park Hotel that after-noon, she made a triumphal entrance, greeted by autograph-seekers and a lineup of teammates clapping and cheering. "No, I haven't got a new technique," she grinned. "My hand slipped when I picked up the pole. It slid along about six inches and then I got a good grip again. And then I threw and it just went."

Four days later, Babe competed again, against Evelyne Hall in the eighty-meter hurdles—another event making its debut as an Olympic competition for women. This race would yield one of the most contro-versial outcomes of the games. Evelyne had held her own against Babe in Evanston, finishing in what looked to be a dead heat. In fact, Evelyne thought she'd won. Now she was lined up next to Babe again, in the Coliseum. Though usually effervescent and gregarious, she felt shaky this afternoon. Coming through the tunnel, out to the field, Evelyne had been so nervous she kept bumping against the concrete walls. When she reached the field and saw the thousands and thousands of spectators, her legs buckled so badly someone had to bring her a chair. Yet when the race began, she exploded into the lead, with Babe late off the mark (hesitating after an initial false start). Babe chased her down, she being the faster runner, Evelyne the more accomplished hurdler. The two cleared the last, fifth hurdle together. On they ran, dead even as their forward feet hit the ground just before the finish line. The officials con-ferred for half an hour as cheering athletes from other countries called out to Evelyne, "You won, you won, you won." Many spectators and sportswriters thought they at least had tied—Damon Runyon wrote, "They hit the tape apparently right together." The officials, in the end, disagreed: Babe had won by a sliver, though both were timed at 11.7 seconds—a new world's record that would stand for seventeen years. Evelyne was deeply disappointed, but—given what had happened at the Evanston trials—not surprised. Said Babe to a reporter, "Sure, I slowed up a little. I just wanted to make it a good race. Win the next event? Well, I hope to. That's what I'm here for."

Babe's third and final event, the high jump, was no less controversial. She and Jean Shiley had tied for first place at the Evanston trials, both breaking the world record as they cleared 5 feet 3 3/16 inches. Now they faced off again in the Coliseum in a classic showdown. Following her coach's orders, Jean had rested all week, abstaining from Olympic events and parties. During that period, more than a few athletes had visited Jean in her Chapman Park Hotel room, begging her to beat Babe, whose relentless self-promotion had become ever more maddening. Jean went to work once the competition started, and so did Babe, still using her unconventional Western roll technique—which the Canadian and German jumpers, all through the heats, had been protesting. One by one the other contenders were eliminated, leaving only Babe and Jean on the field. Both easily eclipsed the existing world record of 5 feet 3¾ inches, and kept going, with a capacity crowd raucously applauding. Both cleared 5 feet 5¼ inches, jointly setting a new world record. Both failed at 5 feet 6 inches. In a jump-off meant to decide who won gold (there were no Olympic ties at the time), both, after a long rest, again cleared 5 feet 5¼ inches. But then—finally—the judges interceded: Babe's last jump, they declared, had been an illegal dive. Though she had been using the same technique in meet after meet, the Western roll left her susceptible to bringing her head over the bar ahead of her legs, which wasn't allowed—and that's what the judges decided she'd done on this jump. Jean, who instead used the standard scissors kick— with her legs and hips clearing the bar first—took the gold. Babe objected: "I haven't ever been ruled out for diving in any meet before. I think they should have at least warned me earlier in the jumping. . . . I jumped as high as she did, or higher." But her pique didn't last. At a party that night honoring Jean's victory, Babe joined in the applause, and later told a sportswriter, "Miss Shiley is a fine jumper and we were certainly flying high, weren't we?"

The outcome, at any rate, did Babe no harm—in fact it helped shape her illustrious future: Outraged at the judges' ruling, Grantland Rice invited Babe to join him and three other equally incensed sportswriters (Braven Dyer, Westbrook Pegler and Paul Gallico) at the Brentwood Country Club for a round of golf. She'd played only a few times before but easily held her own with the men, scoring an eighty-two. Hooked, she would go on to become the century's most celebrated professional female golfer and the best all-around woman athlete of her era.

All told, the seventeen trail-blazing American track and field women dominated, winning five gold medals in six events, setting an Olympic record in each, while also garnering three silvers and a bronze. That American women were relatively new to Olympic track and field events, that European women had been competing for many years, made this achievement all the more remarkable. In his official report, the American Olympic Committee team manager, Fred Steers, called the 1932 US women's track and field team "the strongest aggregation of its kind in the history of athletics."

The twenty American women swimmers and divers, dubbed the "glamour girls" of the games by newspaper headline writers, also shone, selling out the ten-thousand-seat swimming stadium every day. But superstar Helene Madison had to battle all the way. At age nineteen, she held every freestyle record from one hundred yards to a mile, yet before the games she still worried about the competition: "I expect that every existing woman's swim record will be beaten in the Olympics. From what I hear all the entrants are swimming faster than they ever have before. The winners, whoever they are, will have to hang up new world records." Helene proved prescient: in the preliminary and semifinal heats for the hundred-meter freestyle—a race she was expected to own, being the world record holder—three other girls broke the Olympic standard, two of them besting Helene's times. Helene was scared for the first time in her competitive life. She particularly feared Willie den Ouden, a petite fourteen-year-old from Holland, whose qualifying time in her semifinal heat had topped Helene's and set a new Olympic record. In her own heat, Helene had tired in the home stretch and seemed to lack her usual self-confidence. Press reports began suggesting she might not be able to beat Willie in the final on August 8.

As it happened, Helene nearly missed even being in that race. Strolling out to the stadium pool deck just as the clock ticked to 3 p.m., after changing into her swimming suit in the apartment of a friend, she didn't realize she was late until somebody urged her to hurry. Hearing the announcer already calling off the event, she leapt into the pool to get wet and climbed back out just in time to arrange herself for the start. The takeoff was perfect for all six swimmers, who hit the water at the same time, but Helene quickly took the lead, with Willie den Ouden close behind. At the twenty-five-meter mark Helene pulled ahead by a full length. Willie, accelerating, closed within two feet. Again Helene moved a length in front, looking in command. Then, at the seventy-five-meter mark, momentarily disoriented, she swerved against the rope on the right side of the lane, slowing enough for Willie to catch up. As ten thousand spectators in the Los Angeles Swimming Stadium cheered wildly, the two swimmers raced the last twenty meters neck and neck, fighting to the end—before Helene, stroking with championship power, touched the wall a split second ahead, setting a new Olympic record. "After it was all over I cried," she told a reporter. "I was terribly happy about winning because I have been pointing for this race for two years." She purposefully had paced herself: "I took a lead of the field and instead of trying to gain on that, I just tried to keep it. It was much easier for me in the finish. I wasn't exhausted. I'm not tired now."

On August 11, a cheering, overflow crowd of twelve thousand came to see nineteen-year-old Eleanor Holm compete against five other top swimmers in the hundred-meter backstroke final. Two days before, she had broken the world and Olympic records in her blazing semifinal heat, leading by a full length at the end, ahead of two previous titleholders. She didn't quite match that in the final, but she led all the way against fierce competition from the Australian Bonnie Mealing, the two remaining only inches apart until Eleanor launched a blazing sprint finish, with twenty-five meters to go, that clinched first-place gold by almost two yards. The American women springboard divers dominated as well, sweeping their competition, winning all three medals, with Georgia Coleman taking gold—but not before a Hungarian judge required Georgia and Jane Fauntz to change into replacement swimsuits, because the ones they were wearing exposed too much of their backs. ("It made no difference to the officials that the back exposed was pleasing to the eye," grumbled an *LA Times* writer.) Soon after, the American women platform divers also swept the field, this time Georgia Coleman taking silver, and eighteen-year-old Dorothy Poynton gold. Dorothy, competing despite a sprained back wrapped heavily with adhesive tape, clinched the title with a flawlessly executed running swan off the ten-meter platform that drew applause from twelve thousand enthusiastic spectators.

Billy was delighted—both divers were representing the Los Angeles Athletic Club. For all his interests in the games as a promotion of Los Angeles, he also, as the longtime LAAC president, harbored an enduring commitment to the sporting events. The LAAC's respected program of sponsoring and training athletes stretched back to 1913, and now, in the Coliseum, Billy could often be seen at the victory stand. The LA Olympic Games had introduced a new way of presenting medals—

**FIGURE 17.** Diving star Georgia Coleman raises the American flag at the Olympic swimming stadium on July 7, 1932. *Left to right:* Marion Dale, Jennie Crammer, Olive Batch Voight, Georgia Coleman, and Dorothy Poynton. Los Angeles Herald Examiner Photo Collection / Los Angeles Public Library.

rather than distribute them to everyone marching in a long single line at the closing pageant, they were presented in a special ceremony at the end of each event, with the athletes on a pedestal facing the Official Tribune, the winner of gold in the center on a slightly raised platform, the trio's homeland flags waving and a band playing the victor's national anthem. Count de Baillet-Latour, as president of the IOC, would hand up the actual medals, accompanied by two others of his choosing—and for the American victors that would usually be a genial Billy Garland, vigorously congratulating the athletes.

The same afternoon that the women platform divers swept their field, the American women blew away the competition in a 4 × 100-meter freestyle relay race anchored by Helene Madison. Delivering a

**FIGURE 18.** Evelyne Hall, who won the silver medal in the eighty-meter hurdles event, flanked by Douglas Fairbanks and Mary Pickford at the Los Angeles Memorial Coliseum during the 1932 Games. Security Pacific National Bank Collection / Los Angeles Public Library.

remarkable team performance, they led from start to finish, breaking the world record and surpassing the 1928 Olympic record by more than nine seconds—with each of the four swimmers beating the individual 100-meter Olympic record. The next day, a capacity crowd saw one of the most memorable competitions of all time in women's swimming: the 400-meter freestyle pitting Helene Madison against seventeen-year-old Lenore Kight, who had broken the old Olympic record during the Jones Beach trials. Madison started fast but so did Kight, and they remained neck and neck, shoulder to shoulder, the entire eight-length race, never more than a one-foot distance dividing them. Helene was quicker on the turns, a true master, but Lenore countered with greater swimming speed. After trading the lead twice, the two were abreast

FIGURE 19. The US women's championship 4 x 100-meter relay team, after winning gold medals on August 12, 1932. *Left to right:* Josephine McKim, Helen Johns, Eleanor Garatti Saville, and Helene Madison. Security Pacific National Bank Collection/Los Angeles Public Library.

with half a pool length to go, the crowd on its feet screaming and yelling. Five meters from the finish, they were still head to head. Again Helene closed with power. The judges had to study photos and deliberate—before ruling that Helene had won by an inch. Her time was 5:28.5, Lenore's 5:28.6, both well under Olympic and world records. The *Los Angeles Times'* Bob Ray called this "a magnificent race that will never be forgotten by those who saw it." When it was over, Helene swam over to Lenore and embraced her.

That night, she was seen dancing at the Cocoanut Grove with Clark Gable (half a head shorter than her). "Queen Helene," they were calling her. Also, "a majestic bronze figure of femininity." Topping even Babe Didrikson, she had won three Olympic gold medals and now found herself in a whirl of publicity, national radio interviews, and rumors about a possible movie career.

In truth, so did a number of the female swimmers and divers, who, all told, took gold in six of their seven events. The sportswriters covering the games couldn't resist slavering a bit. "An amazing thing dawns upon all those thousands in the stands," wrote *Los Angeles Times* staffer Jean Bosquet. "These girls who give demonstrations on the field below of their speed, strength and stamina have—sex appeal, too. The cheers for the girls of the Olympiad, trim and lovely in their abbreviated costumes, are mighty." Eleanor Holm, he observed, kicked with "lovely legs ... beautiful legs." Dorothy Poynton was "still in her teens, but rounded like nobody's business." Even *The Times'* lone woman sports reporter, Muriel Babcock, got into the game: Evaluating potential screen stars, she wrote, "The dope is that of the women, pretty dark-haired big-eyed Eleanor Holm, backstroke champion of America, is one of the best bets. Miss Holm is considered one of the most beautiful girls of the Olympics.... Josephine McKim is nominated by the writers of The Times sports department as another beauty. Also, Georgia Coleman, as a second Miriam Hopkins.... And Helene Madison." Whether they sought it or not, many of the women athletes drew this kind of attention during the Olympics, in part because they were pioneers, in part because they were remarkable athletes, and in part because the sportswriters found them, as Grantland Rice put it, "easier to look at."

Though they didn't get rated on their looks, the great men athletes also drew accolades for competing at extraordinarily high levels. In track and field, the hundred-meter finals on August 1, featuring the two star African American runners, Eddie Tolan and Ralph Metcalfe, drew particular attention. They were as much trail-blazing pioneers as the women, for only a handful of black athletes had appeared in previous games, in part because most American Olympic contestants were sponsored by local clubs that didn't allow black members. Tolan and Metcalfe both had risen out of their tough, impoverished Midwest childhoods through college athletic scholarships—Eddie at the University of Michigan, Ralph at Marquette University. Yet they were a study in contrasts: Metcalfe was a strong, muscular six-footer, while Tolan, a bit chubby, stood just five feet five inches, wore thick horn-rimmed eyeglasses taped to his head, and ran always with a heavy elastic bandage wrapped around a knee he'd damaged years before, playing football. They had different running styles as well: Metcalfe held back and paced himself, saving for an explosive finish, while Tolan ran as fast as he could from the start. Tolan was the underdog, Metcalfe the NCAA champion who had prevailed at the Palo Alto trials. They roomed together at the Olympic Village, where Eddie would always try to psych out his rival. "Gee, I wish I'd been assigned anywhere else," Ralph told another American athlete at the time. "He's just driving me crazy. All the time he's rattling me."

At the starter's gun for the hundred-meter final, a Japanese runner (Takayoshi Yoshioka) burst into the lead, but at the halfway mark Tolan shot past him, with Metcalfe, as usual, lagging a yard behind. Then, with twenty meters to go, Metcalfe unleashed his ferocious kick, pulling even with Tolan. They ran neck and neck the rest of the way. Eight yards from the tape, four yards, two, one—still they were absolutely even. It looked like another dead tie at the end. "At one yard there was nothing whatsoever to choose between them," wrote Arthur Daley of the *New York Times*. "Neither was there at the tape." The consensus in the press box was that Metcalfe had won, and some reporters, aiming to beat the competition, even sent out stories declaring him the victor. Reportedly, US Olympic team coach Lawson Robertson agreed, saying, "Sure I saw Metcalfe win," as he paid off a bet he'd made on Tolan. Both runners flashed smiles as they returned from the finish line, but it appeared Eddie was congratulating Ralph. Again the judges deliberated at great length, studying both film and still photos of the finish. Two hours passed before they finally decided that Tolan had won the gold by two inches, though both had run the race in 10.3 seconds, an Olympic record and tie with the world record.

This and the eighty-meter-hurdles race between Babe Didrikson and Evelyne Hall would end up being the two closest and most disputed events of the 1932 games. But whatever the ambiguity at this moment, it could not obscure the fact that, for the first time, a black man had won the prestigious hundred-meter race—and another black man had placed second. This was, in truth, the first running victory ever scored by a black man during modern Olympic competition.

Two days later, in the two-hundred-meter race, the underdog Tolan again beat Metcalfe, amid yet more controversy. Though it was impossible to really tell because of their staggered starts, Metcalfe assumed he was securely in the lead until Tolan zoomed past him coming around the curve. Something didn't seem right, and it wasn't: officials later discovered that whoever had designated the starting points in the staggered lanes had accidentally given Tolan at least a one-full-stride advantage over the rest of the field. Yet he'd won by more than that advantage, so the result stood, with Metcalfe ending up in third place, behind his teammate George Simpson, who took silver for an American sweep.

Tolan would be the 1932 games' only double-gold winner in men's track and field events. A grinning Billy Garland presented medals to Eddie and Ralph at the victory stand.

The Japanese men dominated the swimming events, winning five of the six races and taking four seconds and two thirds as well. With a seventeen-swimmer delegation, eleven still in their teens, they stole the show, ending America's long-standing international leadership in aquatics for men. The gold medalist in the 1,500-meter freestyle, Kusuo Kitamura, was at fourteen the youngest male ever to win an Olympic swimming event; the victor of the 100-meter freestyle, Yasuji Miyazaki, was fifteen; the backstroke winner, Masaji Kiyokawa, was nineteen. On the afternoon of August 9, the Japanese 4 × 200-meter-relay team bested the Olympic and world record by a remarkable 37.4 seconds, with three of the team's four swimmers breaking the world record for 200 meters. After the races, and only in private circles, a story circulated that the Japanese men swimmers had been given pure oxygen. This was never confirmed, but when the diver Jane Fauntz asked Buster Crabbe about the rumors, he told her he'd felt disconcerted on the starting block to see an adjacent Japanese athlete with a mark around his nose and mouth as if a suction cup had been recently removed.

As it happened, only Buster Crabbe prevented a Japanese sweep in the swimming events. In the 400-meter freestyle, Buster expected his toughest competition would be the overpowering Japanese, so when the race began, he stuck close to them—not realizing that his greatest threat was France's Jean Taris, who in the heats had tended to fade. Now Taris remained far ahead and showed no signs of slowing. "Suddenly I realized he had probably been faking it in the trial heats," Buster recalled. "So I took off after him." The crowd of twelve thousand roared as ushers and swimmers from all countries—including Olympic champion Johnny Weissmuller—rushed to the side of the pool. Buster kept closing the gap. Bedlam broke loose in the stadium. Buster thought he couldn't make it: "I was maybe 30 seconds from the finish, and I was completely spent. I wanted to stop." He didn't, though. Three yards from the finish line, they were in a dead heat. Buster kicked hard. "The only thing that kept me going was the tremendous noise of the crowd. Everyone was screaming." For good reason—Buster ended up beating Taris by a paper-thin tenth of a second, establishing an Olympic record.

The 400-meter finals in men's track offered one of the most sensational races in the Olympics, pitting the celebrated NCAA champion Ben Eastman of Stanford University against challenger Bill "Wee Willie"

**FIGURE 20.** American divers and swimmers celebrate their gold-medal victories, August 1932. *Left to right:* Michael Galitzan, Clarence "Buster" Crabbe, Helene Madison, and Georgia Coleman. George Watson, Delmar Watson Photography Archives.

Carr, now at the University of Pennsylvania. To just about everyone's surprise, Wee Willie (who stood five feet six inches) had upset Ben twice that July, at the Olympic trials and at a meet in Berkeley, instantly forging a storied rivalry: "Their relative merits have caused more debates than anything in the recent history of American athletics," reported Arthur Daley of the *New York Times*. Ben had dominated for two years, earlier in 1932 becoming the first to run a 440-yard race under forty-seven seconds; Wee Willie, meanwhile, had won every 440-yard and 400-meter race he'd entered. Their race now would definitively determine who reigned—the shorter, dark-haired sprinter Carr, or the lanky, blond pace-runner Eastman. None of the others in the race mattered—these were the quarter-milers of the century.

At the starter's gun, the long-striding Eastman took an imposing lead, but Carr came on strong, beginning to move up, gliding with perfect rhythm. Around the last turn they joined, running neck and neck for some sixty meters, the crowd of seventy thousand roaring them on. Then Wee Willie began to advance, with Ben fighting furiously to keep up. He could not. In a tremendous burst, Carr accelerated near the finish line, hitting the tape going away, four feet ahead of Eastman. They both had broken the world's record, with Wee Willie shaving a full four-fifths of a second off the standard—a remarkable time of 0:46.2. Here, the sportswriters all agreed, was the greatest 400-meter race in history.

The Americans, with an overabundance of confidence, had anticipated sweeping all three medals in the men's pole vault final, but two of their best faltered, including Bill Graber, who'd set a world record at the trials in Palo Alto just weeks before. For the United States, that left only Bill Miller of Stanford in contention for the gold. Heavily favored, he found himself facing surprisingly strong opposition from a young, slightly built Japanese, Shuhei Nishida—who threatened to pull off a stunning upset. Their showdown began at fourteen feet, which Miller easily cleared on his first try. Nishida failed on his first try, and failed again on his second—before smoothly clearing the bar on his third attempt, tying Miller as seventy-five thousand spectators stood and cheered his gutsy performance. Officials raised the bar to 14 feet 1⅞ inches. Both Nishida and Miller failed on their first two tries. Then Nishida failed on his third and last attempt. It was all up to Bill now. He gripped the bamboo pole and stepped to the track's far edge. Athletes and officials elsewhere on the field walked over to observe. Bill studied the runway, looked at the bar and started to run. Step by step he accelerated. Then up he went. The crowd roared as Bill cleared the bar—but going over, his arm hit the rod, which wobbled precariously as Bill fell on his back in the sawdust pit. While everyone watched, the bar stopped wobbling, stayed in place. Spectators and other athletes alike cheered wildly. Bill Miller had won the gold. Shuhei Nishida, standing nearby, studied the now-steady bar, then approached Bill, still lying in the sawdust. Smiling broadly, Shuhei reached out a hand and helped Bill to his feet.

In the twenty-six-mile marathon, held on Sunday afternoon, August 7, the Argentine Juan Carlos Zabala, a twenty-year-old newsboy, turned in one of the most stirring performances of any Olympics. He'd endured a bleak childhood after losing both parents at an early age. While in an orphanage or reformatory (the stories vary), he drew the attention of a track coach who became his foster parent. Before arriving in LA for the

Olympics, Zabala had amazed a crowd in Czechoslovakia by finishing a marathon fourteen minutes ahead of the second-place runner. Yet he had failed even to complete another marathon held six weeks before the Olympics, quitting at the nineteen-mile mark. Slightly built, standing just five feet five inches, weighing 115 pounds, he did not seem to have the needed stamina. From the gun, however, he led the twenty-eight Olympic marathoners out of the Coliseum. Others passed him four times throughout the long run on the spectator-crowded streets of Los Angeles, but he regained the lead each time. During the last two miles heading back into the Coliseum, three runners again challenged him in a fierce battle, and Zabala now held his lead. At twilight, two and a half hours after the start of the race, trumpets sounded in the Coliseum, bringing to their feet seventy thousand spectators, who began peering at the tunnel on the west end of the stadium. Through it darted Zabala. He was still in the lead—though not by much. Three other runners suddenly appeared out of the tunnel: Samuel Ferris of Great Britain, Armas Toivonen of Finland and Duncan McLeod Wright, another Englishman. A more remarkable finish had never been seen in an Olympic marathon. After twenty-six miles, four runners were on the track simultaneously with only three-quarters of a lap left to run—the first time in Olympic history. The others bore down on the leader as Zabala, wan-faced but bravely waving his white polo cap, the crowd's screams in his ears, fought to hold them off. At the end he was staggering, wracked by pain and fatigue—but hold them off he did, falling into the friendly arms of his countrymen at the finish line as he set a new Olympic record. For almost an hour after the race, Zabala stood in the midfield, waving the blue Argentine flag. The American relay racer Hector Dyer later found him in the locker room shower, about to topple over. "You ran to Redondo Beach and I ran a quarter of one lap, but I got a medal too, with three of the fastest runners helping me," Dyer joked. "I don't think you're so smart as I am." Zabala simply shook his head and laughed. Later he said, "I just had to win or die in the attempt. It would never have done to be beaten. I could not have gone back to Argentina." On the victory stand, listening to Argentina's national anthem, he wept.

At the gun in the showpiece 1,500-meter race, a short, slender, twenty-three-year-old Italian named Luigi Beccali started from the blocks as an unheralded long shot, having failed to even make the finals at the 1928 Amsterdam games. The other runners—comprising one of the greatest 1,500-meter fields ever—paid him little attention as they circled the track. The American Glenn Cunningham took the lead at

550 meters and, to the crowd's delight, held it to the start of the last lap. But he did not have enough to finish strong. The final lap was a churning sprint, with several runners trading positions until John Cornes of Great Britain shot to the front, worrying most about holding off Cunningham (who had faded to fourth). With 100 meters to go, few but the Italians seemed to know Beccali was even in the race. He was, though—and at the last turn, after hanging far back for most of the way, he burst past Cornes, accelerating at an astonishing pace in a closing drive rarely seen by a distance runner. Crossing the finish line pulling away, with a six-yard lead and a new Olympic record, a triumphant Beccali tore the tape with his fist. He emerged from his Olympic Village cottage the following morning to find that his teammates had spread rugs across the grass to the road—a royal pathway for him lined by flower-adorned wicker chairs, behind which Beccali's countrymen stood with arms raised in the Fascist salute, calling out, "Luigi! Luigi! Luigi!"

The Irishman Robert Tisdall's presence in the 400-meter hurdles made for one of the most unexpected outcomes at the games. When the Olympic Council of Ireland first received Tisdall's request to be on their team, they sniffed at the astonishing presumption. Tisdall, after all, had never even run a 400-meter hurdle race. He was a competitive all-around athlete in Ireland, but not of international measure. Still, the president of the council, liking his nerve, invited him to participate in the trials in Dublin. There, Tisdall initially failed to qualify, so the council president decided to hold a second trial. This time Tisdall won and set a national record, though it paled compared to international standards. Having made the team, he weathered the two-week journey from Ireland to Los Angeles—only to spend hours napping in his Olympic Village bungalow while his teammates trained vigorously for the games. He must have been saving his energy: once inside the Coliseum, he won his quarterfinal and semifinal heats, in the latter matching the Olympic record. In the 400-meter-hurdle final, Tisdall did even better, opening a huge five-yard lead. But then, as he cleared the last hurdle, he grazed it, stumbled, and almost fell—before regaining his balance and bolting for the tape inches ahead of two other runners. The long-shot Tisdale, running only his sixth race, had beaten the cream of the world's hurdlers, taking the gold medal. (He also broke the world's record, but it didn't count, owing to the hit hurdle.) Douglas Fairbanks promptly invited him to a gala party at Pickfair. Driving a borrowed Cadillac that evening, armed with uncertain directions, Tisdall stopped at an imposing mansion in the hills above LA. At the front door, he asked if this was the Fairbanks residence, and a butler replied, "No, sir, Mr. Charles Chaplin lives here." Eventually, Tisdall arrived at Pickfair—where he found himself sitting next to Amelia Earhart inside a big tent painted to represent the walls of a Norman castle. After dinner, a screen appeared, the lights went out, and everyone watched a preview screening of Fairbanks's next film, *Robin Hood*.

Only two instances of poor sportsmanship marred the games. One, alas, involved the Brazilian water polo team, which did not get to complete its participation in the Olympic Games, despite selling all those coffee beans. In a preliminary match, the Brazilians, furious at a Hungarian umpire's rulings, charged, surrounded, and shouted abuse at the official. "Fists flew and a general riot ensued," the *Los Angeles Times* reported. The melee grew even worse when police slammed Dr. Leo Donath, secretary of the International Swimming Association, into a concrete wall, mistakenly thinking he was part of the brawl. The Brazilians may have had reason to be enraged—the referee, repeatedly booed by the spectators, had called forty fouls on Brazil's team, and only four against Germany (which won, 7–3). Nonetheless, their conduct earned the Brazilians a disqualification from the water polo competition, with three members of the team also barred from further participation in the swimming events.

An even more egregious breach occurred in the five-thousand-meter long-distance run, where the favorite, Finland's Lauri Lehtinen, leading all the way, was suddenly challenged on the final turn by an uncelebrated Oregon runner named Ralph Hill, cheered on by an exuberant crowd of seventy thousand. Lehtinen labored vainly to shake him off. Fifty meters from home, they were virtually abreast. Twice Hill tried to sprint past the Finn—once from the outside, once from the inside—and twice Lehtinen swerved in front of him, cutting him off, forcing Hill to break stride, which gave Lehtinen a two-yard lead. After the second blatant foul, the crowd rose and started angrily booing. At this point, Bill Henry, serving as the public address announcer, spoke out, seeking to calm the spectators: "Remember, these people are our guests." Chastened, the crowd watched quietly as Hill, his energy now depleted, still managed over the last thirty meters to close the gap and lunge at the finish line, seemingly in a dead heat with his opponent. Though their times were identical, setting an Olympic record, the judges, after studying the photo-finish film and deliberating for two hours, ruled Lehtinen had won by two inches. The judges called no fouls, and neither Hill nor American officials filed a protest. The next day, on the victory stand, Lehtinen tried to lift Hill to the gold medalist's dais with him, but the Oregon runner forcibly declined, refusing to divide the honors. Instead Lehtinen pinned a Finnish medal on Hill's sweater before they parted.

The desire to remain a gracious host may have encouraged Billy Garland to look the other way regarding the five-thousand-meter run. What bothered him more, what lingered in his mind for days as the games unfolded, were the two closest, most-disputed races of the Olympics, both pitting American athletes against each other: Evelyne Hall and Babe Didrikson in the eighty-meter hurdles, and Eddie Tolan and Ralph Metcalfe in the hundred-meter dash.

Near the end, as the games were drawing to a conclusion, Billy and AOC president Avery Brundage convened a meeting of Olympic officials and athletes in a conference room at the Biltmore Hotel. Their intent was to review the photographed and filmed finishes of both races, taken by the new photo-finish Kirby camera, introduced at the 1932 games but not yet in official use. Gustavus Kirby, the camera's inventor and a prominent member of the American Olympic Committee, was there along with various Amateur Athletic Union officials. So was Evelyne Hall. First they showed the Tolan-Metcalfe race, then Hall-Didrikson, freezing the film frame by frame, using large pointers to try to pick out which was the final, deciding picture. Eddie was thinner than Ralph, which made their final second tricky to judge. Hall and Didrikson had been in adjoining lanes, both wearing all-white uniforms, which made it hard to tell where Babe's body ended and Evelyne's started. After close examination, the two races looked to Evelyne like dead-even ties—and that's what the Olympic officials in the room concluded as well: "The photographs showed that the two contestants in each case hit the tape simultaneously," Avery Brundage wrote later that year to a *New York Herald Tribune* columnist.

However, that didn't change the outcome. "The finish rule at that time," Brundage explained, "provided that the race was not over until the torso of the competitor entirely crossed the finish line. That is why Tolan and Miss Didrikson were adjudged the winners. Their bodies crossed the line a fraction of an inch before their opponents. After the Olympic Games, the International Federation controlling track and field events for obvious reasons changed this rule. The finish rule now provides that the contestant who breasts the tape first, wins the race. Had the present rule been in effect at the Olympic Games, these two races would have been dead heats and the championships as well as the time would have been shared." Aware of criticism leveled at Olympic officials over this, Brundage added, "We are only human."

In the end, at least the times were shared. On November 21, some three months after the close of the 1932 games, the Amateur Athletic Union, following animated discussion at its national convention, voted to recognize Ralph Metcalfe and Evelyne Hall as coholders of the American records set in their races. Both races, the AAU concluded, had ended in virtual dead heats, with the time of winner and loser less than one-hundredth of a second apart, allowing only the electric camera to identify the victor. The convention's action—urged by Gustavus Kirby, a past AAU president—was unprecedented in the history of amateur athletics in the United States.

The AAU came close to according Ralph Hill the same honor in his five-thousand-meter race against Lauri Lehtinen. The Finn had been timed as hitting the tape in 14:30, a new American and Olympic record, but a separate set of watches had recorded the same figure for Hill. At first the convention, in a morning session, voted to recognize Hill as coholder of the record. But hours later, in an afternoon session, the AAU delegates reconsidered: Where Metcalfe and Hall had hit the tape at virtually the identical instant with Tolan and Didrikson, Hill had finished inches behind Lehtinen. The convention voted unanimously to deny Hill the record.

The games concluded soon after the Biltmore meeting. In the memorable final event on the final day of the games, Japanese aristocrat Takeichi Nishi won the gold medal in the equestrian individual jumping competition, negotiating a twenty-jump course so dangerously difficult that only five of eleven riders completed it. Nishi, fluent in English and French, both a baron and a lieutenant in the Japanese army, had charmed Los Angeles society during his month-long stay before the games started. He would have crossed paths with Billy more than once, for he'd been flooded with invitations to parties—as many as three a night—and he'd accepted them all. But he was a soldier, too, in a world full of mounting tensions and strife. In World War II, Nishi ended up commanding a tank brigade on Iwo Jima, where he died in February 1945 defending the island against the Americans.

By the time the 1932 Olympic Games' Closing Ceremony began at 5 p.m. on Sunday, August 14, it was clear to Billy and everyone else that the Tenth Olympiad had been an astonishing and historic success. Some 1.75 million spectators had spent $1.5 million for tickets, more than double the attendance at any other games. No fewer than sixteen world records had been broken, and two equaled, with existing Olympic records shattered in all but three events, often by multiple contestants in the same event—in the hundred-meter race alone, six different sprinters from five different countries bested the old benchmark. Collectively, four times as many new standards were set as at all other Olympic competitions combined. The first-ever financial surplus had been realized from a celebration of the Olympic Games—more than $1 million, a true fortune in the depths of the Depression and enough to pay off the entire state bond issue. The *New York Times* called the LA games "the most amazing festival of record-breaking of all time."

Billy Garland and some ninety-five thousand other spectators watched now as the Closing Ceremony started with a repeat of opening day: From the Coliseum's tunnel emerged, first, a white-clad figure bearing the banner of Greece. Then, in order, came others carrying the national flags and banners of the competing nations. After marching around the track, they gathered in a semicircle before the Tribune of Honor. Count de Baillet-Latour addressed the crowd, calling on the youth of the world to assemble four years hence in Berlin, saying, "May joy and good fellowship reign and in this manner may the Olympic Torch pursue its way through the Ages." The official Olympic flag of embroidered silk was lowered, folded, and handed to Los Angeles mayor John Porter for keeping over the next four years. As the flag bearers left the field, a choir of fifteen hundred began to sing the Hawaiian song of parting, "Aloha—Farewell to Thee." The crowd, many in tears, joined in. Trumpets sounded; cannons saluted; the band played "Taps." Then, in the darkening stadium, the Olympic torch, which had been glowing nonstop for sixteen days and nights, was quenched.

Only one thing was missing: the athletes. Few appeared on the victory pedestal, for most were on their way home. They'd been departing for days now, driven largely by economic need: they could not afford to linger. Midway through the games a financially strapped American Olympic Committee had informed stunned American athletes that they must, after competing in their events, either check out of the Olympic Village or pay two dollars daily for room and board. H. O. Davis, the builder of the village, had offered to compensate any American athlete who wished to remain until the close of games, but not many had availed themselves of this deal.

No matter, it seems. Wrote Grantland Rice after watching the Closing Ceremony: "The greatest of all Olympic Games had come to the closing curtain. . . . Six weeks ago this Tenth Olympiad was to be one of the big flops of all time. . . . In place of this, it turned out to be the great show of sport, the most successful ever held from the standpoint of records, thrills, attendance and organization." In his syndicated column, Will Rogers reported that he'd "just witnessed the closing of the most impressive and successful Olympic Games ever held." Added the *New York Times:* "Los Angeles put over this $10 million undertaking with a success that its most ardent boosters could hardly have hoped to surpass. The 1932 Olympics set a record, not only in the competition, but from every other standpoint as well, that should stand in the annals of international sports competition long after the marks made here during the past two weeks have been effaced from the books."

Thus ended a celebration of the Olympic Games that can only be described as a great coup for Billy Garland. In a letter dated August 19, President Hoover—who, despite the "pressing business" that kept him from the Olympics, had started a fishing-cruise vacation on August 14—wrote Billy to congratulate him "on the magnificent way you carried through the Olympic Games. Los Angeles has done credit to our whole country, and I deeply appreciate the years of labor which you and your many colleagues have devoted to what is fundamentally a most valuable contribution to our international and national life."

The Tenth Olympiad had far exceeded Billy's highest expectations, though he insisted, "I'm not amazed. In my heart I knew this would happen if we persevered." He took great pride in the belief that the world had approved, and made sure to share the acclaim. "The Olympic Games were of the United States," he told reporters, "not just California or Los Angeles. It was our good fortune to stage them, but the honor for the success must go to the people of the entire country." All the same, Billy could not help but once again exult: "Without boasting and without fear of criticism, I feel that I can say that the games were the finest ever held. Anyone who witnessed the closing ceremony yesterday will understand." At the end of that ceremony, Billy Garland had wept.

# A FOOTING IN THE WORLD

Just as Billy had imagined, the 1932 Olympics gave Americans a reason to hope in the depths of the Depression, offering a beacon of light in a dark world. Here came hints of promise, not the least provided by the record-breaking achievements, the marvelous cast of performers, and the introduction of women and black athletes on the main stage. The LA Olympics ignited extraordinary passions as people across the globe listened to live radio broadcasts and devoured morning headlines. Most memorable and consequential of all, the 1932 games yielded Zack Farmer's pioneering scheme for an Olympic Village, which would provide a blueprint for all later host cities—a model for how athletes from across the world could fraternize and live together. The village proved to be the salvation and crowning glory of the 1932 games. In a letter afterward to Baron de Coubertin, Billy wrote, "The Olympic Village will always remain in my mind as the brilliant jewel of the Xth Olympiad. . . . The Village was one grand triumph."

That village evaporated in the hours after the 1932 Olympics ended, providing a tangible reminder of the illusion underpinning the games. Even as the athletes were moving out and sailing for home, workers were dismantling the village, part of Billy's deal with the Baldwin estate. Not at a financial loss, though—Garland's gang had thought to make money through shrewd recycling. They sold off the 550 cottages singly and in groups (unfurnished for $140, furnished for $215), with many ending up in foreign lands—Copenhagen, Japan, Berlin. (One can still be seen near Olvera Street in downtown LA, another in Malibu.) They also sold eight thousand bedsheets, twenty-four thousand towels, and six thousand pillowcases—all to a laundry. A restaurant chain bought the dishes and silverware. Stoves, pots and pans, roof tiles, doors, flagpoles, furniture—the whole lot went. "After our show," recalled Zack Farmer, "we salvaged everything for 100 cents on the dollar. Well, everything but the paved street. You can't sell a paved street."

Just as the village didn't last, neither did all the feelings of harmony and prosperity. The games had not obliterated the Great Depression or the mounting international tensions. After the games, the Hoovervilles, hunger marches and breadlines continued, as did the rise of Hitler (named chancellor of Germany in January 1933) and the spread of fascism in Italy and Japan. Then, too, attention in the United States turned to a presidential race that would soon mark a momentous shift from the party and politics of Harding, Coolidge and Hoover—Billy's world—to the New Deal of Franklin Roosevelt. "Just witnessed the closing of the most impressive and successful Olympics Games ever held," Will Rogers wrote in his syndicated column on August 15. "Now we go from that into three straight months of political 'hooey.' Records will be broken there, too. You will hear speeches that require more wind than the Marathon race."

A good number of American Olympic athletes, following their glorious hour on stage, living large and treated as celebrities, returned to the grim realities of the Depression. After George Roth, a Californian who won gold in gymnastics, received his medal before sixty thousand cheering fans, he went outside the Coliseum and thumbed a ride home. Broke and unemployed, now without the food he'd been sneaking from the village dining room for his wife and daughter, he had no option but the breadline.

A band and reception committee met Eddie Tolan at the train station when he returned to Detroit with two gold medals, and Michigan governor Wilber M. Brucker declared September 6 "Eddie Tolan Day" throughout the state. But Tolan, walking the streets, vainly struggled to find a paying job. With his parents also long unemployed, he had to give up his enduring dream of becoming a doctor. For a brief time, he appeared in vaudeville, which led the Michigan Amateur Athletic Association to strip him of his amateur status. Eventually, he landed a position in Detroit as a clerk to the Register of Deeds, and later became an elementary school teacher.

Jean Shiley, after winning gold in the high jump over Babe Didrikson, returned home by bus (out of money, she again sold her train ticket) to a stirring reception in Haverford Township, Pennsylvania. She hoped to compete in the 1936 Berlin games and eventually attend medical school, but her first, central concern was to each day earn the money she needed in order to get to her classes at Temple University the next morning. She ended up having to borrow a hundred dollars to finish her senior year there, only to find there were no jobs, even for a world and Olympic champion. Stints as a shoe store salesperson and substitute typing teacher didn't last long (she didn't know how to type when she started that teaching job). She finally landed a position as swim instructor and lifeguard at a country club pool—then belatedly learned it disqualified her from competing in the 1936 Olympics. "The rules said I was a professional by virtue of teaching swimming. . . . They wouldn't permit me even to tryout. I made a special trip to New York to see Avery Brundage. They just said no, and that was it."

Even "Queen Helene" Madison struggled. She did cereal and Camel cigarette endorsements and acted in one forgettable movie, before returning to her home in Seattle. There, after failing in efforts to become a nightclub entertainer, she found work as a hotdog vendor at West Green Lake Beach—the site where she as a young girl began her swimming career. Despite her three gold medals and stack of world records, Seattle would not hire her as a swim instructor—city parks department rules banned women from teaching swimming.

All the same, the Depression did eventually end, and through the games many 1932 Olympic athletes in time found their footing in the world, launching a wide range of successful careers. Babe Didrikson became a world-famous professional golfer. Helene Madison trained as a nurse and opened the Helene Madison Swim School in Seattle before marital issues and health problems sidelined her. The backstroke champion Eleanor Holm—whom Avery Brundage kicked off the 1936 US Olympics team for partying too heartily on the ship steaming to the Berlin games—ended up signing a seven-year contract with Warner Brothers, singing with Art Jarrett's band at the Cocoanut Grove, and swimming in Billy Rose's Aquacades (she also married Jarrett and Rose). Buster Crabbe went on to a successful movie career, starring in a number of popular films in the 1930s and 1940s, including the title role in the serials *Tarzan the Fearless, Flash Gordon,* and *Buck Rogers.* Josephine McKim enjoyed a film and stage career as well, appearing with Buster in *Lady Be Careful* (1936). Evelyne Hall won an athletic scholarship at what is now DePaul University, became recreation instructor of the Chicago Park District, and, eventually, the first athletic supervisor for women and children in Glendale, California, where she served as chair of the Pacific Coast Amateur Athletic Union. Roger Metcalfe, after his disappointments in LA—and some disappointment in the 1936 Berlin games as well, where he had to settle for silver in the hundred-meter dash, running second to the legendary Jesse Owens—went on to succeed in politics, serving as a Chicago alderman and later as a US congressman from Illinois.

The games introduced individual young athletes to the world, and the world to them. Billy Garland's creation, whatever else it did, deeply touched otherwise isolated children of the Depression. Looking back many years later, Jean Shiley, who served as a US Navy officer during World War II, said, "The way I view my time slot is that the Olympics were a microcosm of the world. The many faces of mankind were so different and interesting and such a vital part of our interaction. It changed my whole life forever. I was interested in the history of various nations I had never heard of before. I was interested in their culture, their religion, their music, their mores. The whole world was open to me. I was a little country girl. I was very confined in a very small area with people that were all alike. It just intrigued me and enriched my life so."

The games signified a turning point in the Olympic movement as well. The crowds, the athletic achievements, the innovations, the village—all helped cement LA's 1932 legacy. So did the lifeline Los Angeles provided. The entire Olympics movement had been faltering in the years before 1932. The LA games not only rescued the movement but also provided a model and path forward, demonstrating how to make a profit and attract legions beyond the hard-core sports fans. "It is fortunate," declared the *IOC Official Bulletin,* "that facts have proved how great a mistake was made by those pessimists who for the past several months predicted the failure of the Games of the Xth Olympiad."

The 1932 Olympics also had a significant impact on the development of Southern California, just as Billy Garland had prophesied back in 1922. A total of sixty-two conventions were held in LA during the games, and visitors left behind some $60 million (almost $1.1 billion in 2018 dollars). Many thousands chose to linger in the region for days and weeks after the games—and not all were tourists. Some five hundred registered with a LA Chamber of Commerce committee formed with the purpose of creating business contacts and stimulating international trade. "City Makes New Connections in All Parts of the World," reported an *LA Times* headline. "Industry, Farms and Culture Studied by Visitors."

Undeniably, the publicity surrounding the games made Los Angeles famous—Billy Garland would never again have to pull out a map to show a diplomat the city's location. He and a supportive cadre of sportswriters and publishers marketed the city as much as the games—the culture of Hollywood and movie stars, the geography of mountains and sea and desert, the (mythical) history of mission ruins and Spanish fiestas, the climate of endless sun and mild temperatures, and—above all—the notion of Southern California being a land of unlimited opportunity, a place where dreams can be realized. Even in a city that invented itself chiefly through self-promotion, the games stood out as an unsurpassed example of boosterism—a colossal feat of public relations. In the hours after the games ended, Harry Chandler's *LA Times* rejoiced: "In no other international competition has the name of one city . . . been mentioned so prominently or with so much appreciation as has the name of Los Angeles in the thousands of press dispatches sent out from the Olympic Stadium [Coliseum] to the leading newspapers of the world."

All this had lasting consequences. In the ten years following the Olympics, Los Angeles expanded rapidly: The Original Farmers Market, Union Station, the Griffith Observatory, Los Angeles International Airport, and the nation's first freeway (the Arroyo Seco Parkway) all opened. The Cleveland Rams became the Los Angeles Rams, making the Coliseum their home. Shipbuilding became the primary business of the Port of Los Angeles, employing some 90,000 workers. By 1939 the population of Los Angeles stood at 1.6 million; by 1950 it was more than 2 million, surpassing Detroit to become the fourth-largest city in the country. The Dodgers arrived in 1958, knowing they could play in the Coliseum while constructing their own stadium. The Lakers landed two years later, lured by the newly built Sports Arena financed by the Coliseum Commission.

That did not mean Billy and his colleagues had fully transformed their mirage into reality. The village and playing fields of the Coliseum offered havens of seeming equality, yet Los Angeles itself remained something different, still segregated by race and class through a range of covenants, restrictions and policies. Despite star appearances by Eddie Tolan and Ralph Metcalfe, Los Angeles' downtown and suburban clubs still discriminated against Jews, Catholics and blacks (and would do so well into the 1970s). Of course, Los Angeles was not alone: The 1932 games had unfolded in a country full of racial and social barricades. The members of the Japanese Olympics team learned this firsthand. When they attempted to enter dance halls or classy restaurants in Los Angeles during the 1932 games, they found themselves blocked at the door by hosts saying, "Mexicans are not permitted." Clarifying that they were Japanese, not Mexicans, only made matters worse, leaving the visitors deeply hurt and puzzled.

The full story, though, is more complicated. The Japanese athletes, at the same time, came away with wholly pleasant impressions of the officials and the public at the games. They told of receiving "very kind and fair treatment" from officials and warm enthusiastic support from spectators, who applauded Japanese athletes' success as much as that of Americans—in fact, Japanese athletes drew more American cheers than any other foreign nationality. The Japanese visitors did expect Los Angeles to be a "far finer, more modern city" than they found it, but that simply meant LA was still an evolving outpost. In the end, all could at least agree that Billy Garland had delivered what he'd promised—a big, rousing, blues-chasing party. For better and worse, good and ill, he had propelled Los Angeles into the future. The city, as always, was on its way.

# EPILOGUE

On December 29, 1933, Miss Helen Chandler, Harry's daughter, married John Jewett Garland, Billy's son. The two families were now officially joined, even if it involved the merger of two decidedly different cultures. "There are amusing stories," recalled Billy's granddaughter Gwendolyn Garland Babcock, "about the Garlands and their visiting relatives all stopping at 815 West Adams for a glass or two of champagne before going to what they knew would be a dry reception at the Chandler's home ... in the Los Feliz area." The Chandler household generally seemed austere compared to "the more volatile atmosphere of the Garland house. I remember [my mother] telling me about how the Chandlers, when angry, would hold a grudge and not speak to each other for days, while the Garlands would shout at each other and get all their feelings out in the open, and then forget the whole affair in a matter of hours."

As children, Gwen and her brother would visit their grandparents' home on Sunday mornings, after attending Sunday school at St. John's Episcopal Church. During summers, they would also visit them at Casa Ladera, a rambling three-level home Billy had built at Pebble Beach, near Carmel, in the late 1920s. This is where Gwen best got to know her grandparents. She considered Casa Ladera a dream world, five acres of vegetable and cutting gardens, a croquet course, a putting green, a pine forest and expansive lawns to run on. The house itself, she recalled, included "a wonderful round room" where the family would have cocktails while "surrounded by the posters from the 1932 Olympic Games."

Such nostalgia was understandable: The 1932 Olympics, in a sense, marked the apogee of Billy Garland's influence, and Harry Chandler's as well. Less than three months after the games, Franklin Roosevelt was elected president in a landslide, with California going not just for FDR (the first time the state had gone Democratic in a presidential election since 1916) but also for a Democratic senator. Between 1932 and 1934, Democratic registration doubled in the state. The Depression had continued and deepened, despite Billy's assurances of a quick recovery. In June of 1934, more than 20 percent of California's population was on welfare, and labor strikes were roiling an insistently "open shop" region. Migrants to California—three hundred thousand between 1930 and 1934—were no longer the skilled, well-off midwesterners of the 1920s but, rather, impoverished refugees from the southern Great Plains, including a good number of unattached transients. By late 1935, the Los Angeles Chamber of Commerce, responding to urgings by the police chief, James Davis, was calling for hard-labor "rock pile" penal camps for vagrants. In February 1936, in a city once gloriously renowned for luring immigrants, Chief Davis sent officers to secure the state's borders against undesirable indigents heading to Los Angeles.

Los Angeles, though still a largely Anglo-Saxon city, now had a significant percentage of blacks, Hispanics and Asians. The region's multicultural future was on the horizon. So was a stirring of socialist activism. That, above all, seemed to draw Billy Garland's attention. Upton Sinclair's candidacy for governor of California in 1934 particularly disturbed him, enough so that he spoke out publicly. Asserting that "California today faces destruction through foreign invasion in the guise of Socialism," Billy in late September of 1934 called upon voters to oppose Sinclair, the Democratic Party's candidate: "Remember, you who have chosen real estate as your profession, and you who own real estate in California, that he who has never owned a square foot of realty, who has never paid one dollar in tax on real estate, and who believes all real estate should be owned by the State, has nothing in common with that man who has for years striven to own his own home." Regardless of political affiliation, he concluded, "it is imperative that you and all of your friends cast your votes against the influence which would destroy the bulwark of American liberty and American civilization."

Two matters regarding the Olympic Games and the Olympic movement also aroused Billy's concern in the wake of the 1932 games. Both involved him intimately with Avery Brundage, still the president of the

American Olympic Committee, and both arose from the prospect of the coming 1936 Olympic Games in Berlin.

The first turned on the $1.25-million surplus realized by the Los Angeles Olympic Organizing Committee, unprecedented in Olympic history. Brundage wanted at least some of it assigned to the AOC for use in funding the United States' team at the 1936 Olympics. Billy and his organizing committee thought differently: $1 million should go to pay off the California state bond issue that financed the games, and the balance should be donated to the city and county of Los Angeles, which had absorbed the cost of building the Coliseum and other stadia.

The matter ended up in court, with the AOC filing a "friendly lawsuit" in order to determine whether they had a right to the surplus. But Brundage also kept writing to Billy, and in April 1935 he proposed that a "subscription" from the LA Olympic Organizing Committee, in support of the 1936 Berlin games, would be acceptable in place of handing over the surplus. Billy and his committee did not respond favorably to this idea. The general opinion of his colleagues, Billy reported to Brundage, was that the legal brief filed by the AOC in support of its lawsuit was "so full of downright lies and disgusting claims . . . that any possibility of a subscription is quite out of the question." Billy professed not to have read the brief himself, and to "have no feeling in the premises," but believed his committee's plan to return the surplus to the city, county, and state "is final and cannot be changed." What's more, he wrote, "I am out of pocket myself about $50,000 ($745,000 in 2018 dollars) by reason of bringing the Games to Los Angeles, and that is all I care to invest in Olympic matters for some time to come."

Despite the rhetoric, Billy Garland and Avery Brundage were more friendly allies than angry adversaries. Their connection and their shared values concerning the Olympic movement became particularly evident as controversy mounted regarding America's participation in the Berlin games. This was a decidedly questionable time for both of them.

When the IOC, by mail ballot in 1931, selected Berlin to host the 1936 games, a centrist coalition governed in Germany, led by Chancellor Heinrich Brüning. By early 1933, that had changed: Adolph Hitler was chancellor and the Nazis ruled, holding a plurality in the Reichstag. That March, six Americans in Berlin, five of them Jews, reported assaults by men wearing Nazi uniforms, as anti-Semites roamed the streets, compelling shops to close. Questions soon rose about the advisability of holding the games in Berlin.

On June 7, the IOC met in Vienna to consider whether Berlin should still get the 1936 games—the chief issue being the clash between Nazi dogma and Olympic tenets, which flatly prohibit racial or religious discrimination. Billy Garland attended, part of a sixty-day trip to Europe during which he collected three awards—the Legion of Honor from France, the Cavalier of the Crown from Italy, and the Order of Leopold from Belgium—bestowed in recognition of his efforts on behalf of the 1932 games. At the IOC session, he, together with a second US member, Brigadier General Charles Sherrill, interrogated Theodor Lewald, president of the Berlin organizing committee, asking whether German Jews would be able to try out for, and compete on, the German team. Lewald reassured them that German Jews had this right. Billy, as always the upbeat optimist, thought they'd prevailed.

Upon returning from Vienna, he stopped in Quebec, where he told reporters on July 13 that "a strong attitude was taken by all other countries participating in the committee meetings, and both the German government and the German Olympic Committee have given assurance that Jews will have perfect freedom and facilities to compete." Billy added, "The games cannot and will not be held if any restriction . . . is made. It would be a complete reversal of the whole meaning of the Olympiad." A week later, back home in Los Angeles, he elaborated: "This question arose because of the fact that Germany had declared that no Jewish youth could represent Germany in these Games. . . . At the Vienna meeting Germany was notified that unless the youth of Germany is permitted to participate . . . the XIth Olympiad would be held elsewhere, and that no such restriction or discrimination will be tolerated." Billy again believed they'd persuaded the Germans: "I am happy to say that . . . all the laws regulating the Olympic Games shall be observed. As a principle, German Jews shall not be excluded from the German teams."

Others were not so trusting. At the American Olympic Committee convention in late November 1933, delegates adopted a resolution that threatened a boycott. In early March 1934, the American Jewish Committee held an anti-Nazi rally at Madison Square Garden. The next month, a Jewish member of the AOC, Charles Ornstein, wrote Brundage, arguing it would be "unthinkable" to hold the games in Berlin. He urged Brundage to brief Billy Garland and the other American IOC delegates, so they could raise the issue at the next International Olympic Committee meeting.

On May 15, 1934, the IOC convened that meeting in Athens. Billy once again interrogated Lewald, in what he'd later call a "showdown," and once again Lewald offered reassurances. Upon returning to the United States, Billy, stopping in New York on June 21, declared that Germany had satisfied the IOC that it is living up to "solemn pledges" not to discriminate against Jewish athletes. He seemed now to have firmed up his position, to have dug in his heels in support of the Berlin games. Reflecting the intensity of his faith in the value and importance of the games, he repeatedly defended the Olympic tradition as something separate from politics. "I realize our athletic leaders have been besieged by communications asking us not to participate in the 1936 Olympic Games," he told an Associated Press reporter, "and to use our influence to take the Games away from Germany because of the agitation over the Jewish question." However, "as I see it, the American Olympic Committee must not become involved in racial, sociological or religious controversies of any kind. Regardless of my personal views, the American Olympic Committee is concerned solely with athletic affairs and if the German authorities continue to live up to the pledge they made to the IOC at Vienna in 1933, and which they repeated at Athens this year, namely to respect and observe the Olympic protocol, that is all we can expect."

That evening, the American Jewish Congress expressed its disagreement with Billy's views and the attitude of the International Olympic Committee. Citing a "general skepticism in many countries" about Germany's pledges, the congress's president, Bernard Deutsch, pointed specifically to the AOC's recent decision to postpone accepting an invitation to the Berlin games until Avery Brundage completed an investigative tour through Germany.

Brundage, upon returning from that tour—a one-week stay in Germany, where he relied on translators—delivered his report in late September. He now strongly favored accepting the German invitation. "I was given positive assurances in writing," Brundage told reporters, "that there will be no discrimination against Jews. You can't ask more than that and I think the guarantee will be fulfilled." The next day, the AOC met and, after extended deliberation, resolved unanimously that "in the light of the report of President Brundage and the attitude and assurances of the German Olympic Committee and the representations of the German Government . . . we accept the invitation of the German Olympic Committee."

This did not quell the controversy. New York congressman Emanuel Celler called for hearings, the Anti-Defamation League called for a boycott, and the delegates to the Amateur Athletic Union convention in early December, in defiance of Brundage, voted to postpone accepting the German invitation. By mid-1935, a determined boycott campaign was underway, involving a range of nationally prominent figures and Olympic athletes, including the swimmer Helene Madison, who said, "Fair competition for every eligible athlete in the world . . . is what the Olympic Games stand for. I think America as a leading nation should refuse to compete where sportsmanship is threatened by prejudice." Brundage began heatedly defending his position in newspaper interviews, an international radio broadcast, and a sixteen-page pamphlet published by the AOC. "I have not heard of anything to indicate discrimination against athletes of any race or religion," he said in a statement issued July 26. "This question was answered by assurances from German political and sports leaders. . . . I know of no reason for questioning these guarantees." Unable to stop himself, he added, "The fact that no Jews have been named so far to compete for Germany doesn't necessarily mean that they have been discriminated against. . . . In forty years of Olympic history, I doubt if the number of Jewish athletes competing from all nations totaled 1 percent of those in the games. In fact I believe one-half of 1 percent would be a high percentage."

Billy Garland wrote Brundage soon after: "I have read your interviews in re: Jewish propaganda, printed in all the daily papers, and I think your statements have been dignified, calm and constructive. To be stampeded at this time in the face of wild and vicious utterances through doubtful press reports would be cowardly and unfair. . . . We are in sport alone and not politics."

In mid-October, Billy continued this theme in a letter to Theodor Lewald. The United States, in face of "wide-spread propaganda of hatred by certain influences," should have "the right kind of publicity concerning the XIth Olympiad." The country should know "that the Reich, with the German Olympic Committee, was keeping the pledges." Billy was "deeply impressed with the earnestness and sincerity of the German people in keeping the faith." He was "sorry that so many misrepresentations had been accepted as truth in our country." He was "strong for the Berlin Games, and Mrs. Garland and I are looking forward to being there."

A day later, he wrote as well to the IOC president, Count de Baillet-Latour. He believed that Germany had been "living up to" its pledges, and he had "taken occasion frequently to make known this information." But in the United States "[we] badly lacked the right kind of national publicity" regarding the Berlin games, even though Avery Brundage "has done his utmost to stem the tide of Jewish and Catholic propaganda." As did Brundage, Billy felt "there would be German-Jewish participation at Berlin if the Jews had any outstanding athletes."

The next month, on November 27, one of the two other Americans on the IOC, Ernest Lee Jahncke, a former assistant secretary of the US Navy, openly disputed Billy's view. By then, the Reichstag, on September 15, had enacted the Nuremberg Laws, which excluded German Jews from Reich citizenship and prohibited them from marrying or having sexual relations with persons of "German or related blood" (this prohibition was extended on November 14 to also cover blacks, Gypsies and those who could produce "racially suspect offspring"). Jahncke, in his own letters to Theodor Lewald and Count de Baillet-Latour, which he released publicly, said he opposed American participation in the Berlin games because, "under the domination of the Nazi government the German sports authorities have violated and are continuing to violate every requirement for fair play . . . and are exploiting the games for the political and financial profit of the Nazi regime." He challenged Baillet-Latour directly: "You remind me of my duty as a member of the International Olympic Committee. Therefore I feel sure you will not consider me presumptuous in reminding you of your duty as president of the International Olympic Committee. It is plainly your duty to hold the Nazi sports authorities accountable for the violation of their pledges."

Billy, feeling "intense disappointment" regarding Jahncke, pushed back publicly two days later. Joining with America's third IOC member, Charles Sherrill, he condemned the proposed boycott of the Berlin games, leaving Jahncke isolated in their delegation (though supported by, among others, Zack Farmer). Billy seemed driven by his longing for the nonpolitical Olympic spirit and hospitality that infused the 1932 games in Los Angeles. "To refuse to join with the nations which sacrificed a great deal to come to our celebration of the Games in 1932," he told an Associated Press reporter in Los Angeles, "would reflect on no one as much as the United States." Billy stressed that the games could not become a tool for German political propaganda: "Germany does not run the Games. The host country has two definite duties: preparation of the site for the Games, and selection and training of its team. . . . The organizing committee ceases to exercise any authority with the opening of the games. Chancellor Hitler can no more make a political speech than could have President Hoover at Los Angeles. Those who have prophesied the avalanche of Nazi propaganda at the games simply display their ignorance of the conditions under which the games are held."

Days later, delegates at the AAU annual meeting in New York, in a close vote after heated, bitter debate, finally decided to accept the German invitation. That ended the discussion—Americans would compete in Berlin. When the International Olympic Committee convened its annual session there on July 30, just before the start of the games, the members voted forty-nine to zero—with Billy Garland abstaining—to expel Ernest Lee Jahncke over his public challenge to the IOC's president (the only such ejection in IOC history). As Jahncke's replacement, the IOC elected none other than Avery Brundage—long Billy's ambition. Brundage eventually became president of the International Olympic Committee, a position he held for twenty years, from 1952 to 1972.

For a time after the 1936 Berlin games, Billy Garland's name still popped up in newspaper headlines. There he was in June 1937, back from a two-month tour of the Orient, enthusiastic about the prospects of staging the 1940 Olympics in Japan—something for which he'd strongly campaigned and lobbied. The Japanese were designing a complete Olympic Village modeled after the 1932 village in Los Angeles, Billy noted with appreciation. "Everywhere I went in Japan, I was impressed with the sincere desire of the Japanese to provide the cordial atmosphere which they encountered at Los Angeles in 1932." Billy sounded ready to jump in and help them prepare: "They are planning the construction of some new hotels for 1940 and the famous Imperial Hotel is to be considerably enlarged, but I doubt very much if they can foresee the large numbers of persons planning to visit Japan during the period of the Games. They'll be surprised and, if they're not careful, swamped."

There he was again, a year later, on May 9, 1938, still enthusiastic after returning from another two-month tour of Europe and the Near East. A review of Italy's building activity under Mussolini had impressed him, and a stop in Jerusalem had thrilled him ("It was stirring to find oneself at the Holy Land scenes familiar by name since childhood"). He now had little to say, however, about the 1940 Olympic Games in Tokyo. For good reason: War between China and Japan (the Second Sino-Japanese War) had been underway for nearly a year, Hitler's troops had annexed Austria just two months before, Germany was menacing Czechoslovakia, and the Spanish Civil War continued. Still, Billy clung to his salesman's optimism: "I was one of those who favored Tokyo in the first place, as an extension of the international idea clear around the world. The Games were awarded to Tokyo and the city is going ahead with plans . . . in good faith. Under Olympic Games provisions, then, there is no way the scheduled Tokyo events could be called off unless the Japanese themselves desired to do so. This they certainly don't intend to do. . . . That's all there is to it."

Just two months later, on July 14, news dispatches from Tokyo reported that Japan had cancelled the 1940 Tokyo games because of "the present circumstances"—among them the Chinese war, monetary concerns and army opposition to internationalism. Billy was obliged to respond when called by an *LA Times* reporter: "Inasmuch as I have received no official notification that Japan has suspended the Games . . . I am unable to make a statement concerning a possible substitute site." He couldn't help himself though. When asked if Los Angeles might be selected, he said, "Does Los Angeles want the Olympic Games in 1940?"

Billy did—that much is certain. Instead came Germany's invasion of Czechoslovakia, Japan's bombing of Pearl Harbor, and the United States' entry into World War II.

In 1942, Billy's granddaughter Gwen, at age seven, came down with polio, which obliged her to spend nine months in Children's Hospital in Los Angeles. Billy was a frequent visitor. He played gin rummy with her and taught her dominoes. He was, by then, quite hard of hearing. "My memories of my grandfather are of an elderly, very deaf gentleman," Gwen recalled. "I wonder if years of shooting guns without any protection in the ears was the cause of his deafness."

Billy was seventy-six, and the world he had conjured no longer existed, at least not as he'd envisioned it. Abroad, global war had supplanted Olympic hospitality and understanding. Locally, perpetual growth no longer looked like nirvana in ever more congested and sprawling Southern California cities. All the same, Billy had left his mark—the hand of man. So, of course, had Harry Chandler.

Harry passed on first. By the time he and his wife, Marian, celebrated their fiftieth wedding anniversary on June 5, 1944, he was the largest land baron in Southern California, a partner in countless deals, and a force to be reckoned with by those who meant to oppose or regulate him. When he suffered a fatal heart attack three months later, on September 23, at the age of eighty, his estate was worth an estimated half a billion dollars (more than $12.3 billion in 2018 dollars). Secretive to the end, on his deathbed he reportedly ordered the destruction of all his papers.

Billy lived on to see Germany's surrender, after Hitler's death, on April 29, 1945. He lived to see Japan's surrender on August 15, 1945. He lived to see more than a hundred thousand people gather on October 27, 1945, at the Memorial Coliseum—his most enduring legacy, now a national historical landmark and famed magnet for major events—to celebrate the end of World War II in a "Tribute to Victory."

In Billy's lifetime, the last public attention came on his eighty-second birthday. "Probably no section in the world has such enthusiastic boosters as our Southern California," read a *Los Angeles Times* article on March 30, 1948. "So today we present the daddy of them all, the man who brought the world to Los Angeles in 1932, Col. William May Garland. . . . Tomorrow Garland will celebrate his 82nd birthday. The colonel and his family will have a quiet celebration at their Pebble Beach home." Though not lacking in awards, the *Times* added, "the honor that Col. Garland probably cherishes most of all came in 1934. That year he was voted the James E. Sullivan Award for outstanding contributions to sports, the only non-athlete to be thus honored by sports editors and sports leaders of the land."

Almost to the end, Billy remained an active member of the International Olympic Committee, though he was never able to attend another Olympiad after the 1936 Berlin games. World War II precluded Olympic celebrations in 1940 and 1944, and as the time for the 1948 games in London approached, Billy reluctantly wrote an IOC colleague to say he could not be there: "My doctor has just given me news which makes me very sad. His verdict is that I cannot attend the Olympic Games next month in London which I had hoped to witness with Mrs. Garland. My son, John Jewett Garland . . . will however be present at the Dorchester Hotel with his charming wife, Helen." Billy added that he felt it fitting to resign his IOC post "in place of a younger man." For that replacement, he urged the IOC to accept his son John, which it did. Billy, who had not seen a Republican in the White House since Hoover in 1932, remained hopeful in this letter: His son John would soon serve as a delegate to the Republican National Convention in Philadelphia, where "their choice of a nominee will probably be the next President of these United States."

Billy Garland did not live to see Harry Truman elected president. He died at age eighty-two, on Sunday, September 26, 1948, in the Monterey Community Hospital, from pneumonia exacerbated by chronic bronchitis and a gangrenous gall bladder. The next day, the Los Angeles City Council adjourned out of respect for the memory of the man who "brought the 1932 Olympic Games to Los Angeles, and led scores of other community projects." The *Los Angeles Times,* in an editorial titled "William May Garland, a Great Influence," observed, "Nearly every aspect of this community's life owes something to William May Garland—our street improvements, our harbor, our airways, our business and industry. His death at 82 closes a career of singular usefulness." Paul Zimmerman, the *LA Times* sports editor at the time, wrote, "Certainly Col. Garland was a man who walked with kings, yet kept the common touch." Avery Brundage sent flowers and released a statement: "It was only his perseverance and personal charm that finally convinced the Europeans that the Games could be properly stated in California. . . . He also originated the Olympic Village. . . . I have lost one of my closest friends."

Private funeral services were conducted on Friday, October 1, at the family home on West Adams that Billy had built nearly a half century before. Relatives, friends and a range of government, civic and business leaders (among them Acting Governor Goodwin Knight, Chairman Raymond Darby of the LA Board of Supervisors, Mayor Fletcher Bowron and Harry's son Norman Chandler) listened to Reverend George Davidson of St. John's Episcopal Church comfort the family: "In all these things we are more than conquerors, through Him who loved us." Inurnment followed at the nearby Pierce Bros. Chapel of the Pines in the West Adams District.

The next year, in Billy's honor, civic leaders placed a bronze bas-relief plaque in the Memorial Court of Honor at the historic Los Angeles Coliseum Peristyle. It featured his content, smiling profile, and it described Billy as a pioneer and "guiding spirit of the Games of the Xth Olympiad." The plaque remains there today and at its bottom reads, "If you seek his monument, look about you."

# ACKNOWLEDGMENTS

Assembling a nonfiction chronicle such as this, one derived almost entirely from archival research, has left me deeply indebted to the wonderful people who maintain the superb libraries of Southern California. Most particularly, I thank Wayne Wilson and Michael Salmon at the LA84 Foundation Library. Created with a share of the 1984 Olympic Games surplus, LA84 among many other activities maintains the world's premier Olympic and sports library collection, and I was fortunate to have unfettered access to the library's boundless resources. I was fortunate as well to have Wayne and Michael serving as gracious, patient, and always helpful guides. They provided a wealth of documents, constant advice and invaluable support, fielding my unending flow of queries and requests over a number of years.

I'm obliged as well to Anne Blecksmith, head of reader services at the Huntington Library; Sue Luftschein, head of special collections at USC Libraries Special Collections, Doheny Memorial Library; and Dale Ann Stieber, special collections librarian, Occidental College Library. They and their staffs, with warmth and enthusiasm, tracked down and rolled out all manner of obscure documents that proved invaluable to my project.

I also thank Matthew Roberts, a former research librarian at the UC Irvine Library who, until his departure, supported the UCI Literary Journalism Program. Whenever I hit a roadblock in my research, Matt happily came to my rescue, searching for and finding obscure documents and articles from long ago.

A very special thanks goes to Gwendolyn Garland Babcock, the granddaughter of both William May Garland and Harry Chandler. I am fortunate indeed that Gwen Babcock has made a yearslong project out of the genealogical study of her extended family, resulting in a superbly researched and written family history. Over lunch one afternoon at her home, she graciously gifted me with a bound copy of one volume in this history, titled *The Ancestry of John*

*Jewett Garland* (which is available at babcockancestry.com). I am deeply indebted to Gwen Babcock and thank her, with much appreciation, both for her wonderfully realized family history and for her warm support of my project.

I thank as well UC Irvine's Humanities Commons for a publication support grant. This generous funding helped me during my research and my pursuit of long-ago photos of Los Angeles. I am indebted also to Carol De Riggi Peterson, whose design sense and mastery with photos provided the support I sorely needed in pulling together an art program for this volume. To those who kept me functioning physically—Janet at Massage Place; Leffel and Veronica at Core Conditioning; Stu, Janet, and Renee at LA Valley College Aquatics Center—I offer my abundant appreciation.

Once the research is completed, the writing—and rewriting—begins. I am deeply indebted to Reed Malcolm, my editor at UC Press, for his ceaseless support and superb editing advice. His enthusiastic belief in my project inspired me to keep improving my manuscript. So did the insightful and meticulous work by Bonnie Hurd, a truly gifted and caring copyeditor. I thank as well Archna Patel and Dore Brown at UC Press for their warm support in shepherding me through the publication process.

My regard and appreciation for my agent, Kathy Robbins, knows no bounds. Throughout this project she encouraged, championed and challenged me all at once. She greatly improved both my spirit and my prose.

My wife, Marti Devore, as always put up with me. But she did way more than that: she served as my invaluable research partner. Her skills at roaming the internet, and her excitement about what she was finding, helped me enormously. I could not have written this book without her. Marti's love, support and tolerance make it all possible.

# NOTES AND SOURCES

**PROLOGUE**

My account of the 1932 Tournament of Roses parade derives from a number of *Los Angeles Times* articles, including "Rose Tournament Today to be held Rain or Shine," January 1, 1932; "New Year's Rain Due Here Today," January 2, 1932; "Beauty and Glory Join in Rose Parade Epic," January 2, 1932; and "Floats Entrance Throngs," January 2, 1932.

Here and elsewhere, my account of the 1923 International Olympic Committee (IOC) meeting in Rome derives largely from a thirty-four-page letter Billy wrote to his wife, Blanche, titled "Story of the Origin of the Xth Olympiad Held in Los Angeles, California in 1932," which I obtained at the LA84 Foundation Library. I also draw from *Olympic Memoirs* by Pierre de Coubertin and from *The IOC Sessions, 1894–1955*, by Wolf Lyberg. I draw as well from news accounts on April 10, 1923, in the *Los Angeles Times* ("LA Awarded 1932 Olympic Games: Garland Wins Long Struggle") and the *New York Times* ("LA Gets Olympics of 1932"). Robert Barney offers an account of this IOC meeting in "Resistance, Persistence, Providence: The 1932 Los Angeles Olympic Games in Perspective."

A reference to "Garland's folly" appears on p. 11 in *The X Olympiad* by Ellen Galford, an official account of the 1932 games jointly published by the International Olympics Committee, the United States Olympic Committee, 1st Century Project, and World Sport Research and Publications.

Accounts of the confrontation in a Los Angeles Athletic Club meeting room appear in two articles by Al Stump, "The Olympics That Almost Wasn't" and "1932, the 'Hopeless' Dream of William May Garland." Stump was an author and sportswriter for the *Los Angeles Times* and *Los Angeles Herald Examiner*. He does not indicate his sources, but I have reason to believe they included Bill Henry, a former sports editor at the *Times* who was present in the LAAC conference room and intimately involved in organizing the 1932 games. Strong corroboration of this LAAC showdown comes in a letter Billy Garland wrote to Bill Henry on May 23, 1933, referring to "one noon in the LAAC" when "you and Harry Chandler rallied to my assistance." This letter is reproduced on p. 48 of *Behind the Headlines with Bill Henry, 1903–1970,* edited by Patricia Henry Yeomans.

### CHAPTER 1. BILLY'S MIGRATION

My accounts here and elsewhere of Billy's early history derive from multiple sources. Chief among them is *The Ancestry of John Jewett Garland,* an extensive genealogical study compiled by Billy's granddaughter, Gwendolyn Garland Babcock. Other sources include biographical sketches published by the International Olympic Committee, the National Association of Realtors, and Los Angeles County, and the obituary of Billy published in the *Los Angeles Times* on September 27, 1948, "Civic Leader W. M. Garland Dies at 82."

My account of the boom and bust in Los Angeles during the 1880s draws from multiple sources, including *City of Quartz* by Mike Davis; *Southern California: An Island on the Land* by Carey McWilliams; *Inventing the Dream* by Kevin Starr; *Los Angeles: City of Dreams* by Harry Carr; *Paradise Promoted* by Tom Zimmerman; *Los Angeles: The Enormous Village, 1781–1981* by John Weaver; *Los Angeles in the 1930s,* by the Federal Writers Project of the Works Progress Administration; *The Powers That Be* by David Halberstam; and "The Great Real Estate Boom of 1887," by J. M. Guinn.

Billy published his ode, "Real Estate, the Basis of All Wealth," in the *Realty Blue Book of California.* I first learned that Billy became Henry Huntington's "primary real estate broker" from "The Promise and Principles of Real Estate Development in an American Metropolis: Los Angeles 1903–1923," a PhD dissertation by Laura Redford. Huntington's belief that Los Angeles would become "the most important city" appears in Carey McWilliams's *Southern California: An Island on the Land,* p. 123.

### CHAPTER 2. LA ON THE CUSP

Billy's marriage to Blanche is chronicled in Gwendolyn Garland Babcock's *The Ancestry of John Jewett Garland.* I rely also on "Garland-Hinman: Brilliant Wedding Last Evening in St. John's Church," published in the *Dunkirk Evening Observer* on October 13, 1898, which Gwendolyn Babcock reproduces in her study.

Early acclaim for the Van Nuys Hotel appeared in a *Los Angeles Times* article on September 22, 1896, headlined "The Grand Hotel: It Will be Opened Early in the New Year." For my account of the more "raucous" side of the Van Nuys Hotel, I draw from a number of *Los Angeles Times* articles: "Bell Boy Killed," January 3, 1900; "Van Nuys Guests Robbed by Bell Boy," March 28, 1901; "Nimble Burglar," January 17, 1902; "Too Many Napkins: Hotel Waiter's House Raided by Police," August 20, 1900; "Thieving Bell Boy," February 18, 1898; "Fell Three Stories: Charles Gamble Killed in an Elevator Shaft," March 4, 1897; "Dies in a Hallway," February 21, 1902; "Carved with Bread Knife: Bloody

Fracas at Van Nuys Hotel," August 1, 1902. I also learned about this dimension of the Van Nuys Hotel from "Death at Hotel Barclay: Behind the Beautiful Façade, Gruesome Slayings and Bloody Accidents," an account by Hadley Meares that appeared on the Curbed LA website (la.curbed.com) on October 20, 2017. (Hotel Barclay is the current name for the former Van Nuys Hotel.)

My report about the rise of the LA Chamber of Commerce and the Merchants and Manufacturers Association, the battle over the San Pedro deepwater harbor, and the emergence of exclusive private clubs draws from multiple sources, including *City of Quartz* by Mike Davis; *Southern California: An Island on the Land* by Carey McWilliams; and *Inventing the Dream* by Kevin Starr.

Billy's remarks about President McKinley came in a *Los Angeles Herald* article on July 21, 1900, "Success of McKinley: Republicans Assured." His remarks about business prosperity came in a *Los Angeles Herald* article on October 30, 1902, "East is Prosperous, Sales Increasing."

My account of the formation of the Los Angeles Realty Board (LARB) draws from "The Promise and Principles of Real Estate Development in an American Metropolis: Los Angeles 1903–1923," a PhD dissertation by Laura Redford. My account of LARB's first banquet at the Del Monte Tavern draws from "Good Boosters Are the Realty Men: Enthusiasm at First Banquet of Organized Board," *Los Angeles Times*, July 16, 1903.

My chronicle of the *Crocker v. Garland* lawsuit draws from a number of newspaper articles, beginning with "Sizzling Lawsuit Against W. M. Garland: Accused of Having 'Jobbed' Certain Clients," *Los Angeles Times*, April 23, 1903. Others include "Charge Fraud in Realty Sale," *San Francisco Call*, April 23, 1903; "Garland Forced to Confess Deception," *Los Angeles Times*, October 7, 1903; "Tells of Real Estate Values: Garland Kept on Stand Another Day," *Los Angeles Herald*, October 8, 1903; "Lawyer Meets Shrewd Witness," *Los Angeles Herald*, October 9, 1903; "Judge VM Fleet on Witness Stand Gives His Version of a Famous Interview: Visit to Garland was intended as a Surprise," *Los Angeles Herald*, October 11, 1903; "Masterful Argument Made by George Denis in the Famous Garland Case: Character of Defendant at Stake," *Los Angeles Herald*, October 15, 1903; "William M. Garland's Conduct Promptly Vindicated by a Jury," *Los Angeles Herald*, October 16, 1903; "More Trouble for Garland: Another Fraud Suit Against Real Estate Man," *Los Angeles Times*, October 18, 1903; "Garland Hard Hit by Court: Jury's Verdict Set Aside and New Trial Ordered," *Los Angeles Times*, March 6, 1904. I could find no news articles on the case after this one on March 6, but a search of court records yielded the Second Appellate District ruling denying Billy Garland's appeal: Civil No. 227, Second Appellate District, July 9, 1906, Henry J. Crocker et al., *Plaintiffs and Respondents v. William M. Garland, Defendant and Appellant.*

My account of the LARB banquet at the Angelus Hotel derives from "Real Estate Men Feast and Boost," *Los Angeles Herald*, January 25, 1907. The report about Billy and Blanche's inheritance draws from "Big Bequest Comes Hither: Will of Marshall Hinman is Filed for Probate," *Los Angeles Times*, June 18, 1907. The story about Billy's handshake with Avery Brundage appears in a "Bill Henry Says" column in the *Los Angeles Times*, July 23, 1933.

The summary of Billy's community activities draws from a number of *Los Angeles Herald* articles: "Will Treat Orphans to Long Auto Rides," September 28, 1906; "Gov. Gillet Names Staff Officers," April 28, 1907; "Realty Dealers Show Humanity," June 30, 1907; "Billy is to Appear as good old St. Nick for 650 poor children," December 20, 1913.

My report on the pioneering Los Angeles International Air Meet at Dominguez Field derives from a number of *Los Angeles Times* articles, among them: "Men or Money May Soon Fly," November 16, 1909; "Various Types of Aeroplane," December 12, 1909; "Aerial Advertising," January 20, 1910; and "Ample Room to View Flights," January 20, 1910. I draw also from "Paulhan Captures Los Angeles Honors," *New York Times*, January 21, 1910. Tom Zimmerman describes the meet in *Paradise Promoted* (pp. 142–47), as does Kevin Starr in *Inventing the Dream* (p. 125). My account of Billy's airplane ride with Walter Brookins draws from "Garland and Garbutt Soar with Brookins," *Los Angeles Herald*, December 30, 1910.

My knowledge of Billy's early autos comes from Gwendolyn Babcock's *The Ancestry of John Jewett Garland*. My account of his dispute with the Ventura County Board of Supervisors draws from "Writes Letter to Supervisors," *Los Angeles Herald*, July 14, 1906. My chronicle of Billy's Moosehead Lake auto journey derives from Gwendolyn Babcock's *The Ancestry of John Jewett Garland* and a number of newspaper articles, including "Pierce-Arrow Record Drive," *Los Angeles Times*, May 28, 1911; "W. M. Garland Gives Farewell Dinner; Starts 4,000 Mile Auto Trip Today," *Los Angeles Herald*, June 11, 1911; "Garland Flees From Own Coin; Farmer Pursues Angeleno; Realty Broker Touring Iowa Drops $6,500 on Road; Speeds On," *Los Angeles Herald*, July 4, 1911; "Maine Trip Fine; Realty Board President Delighted with Splendid Cross Continent Run in Automobile," *Los Angeles Herald*, July 28, 1911.

My account of the "Gardens of Magic" party for five thousand delegates from the National Association of Real Estate Boards (NAREB) derives from "Five Thousand Persons in Gardens Of Magic: Lawn Fete for Convention Visitors Our Most Spectacular Function," *Los Angeles Times*, June 24, 1915. Laura Redford also describes this event in "The Promise and Principles of Real Estate Development in an American Metropolis: Los Angeles 1903–1923." Kevin Starr (*Inventing the Dream*) and Tom Zimmerman (*Paradise Promoted*) both discuss how the early movies effectively promoted Los Angeles.

My report on Billy's resistance to movie censorship draws from "Abolish Movie Censors, Urge Businessmen: Big Organizations Back Film Industry in Fight to Dissolve Board," *Los Angeles Herald*, January 7, 1916. My report on Billy's opposition to prohibition draws from two *Los Angeles Herald* stories: "Business Men Form Prosperity League," March 28, 1916; "Retain State Prosperity, Slogan of League," March 29, 1916.

Billy's election to the NAREB presidency, and his warm salute back in Los Angeles, is recounted in "Garland is Elected Realty Board Head," *Los Angeles Herald*, July 28, 1917, and several *Los Angeles Times* stories: "Realty Boards' Chief Returns: National President Garland Back from Convention," August 10, 1917; "Tribute is Paid Real Live Wire," August 24, 1917; "Business Men Honor Garland," August 23, 1918. Billy's election to the LAAC presidency is reported in "Garland Heads Athletic Club," *Los Angeles Times,* August 30, 1918. Doris H. Pieroth describes the LAAC's coaching program for young athletes in *Their Day in the Sun,* p. 61.

### CHAPTER 3. THE QUEST

Billy Garland describes his meeting with the five publishers in his memoirlike letter to his wife, Blanche, "Story of the Origin of the Xth Olympiad Held in Los Angeles, California in 1932." The "Certain Signs of Dawn" headline appeared in the *Los Angeles Times* on November 2, 1918.

My account of Harry Chandler's background and early years in Los Angeles derives from multiple sources, including an unusual personal memoir Harry wrote and published on page one of the *Los Angeles Times* on December 4, 1941 (the paper's sixtieth-anniversary edition), titled "Harry Chandler, 'Oldest Employee,' Has Seen This City Transformed." Other sources: "Harry Chandler Called by Death," *Los Angeles Times,* September 24, 1944; *The Ancestry of John Jewett Garland* by Gwendolyn Babcock; *Thinking Big* by Robert Gottlieb and Irene Wolt; *The Powers That Be* by David Halberstam; *Material Dreams* by Kevin Starr; *Southern California: An Island on the Land* by Carey McWilliams; and *Privileged Son* by Dennis McDougal (who on p. 89 describes Harry hollering "Whoa" to stop his car). Carey McWilliams details the newspaper war over the selling of retail advertising in the introduction to *Southern California: An Island on the Land.*

Billy Garland traces some of the California Fiestas Association's early steps in his "Story of the Origin of the Xth Olympiad Held in Los Angeles, California in 1932." I draw also from "Resistance, Persistence, Providence," by Robert Barney, and "Power without Authority: Los Angeles' Elites and the Construction of the Coliseum," by Steven A. Riess. Billy's public call for "upbuilding," a "great hotel," and resistance to Bolshevism was reported in "Local Realtors Honor Garland," *Los Angeles Times,* March 6, 1919, and in "Future of Prosperity," *Los Angeles Herald,* March 6, 1919. He expanded on these themes in "Garland Realtor Asks Immediate Campaign of Expansion in All Lines of Business," *Los Angeles Herald,* March 8, 1919.

My account of Billy's continued campaign for "upbuilding" throughout 1919 draws from "Million Homes are Needed in Country," *Los Angeles Times,* June 25, 1919; "Hear Fiestas Com. Report on Need of Big L.A. Auditorium," *Los Angeles Herald,* September 6, 1919; "Plans Laid to Aid New L.A. Industries," *Los Angeles Herald,* October 27, 1919; "$588,888 for L.A. Fiestas Planned: New Organization of Business Men Aims at Bringing Many Tourists to So. Cal.," *Los Angeles Herald,* November 12, 1919; "Garland Predicts 2 million LA People in 1949," *Los Angeles Herald,* November 28, 1919. Steven A. Riess describes the initial call for a seventy-five-thousand-seat stadium in "Power without Authority."

Billy Garland traces some of the Community Development Association's early steps in his "Story of the Origin of the Xth Olympiad Held in Los Angeles, California in 1932." I draw also from other sources, including "Resistance, Persistence, Providence," by Robert Barney, and "Power without Authority," by Steven A. Riess.

Billy Garland describes his 1920 trip to Antwerp in "Story of the Origin of the Xth Olympiad Held in Los Angeles, California in 1932." I draw also from newspaper accounts, including "Two LA Men Go to Get Next Olympiad: Garland and Weaver Soon to Sail for Belgium to Urge LA for Contest," *Los Angeles Herald*, July 14, 1920, and "Los Angeles Owes Debt to Himrod and Garland for Securing Olympics," *Los Angeles Times*, March 6, 1932. I draw as well from *The IOC Sessions, 1894–1955*, by Wolf Lyberg. Robert Barney writes about the trip in "Resistance, Persistence, Providence," as does Steven A. Riess in "Power without Authority." Billy reports on the outcome of his visit to the IOC in "Story of the Origin of the Xth Olympiad Held in Los Angeles, California in 1932." So does Pierre de Coubertin in his *Olympic Memoirs*.

Billy's wily cablegram from Antwerp is reported in "Olympiad Here if Bonds Carry," *Los Angeles Times*, August 29, 1920. Billy describes his response to the bond issue's defeat in "Story of the Origin of the Xth Olympiad Held in Los Angeles, California in 1932."

### CHAPTER 4. A FOOT IN THE DOOR

Billy describes the plan to finance the Coliseum privately in "Story of the Origin of the Xth Olympiad Held in Los Angeles, California in 1932." Others also tell this tale. The most thorough account is in Steven A. Riess's "Power without Authority." He discusses the Coliseum's ambiguous provenance there, as does Kevin Starr in *Material Dreams*, p. 110.

Billy quotes from Sloan's letter in "Story of the Origin of the Xth Olympiad Held in Los Angeles, California in 1932." Billy's letter to Coubertin on March 24 is in the William May Garland Collection at the LA84 Foundation Library. So is Coubertin's letter to Billy on April 22.

My description of Coubertin's "masterly coup d'état" derives from *Olympic Memoirs* by Pierre de Coubertin and from *The IOC Sessions, 1894–1955*, by Wolf Lyberg. My account of the brouhaha at the 1921 IOC session draws from several sources. Among them: *Report of the American Olympic Committee, Seventh Olympic Games, Antwerp, Belgium, 1920*, pp. 432–36, and "American Olympic Report is Disliked," *New York Times*, January 4, 1922. I draw also from two accounts by Robert Barney, in "Resistance, Persistence, Providence" and "William Garland and California's Quest to Host the Olympics," in *The World of Games: Political, Social and Educational Aspects*, pp. 144–52.

The extended exchange of letters between Garland and Coubertin in the months after the 1921 IOC session are in the Garland Collection, LA84 Foundation Library.

### CHAPTER 5. THE HAND OF MAN

Frederick Lewis Allen's *Only Yesterday* helped me understand the cultural uprising and political currents of the 1920s. Lynn Dumenil's *Modern Temper* also provided useful insights.

Among others, Kevin Starr *(Inventing the Dream)* and John Buntin *(L.A. Noir)* write about Theda Bara.

Among others, David Halberstam, in *The Powers That Be,* writes about Harry Chandler's instinct for developing lucrative subdivisions. Among others, Dennis MacDougal, in *Privileged Son,* writes about Billy and Harry underwriting Donald Douglas and Harris "Pop" Hanshue.

My account of the Fatty Arbuckle scandal derives from multiple sources, including a number of *Los Angeles Times* stories: "Arbuckle Jailed for Murder; Bail is Denied," September 11, 1921; "Jury Adjourns Without Indicting Film Comedian," September 13, 1921; "Athletic Club Ousts Arbuckle," September 13, 1921; "Arbuckle Indicted," September 14, 1921; "Girl's Death Caused by Arbuckle Jury Finds," September 15, 1921; "Chronology of Arbuckle Case," September 15, 1921; "Arbuckle Out on Bail; Held for Manslaughter," September 29, 1921; "Arbuckle Is Not Guilty, Jurors Decide Quickly," April 13, 1922. I draw also from "Arbuckle is Jailed on Murder Charge in Woman's Death," *New York Times,* September 12, 1921. I draw as well from "West Adams and the Movies" by Danny Miller, published in the December 2005 issue of *West Adams Matters,* the newsletter of the West Adams Heritage Association. Kevin Starr writes about the scandal in *Inventing the Dream,* pp. 325–27.

Billy's warning about an overheated real estate market appeared in "Boom Danger Threatens City," *Los Angeles Times,* December 24, 1922. The intense response to it is described in "Warning From Garland Stirs Hot Discussion," *Los Angeles Times,* December 31, 1922. Steven Treffers tells the story of Victor Girard in "How a Visionary Scoundrel Created Woodland Hills in the 1920s."

Coubertin's letter to Billy in the spring of 1922, notifying him that he'd been elected a member of the IOC, is in the Garland Collection, LA84 Foundation Library. Billy describes his trip to Paris for the 1922 IOC session in "Story of the Origin of the Xth Olympiad Held in Los Angeles, California in 1932." The extended exchange of letters between Billy and Coubertin during the second half of 1922 is in the Garland Collection, LA84 Foundation Library.

## CHAPTER 6. ROME, 1923

Billy describes his trip to Rome for the 1923 IOC session in "Story of the Origin of the Xth Olympiad Held in Los Angeles, California in 1932." I draw also from newspaper accounts, among them "LA Awarded 1932 Games: Garland Wins Long Struggle," *Los Angeles Times,* April 10, 1923, and "LA Gets Olympics of 1932," *New York Times,* April 10, 1923. I draw as well from *Olympic Memoirs* by Pierre de Coubertin and *The IOC Sessions, 1894–1955,* by Wolf Lyberg.

In Billy's accounts of the 1923 IOC session, in "Story of the Origin of the Xth Olympiad Held in Los Angeles, California in 1932" and a radio address to the nation on September 14, 1930, he would describe the IOC first voting for America, then selecting Los Angeles. So would the Los Angeles Olympic Organizing Committee (LAOOC) in its May 1930 *Olympic.* But Coubertin, in a private letter to Billy, later disputed that the IOC first voted for the country, then for Los Angeles, pointing out that the IOC always selects a city. Billy almost certainly had it wrong.

Billy describes his visit to the Quirinal Palace, his encounter with Mussolini, and his visit with the pope in "Story of the Origin of the Xth Olympiad Held in

Los Angeles, California in 1932." Billy's exchange of letters with Coubertin after the 1923 IOC session is in the Garland Collection, LA84 Foundation Library.

The LARB banquet honoring Billy is described in "Realty Men Give Natal Day Affair: Garland is Welcomed at Annual banquet of Local Land Agents," *Los Angeles Times,* June 7, 1923. Billy's recognition as "most useful citizen of 1923" is reported in "Garland is 'Most Useful,'" *Los Angeles Times,* June 19, 1923.

My account of the banquet celebrating the opening of the Biltmore Hotel draws from two *Los Angeles Times* stories published on October 3, 1923, "Biltmore Is Formally Opened by Gay Throng" and "Biltmore Ball Brilliant." My report of the LA Chamber of Commerce luncheon at the Biltmore derives from "Population of Million Within City," *Los Angeles Times,* November 23, 1923.

"Real Estate, the Basis of All Wealth" by William May Garland appeared in the *Realty Blue Book of California.* "Mixing Games and Business Profitably" by William May Garland appeared in *Southern California Business.*

### CHAPTER 7. THE GREAT MIGRATION

Among others, Kevin Starr *(Material Dreams)* and Carey McWilliams *(Southern California: An Island on the Land)* have written penetrating accounts about Southern California's dramatic evolution in the 1920s. "The Soul of the City" editorial appeared in the *Los Angeles Times* on June 24, 1923.

My account of the Liberty Hill demonstrations draws from a number of *Los Angeles Times* stories, including "Nab Wobblies in Night Raid: 'Liberty Hill' Gathering is Surprised by Police," May 13, 1923; "Reds Attack Harbor Jail: Wobblies Are Arrested After Demonstrations," May 14, 1923; and "Reds at the Harbor," May 14, 1923. Kevin Starr writes about the Liberty Hill demonstrations in *Endangered Dreams,* pp. 28, 51–52.

Laura Redford describes NAREB's new national policy on class and racial segregation in "The Promise and Principles of Real Estate Development in an American Metropolis: Los Angeles 1903–1923." Danny Miller writes about the West Adams neighborhood's restrictive covenants in "West Adams and the Movies." My account of the restrictive, nativist immigration acts of the 1920s draws from "The Immigration Act of 1924 (The Johnson-Reed Act)," Office of the Historian, U.S. Department of State; James J. Davis, secretary of labor, "Nation Faces Menace of Immigrant Inundation," *Los Angeles Times,* March 9, 1924; Vivian Yee, "In Trump's Immigration Remarks, Echoes of a Century-Old Racial Ranking," *New York Times,* January 13, 2018. Mike Davis, in *City of Quartz,* insightfully reports on discrimination against Jews, Catholics and blacks in Los Angeles.

Billy's letter to Coubertin, hailing Coolidge's reelection, is in the Garland Collection, LA84 Foundation Library. Billy saw the report of the Dutch wavering over the 1928 games in "Olympic Contests to Los Angeles," *Los Angeles Express,* November 14, 1924. His exchange of letters with Coubertin about this matter is in the Garland Collection, LA84 Foundation Library. The report about Los Angeles possibly taking over the 1928 games appeared in "Next Olympics in California," Associated Press, December 7, 1924.

Al Stump tells the story of Billy's decisive telegram in "The Olympics That Almost Wasn't." Robert Barney recounts it as well in "Resistance, Persistence, Providence."

## CHAPTER 8. PROTECTING THE IMAGE

Billy's optimism for the 1932 games is reported in "William Garland Returns from Europe with Bright Outlook for 1932," *Los Angeles Times,* July 18, 1926.

My account of the Los Angeles County political warfare between the supervisors and the district attorney draws from a number of *Los Angeles Times* stories. Among them: "Keyes Charged with Felony; Supervisors Under Arrest," October 5, 1926; "Supervisors Say Charges Part of Plot," October 5, 1926; "Keyes Charges Intimidation in Board's Action," October 5, 1926; "Webb Starts Keyes Inquiry," October 6, 1926; "Eight Los Angeles County Officials in Court Tomorrow: Supervisors to Answer Charges of Conspiracy," October 17, 1926; "Dirty Politics," October 28, 1926; "The Plot That Failed," December 9, 1926. I draw also from Roger M. Grace, "District Attorney's Criminal Action against Supervisors Fizzles," *Metropolitan News Enterprise,* October 3, 2007. Tom Sitton offers a comprehensive look at Kent Kane Parrot in "Did the Ruling Class Rule at City Hall?," a chapter in *Metropolis in the Making,* a book he coedited with William Deverell. John Buntin writes about Parrot in *L.A. Noir* (pp. 25–30), as do Robert Gottlieb and Irene Wolt in *Thinking Big* (p. 199).

Billy expressed his dismay over the LA County political fracas in W. M. Garland, "As to Our County Supervisors," *Los Angeles Times,* October 22, 1926. Though Billy wrote this in the form of a signed letter "to the Editor of the Times," it ran in the newspaper as a two-column-wide commentary.

Among many others, Kevin Starr has written about the Hollywood scandals of the 1920s, in *Inventing the Dream,* pp. 324–30.

My account of the plague outbreak in Los Angeles derives from multiple sources. William Deverell offers a comprehensive chapter on the outbreak in *Whitewashed Adobe: The Rise of Los Angeles and the Remaking of Its Mexican Past,* and Frank Feldinger expands that report in *A Slight Epidemic: The Government Cover-Up of Black Plague in Los Angeles.* I draw also from "Plague in Los Angeles, 1924–25," a bound manuscript produced by the California State Board of Health, copy in the Huntington Library; "The Pneumonic Plague in Los Angeles" by Emil Bogen; "The Pneumonic Plague Epidemic of 1924 in Los Angeles" by Arthur Viseltear; "The Plague Epidemic" by Helen Martin; and California State Board of Health, *Weekly Bulletin,* November 8 and 15, 1924. I draw as well from a number of *Los Angeles Times* articles: "Nine Mourners at Wake Dead," November 1, 1924; "Fourteen in Funeral Party Dead," November 2, 1924; "State to Fight Disease," November 4, 1924; "Disease Hazard End Seen," November 5, 1924; "Malady Outbreak Traced," November 5, 1924; "Disease Spread Checked," November 6, 1924. The *New York Times* also covered the outbreak: "Pneumonic Plague Seen in 14 Deaths," November 2, 1924; "Pneumonic Plague Takes 7 More Victims," November 3, 1924; "Los Angeles Halts Plague," November 5, 1924; "Three Plague Deaths and Four New Cases In Los Angeles As Epidemic Revives Again," November 7, 1924. So did the *Washington*

*Post:* "Pneumonic Plague is Feared After 13 Die in Los Angeles," November 2, 1924; "Plague Causes 21st Los Angeles Death," November 3, 1924. Cecilia Rasmussen took a look back at the outbreak in her article "In 1924 Los Angeles, a Scourge from the Middle Ages," *Los Angeles Times,* March 5, 2006.

The November 3 meeting in Mayor Cryer's office is described in the State Board of Health's "Plague in Los Angeles, 1924–25." William Deverell writes about it in *Whitewashed Adobe,* p. 184. At the USC Special Collections in Doheny Memorial Library, I reviewed the minutes and the stenographer's reports for LA Chamber of Commerce Board of Directors meetings held during the outbreak; these include sessions on October 30, November 6, November 13, and November 26 of 1924. The stenographer's report provided me with the quoted dialogue I used in reconstructing Harry Chandler and George Young's visit on November 13.

My account of E. L. Doheny's involvement in the Teapot Dome scandal derives from multiple sources. Margaret Leslie Davis offers a comprehensive section on it in *Dark Side of Fortune,* her biography of Doheny. Frederick Lewis Allen discusses it in *Only Yesterday,* as does Kevin Starr in *Material Dreams.* I draw also from a number of *Los Angeles Times* articles: "Trial of Fall and Doheny in Oil Case Opens Today," November 22, 1926; "Doheny in Relapse: Oil Trial Again Postponed," December 8, 1926; "Evil Denied by Doheny: Dramatic Story Told on Stand," December 10, 1926; "Secrets of Navy Safe: Wilbur Balks on Oil Trial Stand," December 11, 1926; "Fall-Doheny Case Will Go To Jury This Week," December 12, 1926; "Fall, Acquitted, Faces New Plot Charge Today: Government Prepares to Press Case Involving Sinclair: Doheny Jubilant," December 17, 1926; "Finale Near in Oil Trial," December 15, 1926. I draw as well from *New York Times* reports: "Doheny Declares Robison Said Japan Had Mobilized; Defends His Loan To Fall," December 10, 1926; "Oil Man Cross-Examined: Defendant Admits the Security for $100,000 Has Only $3,300 Value," December 11, 1926; "Oil Trial Evidence Is Ended Abruptly," December 12, 1926.

Frederick Lewis Allen describes the business community's resistance to the Teapot Dome prosecutions in *Only Yesterday,* pp. 133–36. The *New York Times'* denunciation of "scandal mongers and assassins of character" appeared in a fiery, lengthy editorial on March 31, 1924, titled "Signs of Returning Reason." Doheny's testimony about his son learning something "even if he had been held up on the way" was reported in "Oil Man Cross-Examined: Defendant Admits the Security for $100,000 Has Only $3,300 Value," *New York Times,* December 11, 1926. Doheny's triumphant return to Los Angeles is chronicled in "Greeting Touches Doheny: Oil Magnate Visibly Affected as Crowd of Friends Gives Tumultuous Welcome on Arrival," *Los Angeles Times,* December 22, 1926.

Billy Garland's role as toastmaster and committee chairman for Doheny's appreciation banquet is reported in "Plans Given in Honor of E. L. Doheny," *Los Angeles Times,* January 9, 1927. Margaret Leslie Davis describes the banquet in *Dark Side of Fortune,* p. 212. Not everyone in Los Angeles embraced the notion of treating Doheny as a conquering hero. On January 19, 1927, nine days after the banquet, local attorney Nathan Newby, at a City Club luncheon, denounced Doheny and the prominent citizens who lionized him. To his shouted question, "I ask you, fellow citizens, shall we let the word go out to the world that Los Angeles approves the characterization of Edward L. Doheny as 'the greatest patriot'?" the crowd of three hundred yelled back, "No! No! Never!" See "Doheny Flayed At City Club," *Los Angeles Times,* January 20, 1927.

### CHAPTER 9. A BOLT FROM THE BLUE

My account of Zack Farmer's alarming report and the CDA's near abandonment of the games derives from a letter Billy Garland wrote to Avery Brundage on February 7, 1936, to which he attached a copy of the Farmer report. The letter and report are on microfilm in the Avery Brundage Collection, Box 56, LA84 Foundation Library. Robert Barney also writes about this event in "Resistance, Persistence, Providence."

Jules Tygiel's *The Great Los Angeles Swindle* is the definitive chronicle of the Julian Petroleum Corporation scandal. Dennis McDougal writes about it in *Privileged Son* (pp. 131–34). I draw as well from "True Bills Due in Julian Case," *Los Angeles Times,* June 23, 1927; "The Julian Mess," *Los Angeles Times,* June 23, 1927; Roger M. Grace, "Ex-District Attorney Asa Keyes Becomes Prisoner No. 48,218 at San Quentin," *Metropolitan News-Enterprise,* November 13, 2007; "Asa Keyes Is Dead; Noted Prosecutor," *New York Times,* October 19, 1934.

Those who have written about Mayor Cryer appointing James Davis police chief in 1926 as a means to appease Chandler and the city's business elite include Robert Gottlieb and Irene Wolt in *Thinking Big* (p. 199), Tom Sitton in "Did the Ruling Class Rule at City Hall in 1920s Los Angeles?" (p. 312), and John Buntin in *L.A. Noir* (pp. 29–30). Gottlieb and Wolt report on Billy Garland and Harry Chandler turning out at a celebration to honor the new chief, as did the *Los Angeles Times:* "New Chief Honored at Breakfast: Officialdom of Southland Gathers at Function for Incoming Police Head," March 20, 1926.

My account of Christine Collins's ordeal and the Wineville Chicken Coop Murders draws from a number of *Los Angeles Times* reports: "Police Widen Hunt for Boy," April 5, 1928; "Two Hundred Policemen Today Start New Hunt for Collins Boy," April 10, 1928; "Collins Youth Found in East," August 5, 1928; "Kidnapped Collins Lad Returned to Mother's Arms," August 19, 1928; "'Kidnapped' Boy Tells Hoax," September 20, 1928; "Enigma Boy Identified," September 21, 1928; "Mrs. Collins Accuses Jones," September 25, 1928; "Collins Hoax Comes to End," October 3, 1928; "Council Calls Davis and Jones," October 25, 1928; "Capt. Jones Refuses to Testify Before Council Committee," October 26, 1928; "Jones Suspended By Board," November 20, 1928; "Mrs. Collins' Suit Heard," July 10, 1929; "Ordeal Traced by Mrs. Collins, July 11, 1929; "Hoax Discussed in Collins Suit," July 13, 1929; "The Other Son," October 19, 2008. Anthony Flacco writes about the Wineville Murders in *The Road out of Hell.* A fictional version of Christine Collins's experience was depicted in the 2008 film *The Changeling,* starring Angelina Jolie; Clint Eastwood directed, based on research and a screenplay by the former journalist J. Michael Straczynski.

My account of Billy beating the drums for the games and the Olympic bond issue draws from "Olympiad Aids Dutch Wealth," *Los Angeles Times,* September 7, 1928; "Olympics Success Forecast," *Los Angeles Times,* September 22,

1928; and "Voters urged to Pass \$1 Million Bond Issue, *Los Angeles Times,* November 4, 1928. Al Stump, in "The Olympics That Almost Wasn't," reports on Billy's "the hell you will, sir," challenge to Avery Brundage, as does Robert Barney in "Resistance, Persistence, Providence."

### CHAPTER 10. PLANTING A SEED

Coubertin's confidential February 1929 letter to Billy is in the Garland Collection, LA84 Foundation Library.

The Greystone murder-suicide has been widely chronicled. My account derives from multiple sources, including *Me Detective* by Leslie T. White (the DA's investigator at the murder scene); *Dark Side of Fortune* by Margaret Leslie Davis; "We Shall Never Know: Murder, Money and the Enduring Mystery of Greystone Mansion," by Hadley Meares, KCET.org, July 25, 2014; "Vintage Noir: The Tragedy at Greystone," by Benjamin Welton, crimemagazine. com, May 16, 2013; "Cracking the Cassidy Case," by Robert F. Moss, Criticism and Scholarship: The Raymond Chandler web site, palmettonewmedia. com. I draw also from a number of *Los Angeles Times* stories, including "Doheny Murder Inquiry Discloses Controversy," February 18, 1929; "Doctor Asserts Madness Caused Double Death," February 18, 1929; "Investigators Seek to Reconstruct Death Tragedy at Palatial Home," February 18, 1929; and "No Inquest on Doheny: Officials Close Inquiries," February 19, 1929.

Dr. Fishbaugh's account of his Saturday afternoon visit with Hugh Plunkett appears in "Doctor Asserts Madness Caused Double Death," *Los Angeles Times,* February 18, 1929. Dr. Fishbaugh's account of his late Saturday night experience at the Greystone Mansion appears in "Doheny Murder Inquiry Discloses Controversy," *Los Angeles Times,* February 18, 1929. Leslie White wrote about his investigation at the Greystone Mansion, and his visit with DA Fitts, in a chapter of *Me Detective,* pp. 109–11.

My account of Billy at the IOC meeting in Lausanne in April 1929 draws from *The IOC Sessions, 1894–1955,* by Wolf Lyberg, and from "Garland Goes to Europe for Olympic Meet," *Los Angeles Times,* March 30, 1929. My report of Billy's visit with President Hoover after the IOC meeting draws from "Olympic Games Bid for Hoover," *Los Angeles Times,* June 8, 1929. My description of Billy's clash with Mayor Cryer over the CDA's continued management of the Coliseum draws from "Stadium Lease Disfavored," *Los Angeles Times,* June 1, 1929; and "Olympic Games Booster Home: Garland Returns from Switzerland Meet," June 12, 1929. Steven A. Riess writes about this conflict with Mayor Cryer in "Power without Authority: Los Angeles' Elites and the Construction of the Coliseum."

### CHAPTER 11. THEN CAME THE CRASH

My account of Marshall Hinman, the Brooks Locomotive Works, and the Panic of 1873 derives from Gwendolyn Babcock's *The Ancestry of John Jewett Garland.* In her chapter on Marshall Hinman (pp. 78–81), she quotes extensively from Hinman's talk at the testimonial dinner in 1901.

Al Stump reports on Billy's postcrash promotional shuttle trips to Europe in "The Olympics That Almost Wasn't." So does Ellen Galford in *The X Olympiad*, likely drawing from Stump. The LA Olympic Organizing Committee's methods of promoting the games through a press office are described in *Official Report, the Games of the Xth Olympiad, Los Angeles 1932*, by the Xth Olympiade Committee.

Billy's signing and sending of invitations is reported in "Nations Invited to Games Here," *Los Angeles Times*, February 5, 1930; and American Olympic Committee (AOC), *Olympic News*, April 1930. Billy's meeting with President Hoover is described in "Garland Talks to President," *Los Angeles Times*, March 19, 1930.

My account of the athletes' early training and competition, their eyes on the 1932 games, draws largely from the AOC, *Olympic News*, March 1930 and April 1930 editions. Frank W. Blankley, chairman of the National AAU Swimming Committee, offered his remarks in the AOC, *Olympic News*, April 1930.

My account of Helene Madison's background draws from a range of sources. Among them: "Helene Madison (1913–1970)," by Alan Stein, HistoryLink. org; "Queen Helene Through Racing—It Costs Too Much To Be Champion," *Los Angeles Times*, August 9, 1932; "Helene Madison, Record Swimmer," *New York Times*, November 27, 1970; AOC, *Olympic News*, April 1930. Doris Pieroth writes about Helene's early years in *Their Day in the Sun: Women of the 1932 Olympics* (pp. 72–73). Helene's father talks about her triumphant return to Seattle in "Queen Helene Through Racing—It Costs Too Much To Be Champion," *Los Angeles Times*, August 9, 1932.

#### CHAPTER 12. BERLIN, 1930

My account of the Berlin 1930 IOC session and Olympic Congress derives from a range of sources: "Meeting of the IOC, Berlin 22–24 May, 1930," *Official Bulletin of the International Olympic Committee*, no. 16 (July 1930); "Olympic Congress of Berlin 25th–30th May, 1930, *Official Bulletin of the International Olympic Committee*, no. 16 (July 1930); AOC, *Olympic News*, April 1930, June 1930, July 1930; LAOOC, *Olympic*, May 1930, September 1930, April 1931; *The IOC Sessions, 1894–1955*, by Wolf Lyberg; "Minutes of International Olympic Committee Congress at Berlin," in AOC, *Olympic News*, June 1930. I draw also from a number of *Los Angeles Times* articles: "Garland Off to Berlin Meeting," May 9, 1930; "Olympic Stage Set: Plans for 1932 Games Detailed," May 22, 1930; "Olympic Congress Opens," May 26, 1930; "Olympic Plans Advance," May 27, 1930. Robert Barney writes about the Berlin Congress in "Resistance, Persistence, Providence."

In the wake of Billy's report to the Berlin Congress about reduced expenses, a per-athlete cost of "approximately $400" was reported in LAOOC, *Olympic*, May 1930; and AOC, *Olympic News*, June–July 1930. Two years later, after the games, the LAOOC *Official Report* revised that to "$500 or less." Zack Farmer's comments about resistance to the idea of the village are reported by Al Stump in "The Olympics That Almost Wasn't" and by Jerry Belcher in "LA's '32 Olympics—Bright Days amid Dark Times," *Los Angeles Times*, May 21, 1978.

My account of Billy's cautionary cable to the LA Board of Supervisors, and its effect on city leaders, draws from "Losing Olympic Games Hinted," *Los Angeles Times,* May 25, 1930; and "Fund Provided for Coliseum," *Los Angeles Times,* May 27, 1930. The IOC decision in Berlin to allow female athletic participation is reported in "Fair Athletes Win Argument," *Los Angeles Times,* May 30, 1930.

My account of Billy's triumphant return home after the Berlin Congress, and talk at the Breakfast Club, draws from several *Los Angeles Times* articles, including "Garland Home, Well Pleased," July 17, 1930; "Garland Paints Olympic Glory," July 18, 1930; "Olympic Game Prospects," July 18, 1930. I draw also from "The Strangest Club in Los Angeles, the L.A. Breakfast Club," by James Bartlett, KCET.org, March 16, 2017.

My account of the athletes' achievements in the summer of 1930 derives from a range of newspaper stories that ran in July 1930, among them one about Eddie Tolan breaking the hundred-meter world record while running uphill: "Dash Time Bettered by Tolan: Michigan Flyer Sets New Figure for 100 Meters," *Los Angeles Times,* July 2, 1930. I draw also from the AOC, *Olympic News,* July 1930 and August 1930 editions, and from Doris Pieroth's report in *Their Day in the Sun.*

### CHAPTER 13. A SACRED DUTY

Billy's nationwide radio address is described and reproduced in the AOC's *Olympic News,* October–November 1930 edition. Billy's exchange of letters with Coubertin in September and October of 1930 is in the Garland Collection, LA84 Foundation Library. Coubertin's reminder that "the IOC chooses a city, not a nation," conflicts with Billy's account of the 1923 IOC session in "Story of the Origin of the Xth Olympiad Held in Los Angeles, California in 1932." Billy's version is repeated in the May 1930 edition of the LAOOC, *Olympic.*

Billy's February 1931 proposal for the immediate relief of the unemployment situation in Southern California was reported in "Construction Held Panacea," *Los Angeles Times,* February 8, 1931. For my account of Billy's trip to the IOC annual session in Barcelona in April 1931, I draw from "Olympics Envoy Off for Spain," *Los Angeles Times,* April 10, 1931; "Minutes of the IOC General Session, Barcelona, 1931," in *IOC General Session Minutes, 1884–1989;* and AOC, *Olympic News,* May–June 1931 edition. Billy's claim that three thousand athletes from forty-eight countries would compete in the 1932 games was reported in "Olympic Games Fervor Swells," *Los Angeles Times,* July 3, 1931.

My account of the athletes' achievements in the summer of 1931 draws from a number of *New York Times* articles. Among them: "World's Mark Set by Miss Didrikson," July 26, 1931; "235 Compete Today in Women's Meet," July 25, 1931; "Women's Stars Meet on Track Saturday," July 19, 1931; "A.A.U. Title Meet Will Start Friday," June 28, 1931; "High Hurdle Mark Lowered by Beard," July 5, 1931; "Crabbe Retains Title," July 15, 1931; "Title Swim Meet Opens Wednesday," July 12, 1931; "Diving Title Kept by Miss Coleman," July 20, 1931; "Miss Madison Clips 500-Meter Record," July 27, 1931; "Miss Holm Breaks World Swim Mark," July 20, 1931. I draw also from "Tolan Defeats Wykoff at Vancouver: Colored Star Breaks Mark," *Los Angeles Times,*

August 23, 1931. Doris Pieroth writes about the women athletes' events in *Their Day in the Sun.*

My account of LA's 150th birthday celebration draws from a number of *Los Angeles Times* articles, including "City Acclaims LA Fiesta Opening in Colorful Pageant: Queen Crowning Cheered by Throng of 87,000," September 5, 1931; "Throngs View Gala Pageant," September 5, 1931; and "Downtown's Fiesta Began as a Multicultural Celebration," April 27, 2003. John Weaver writes about this fiesta in *Los Angeles: The Enormous Village, 1781–1981*, pp. 109–11.

The official Olympic Campaign for Funds launch on October 1, 1931, was reported in AOC, *Olympic News,* September–October 1931 edition. President Hoover's official acceptance of an invitation to open the games was reported in "President Will Open Olympics," *Los Angeles Times,* October 11, 1931; and in AOC, *Olympic News,* September–October 1931 edition.

Billy's ecstatic response to Hoover's acceptance, and Mayor John Porter's announcement of plans for the greatest banquet ever held in America, appear in "Porter, Garland Tell Plans for Banquet of 10,000, Big Reception." This article ran on October 11 in a Los Angeles newspaper. I found a reproduction of the story, without an identifying newspaper's name, in the Avery Brundage Collection at the LA84 Foundation Library. My search of databases beyond the *LA Times* did not identify which newspaper published the story. I deduce it appeared in the *Herald.*

Talk across Europe of postponing the 1932 games was reported in "Suggest Olympics Should Be Put Off," *New York Times,* September 24, 1931. My account of hunger marchers demonstrating at the state capitol in Sacramento draws from a number of *Los Angeles Times* articles, including "Reds Foiled by Rolph: Capitol March's Aim Fails," January 8, 1931; "Sacramento Rioters Battle with Police," February 11, 1931; "Rolph Cancels Hunger Parade," December 24, 1931; and "City to Permit Hunger March," December 30, 1931. Al Stump writes about the "groceries not games" demonstrations in "The Olympics That Almost Wasn't," as does Robert Barney, citing Stump, in "Resistance, Persistence, Providence." Al Stump writes about Billy calling for a "a big, rousing, blues-chasing party" in "The Olympics That Almost Wasn't."

### CHAPTER 14. DESPERATE HOURS

I draw from multiple sources for the figures that document the harsh economic conditions at the start of 1932, including "U.S.A.—1932," by Burt Reiner. Billy's optimism and insistence that the Depression was ending appeared in two *Los Angeles Times* articles, "Garland Olympics Optimist," February 21, 1932; and "Easterners Profit Most in Realty Bargains Here," February 28, 1932. Billy's radio talk urging "all Californians to return to habit" was reported in "Normal Spending Sought by Bank," *Madera Tribune,* June 20, 1932. My description of Billy's sixty-sixth birthday party at the Los Angeles Athletic Club draws from "Garland Given Birthday Fete: Widely Known Civic Leader Receives High Honor," *Los Angeles Times,* April 1, 1932.

My account of the Bonus Army draws from multiple sources. Among them are a number of *New York Times* stories: "'Bonus Army' Moves Slowly Over

Indiana," May 27, 1932; "Western Bonus Army Moved Through Ohio," May 28, 1932; "Bonus Army Moves Into Maryland," May 29, 1932; "Bonus Army Invasion New Capitol Worry," May 11, 1932; "Bonus Hikers Begin Lobbying in House," June 1, 1932; "Capital Asks Funds to Feed Bonus Army," June 2, 1932; "Veterans Here Off to Capital as House Forces a Bonus Vote," June 5, 1932; "Capital Faces Siege of 8,000 Veterans," June 6, 1932; "Bonus Army Rallies For Parade Tonight," June 7, 1932; "7,000 in Bonus Army Parade in Capital, Orderly But Grim," June 8, 1932; "Bonus Army Asked to Leave Capital; Veterans Refuse," June 9, 1932; "Bonus March Held an 'Escape Gesture,'" June 9, 1932; "Capital Asks States to Halt Bonus Trek; Epidemic is Feared," June 10, 1932; "Bonus Ranks Grow; Capital Seeks Help," June 12, 1932; "Eager 'Army' Waits Bonus Vote Today," June 13, 1932; "House Forces Vote on the Bonus Today; 'Antis' Muster 175," June 14, 1932; "Bonus Bill Passes in House, 209–176; Senate to Rush Vote," June 16, 1932; "Bonus Bill Reported Adversely, 14 to 2; Camp Morale Sags," June 17, 1932; "Vote on the Bill is 62–18: City at High Tension as Hundreds Camp in Plaza," June 18, 1932; "Reds Urge Mutiny in the Bonus Army," June 19, 1932; "Urges Congress Aid for the Bonus Army," June 21, 1932; "6,000 in Bonus Army Jam Capitol Steps," July 3, 1932; "Bonus Army Boos Hoover at Capitol," July 6, 1932; "Bonus Army Begins an All-Night Siege," July 13, 1932; "Bonus Siege Brings A Call for Marines," July 15, 1932; "Drive Bonus Pickets From White House; Police Isolate Area," July 17, 1932. Burt Reiner writes about the Bonus Army advance on Washington in "U.S.A.—1932." Steve Harvey takes a look back at it in "The Bonus Marchers' Protest," *Los Angeles Times,* April 25, 1971.

Among others, Frederick Lewis Allen writes about difficult conditions abroad in *Only Yesterday.* So does David Guiney in *The Friendly Olympics.* Al Stump describes the "mounting sense of trepidation" about the 1932 games in "1932, the 'Hopeless' Dream of William May Garland" and "The Olympics That Almost Wasn't." Ellen Galford, drawing from Stump, does so as well in *The X Olympiad.* Allen Guttmann refers to the silence from other countries in *The Olympics: A History of the Modern Games,* p. 50. Bill Henry and Patricia Henry Yeomans report on open speculation that the games wouldn't be held in *An Approved History of the Olympic Games,* p. 155. These accounts and others like them stand in sharp contrast to the boosters' claims during this period, as printed in the AOC's *Olympic News* and the LAOOC's *Olympic.*

My account of the American Olympic Committee's struggle to raise funds for its team, and Avery Brundage's pessimism, draws from "Brundage Orders Team Reductions: Lack of Funds is Reason," *New York Times,* May 27, 1932; and "Melting Resources: A Historical Analysis of the 1932 Olympic Winter and Summer Games," by Jonathan Robert Paul. Al Stump describes the suspension of Olympic superstar Paavo Nurmi, and Billy's response, in "1932, the 'Hopeless' Dream of William May Garland" and "The Olympics That Almost Wasn't."

Accounts of the confrontation between Billy Garland and his committee in a Los Angeles Athletic Club meeting room appear in two articles by Al Stump, "The Olympics That Almost Wasn't" and "1932, the 'Hopeless' Dream of William May Garland." Billy, confirming, wrote about this LAAC showdown in a letter to Bill Henry dated May 23, 1933, in which he refers to "one noon in the LAAC" when "you and Harry Chandler rallied to my assistance." This letter is reproduced on p. 48 of *Behind the Headlines with Bill Henry, 1903–1970*, edited by Patricia Henry Yeomans. I believe Henry was the source for Stump's report. Stump described Billy ordering two million tickets in "1932, the 'Hopeless' Dream of William May Garland."

## CHAPTER 15. COMPETING NARRATIVES

My account of the design and building of the Olympic Village derives from multiple sources. Chief among them is *Official Report, the Games of the Xth Olympiad, Los Angeles 1932*, published by the Xth Olympiade Committee (the LAOOC). Others include Duncan Aikman, "Making the Olympic Games Alibi-Proof," *New York Times*, June 19, 1932; and "Olympic Village," in *Canada at the Xth Olympiad 1932*, edited by W. A. Fry (which I came across in the archives of the LA84 Foundation Library). Mark Dyreson writes about the Olympic Village, citing Aikman's *New York Times* story, in "Marketing National Identity: The Olympic Games of 1932 and American Culture," pp. 23–48.

My account of late interest developing owing to reduced steamship and railroad fares draws from "Official Report, the Games of the Xth Olympiad"; *Canada at the Xth Olympiad 1932*, edited by W. A. Fry; and Ellen Galford, *The X Olympiad*. My description of the women athletes attracting interest, and the support of Kirby and Brundage, draws from "Official Report, the Games of the Xth Olympiad"; Ellen Galford, *The X Olympiad*; Allen Guttmann, *The Olympics: A History of the Modern Games*. My report of mounting boosterism for the games in the summer of 1932 derives from a number of *Los Angeles Times* articles. Among them: "Speakers Cite Game Benefits," June 3, 1932; "Whole State Sends Card Inviting World to the Games," June 5, 1932; "Work Speeded as Games Near," June 5, 1932; "Olympic Plans Complete," June 9, 1932; "Nations Parade to be Greatest," June 19, 1932; "Games' Closing to be Colorful: Demand for Tickets Swells as Time Approaches," June 26, 1932.

My account of the competing narratives during the summer of 1932 draws from "Los Angeles Calm as Olympics Near," *New York Times*, May 1, 1932; and Al Stump, "The Olympics That Almost Wasn't." I found Avery Brundage's "for your eyes only" letter to Zack Farmer in the Avery Brundage Collection at the LA84 Foundation Library, Box 56.

My description of mounting tensions at the Bonus Army encampment derives from "Vote on the Bill is 62–18: City at High Tension as Hundreds Camp in Plaza," *New York Times*, June 18, 1932; "Reds Urge Mutiny in the Bonus Army," *New York Times*, June 19, 1932; "The Bonus Marchers' Protest," *Los Angeles Times*, April 25, 1971.

My report on President Hoover cancelling his trip to the games draws from "President's Trip Off; Hoover Cannot Open Olympics," *Los Angeles Times*, June 19, 1932; Al Stump, "The Olympics That Almost Wasn't"; Allen Guttmann, *The Olympics: A History of the Modern Games*, p. 50. Al Stump writes about Billy's "haunted nights" in "The Olympics That Almost Wasn't."

## CHAPTER 16. PLAYING HIS CARDS

My account of Billy getting Mary Pickford and Douglas Fairbanks to promote the games derives from several *Los Angeles Times* articles, including "Radio Plea Arranged for Games—Pickford and Fairbanks Worldwide Broadcast," June 27, 1932; "Olympic Radio Plan Complete—Mary and Doug Introduce Athletes," June 30, 1932; and "Doug and Mary Go on Air—Invite in Great Program," July 7, 1932. I draw also from "Douglas Fairbanks and the Birth of Hollywood's Love Affair with the Olympics," by Rusty Wilson. Kevin Starr writes incisively about Pickford and Fairbanks's hold on their fans in *Inventing the Dream*, pp. 337–38. Doris Pieroth, working off of a tape transcription, quotes from Mary's Hollywood Bowl speech in *Their Day in the Sun*, p. 85.

My summary of athletes preparing for the Olympic trials draws from the Olympian Oral Histories archive at the LA84 Foundation Library (interviews of Evelyne Hall and Jean Shiley, conducted by George Hodak); "Fair Mermaids Crack Records," *Los Angeles Times,* July 17, 1932; and Doris Pieroth, *Their Day in the Sun.* My account of the walkout by five Los Angeles Athletic Club women athletes derives from "Coast Mermaids Fly to Olympic Trials," *Chicago Herald Examiner*, July 6, 1932; and "Girl Aquatic Team Hikes East by Air," Associated Press, July 6, 1932. A playfully posed photo of Georgia Coleman, Josephine McKim, and the three other women athletes, all in bathing suits, carrying hobo bundles over their shoulders, appeared in the *Philadelphia Inquirer* on July 3, 1932, with a caption reading, "Give Us a Ride, Mister; We Want to Try Out for the Olympics." The athletes, the caption added, "are getting in training for the open road, so that if they have to hitchhike their way to New York for the Olympic tryouts they will have some experience in the art." Doris Pieroth, drawing from these same sources, writes about this incident in *Their Day in the Sun*, pp. 62–63.

My account of the Olympic trials derives from a range of sources, including a number of *Los Angeles Times* stories. Among them: "Crabbe and Kalili Win Places on Swim Card," July 15, 1932; "Georgia Coleman Dethroned in National Diving Trials," July 16, 1932; "Fair Mermaids Crack Records," July 17, 1932; "Wykoff, Dyer, Kiesel Get Olympic Berths," July 18, 1932; "Ben Pestered to Failure," July 19, 1932; "I Could Feel 'Twas My Day: Bill Graber Tells of His Great Triumph," July 18, 1932; "Babe Didrikson Steals Shows as Women's Track and Field Championships Are Staged," July 17, 1932; "Yanks Picked to Win Games," July 17, 1932; "Records Don't Worry Babe," July 19, 1932. I draw also from "Miss Didrikson, the One-Girl Track Team, Heads U.S. Squad of 16 Named for Olympics," *New York Times,* July 18, 1932; and from *Report of the American Olympic Committee: Games of the Xth Olympiad*, edited by Frederick W. Rubien. Doris Pieroth, in *Their Day in the Sun,* provides a comprehensive chronicle of the women athletes' achievements at the trials. Ellen Galford reports on selected events in *The X Olympiad.*

My account of Glenn Cunningham's background draws from several sources, including "Cunningham Calls It A Career," kuhistory76.com, the University of Kansas history website. In his oral history in the LA84 Foundation Library archives, Olympic teammate William Chisholm talks movingly about Cunningham's terrible accident at age eight and his heroic process of recovery.

My description of Babe Didrikson's conduct and accomplishments derives from the news stories about the Olympic trials listed above, Doris Pieroth's *Their Day in the Sun*, Ellen Galford's *The X Olympiad*, and *"Whatta Gal": The Babe Didrikson Story*, by William Oscar Johnson and Nancy P. Williamson. My extended profiles of Evelyne Hall and Jean Shiley draw largely from their oral histories in the Olympian Oral Histories archive, LA84 Foundation Library; both interviews were conducted by George A. Hodak in the fall of 1987. Babe Didrikson's "We will win" claim appeared in "Records Don't Worry Babe—Those Foreign Girls Can't Beat Me," *Los Angeles Times*, July 19, 1932.

## CHAPTER 17. A LUSH NEW WORLD

My account of the sudden, skyrocketing interest in the games in July 1932 draws from "Border Ruling Due to Games—Gates Remain Open Longer," *Los Angeles Times*, July 12, 1932; "Interest in Olympics Rises," *New York Times*, July 12, 1932; "Los Angeles Opposes Olympiad Night Life; Protests Opening Border to Mexico," *New York Times*, July 12, 1932; "Olympic Mark Set by Ticket Demand: More than 854,000 Already Sold," *New York Times*, July 17, 1932; "News Writers to See Sights," *Los Angeles Times*, July 17, 1932; "The Call of the Olympiad: 36 Nations Have Answered Call," *Los Angeles Times*, July 17, 1932. The report of seven hundred Texans leasing an entire hotel appears in "Olympic Sale Goes Over 1,300,000 Mark," *New York Times*, July 21, 1932. Among others, Al Stump writes about this upsurge in "The Olympics That Almost Wasn't," as do Ellen Galford in *The X Olympiad* and Doris Pieroth in *Their Day in the Sun*.

The story of the Brazil team's selling of coffee beans appears in a number of accounts, with the precise details often varying. I chiefly rely on "Only 24 of Squad Able to Quit Boat," *New York Times*, by Arthur Daley, July 23, 1932, which seems comprehensive and grounded. But David Guiney, in *The Friendly Olympics* (pp. 70–71), suggests the Brazil coffee bean story has been embellished over time. Ellen Galford tells of South Africa and Australia's efforts to send athletes to the 1932 Games in *The X Olympiad*, pp. 29–30.

My description of various foreign teams arriving in Los Angeles draws from a number of *Los Angeles Times* articles. Among them: "Germans Given Big Welcome," July 22, 1932; "Italian Olympic Team Gets Riotous Welcome," July 18, 1932; "Brisk Week-End on Port Docket: Many Athletes and Visitors Coming to Olympiad," July 22, 1932; "Greeks Carrying On: Five Athenians Here for Olympics," July 24, 1932. Doris Pieroth reports on these arrivals in *Their Day in the Sun*, pp. 85–89.

My account of the American team members' journeys to Los Angeles derives from "Train To Leave Monday: 17-Car Olympic Special to Carry More Than 100 Athletes," *New York Times*, July 15, 1932; "U.S. Stars Depart For Coast Games," *New York Times*, July 19, 1932; and Frederick W. Rubien, *Report of the American Olympic Committee, Games of the Xth Olympiad, Los Angeles, California, July 30–August 14, 1932*, p. 43. My report of the women's track and field team's train ride also draws from the oral history testimony of Evelyne Hall and Jean Shiley. Doris Pieroth reports on this train journey in *Their Day in the Sun,* pp. 46–47, as does Ellen Galford in *The X Olympiad,* p. 108. Tidye Pickett's experience at the Brown Hotel is described in Ron Grossman, "Tidye Pickett: Chicago Track Star Was First African-American Female Olympian," *Chicago Tribune,* August 19, 2016.

The arrival of the American women athletes in LA is reported in "All Records 'To Go Boom,'" *Los Angeles Times,* July 23, 1932; and Grantland Rice, "Greatest Sport Show Ever Held in World," *Los Angeles Times,* July 7, 1932. In Frederick W. Rubien, *Report of the American Olympic Committee, Games of the Xth Olympiad, Los Angeles, California, July 30–August 14, 1932,* p. 32, the chairman of the American Olympic Finance Committee, George W. Graves, writes about enlisting the support of journalists: "The A.O.C. Chair solicited the cooperation of sports writers of the PRESS and many leading magazines . . . and they were later organized into an A.O.C. PRESS COMMITTEE with GRANT-LAND RICE as CHAIRMAN. Their articles greatly assisted our work and were deeply appreciated." (The words in small caps are his.)

Skyrocketing ticket sales are reported in "Olympic Sale Goes Over 1,300,000 Mark: All Attendance Records Exceeded," *New York Times,* July 21, 1932. Vice President Curtis's imminent arrival is hailed in "VP Curtis To Open Olympics; Hoover Unable to Leave Post," *Los Angeles Times,* July 20, 1932. The *Los Angeles Times* emotional editorial, "The Call of the Olympiad," appeared on July 17, 1932.

### CHAPTER 18. A PARALLEL UNIVERSE

Among others, *Los Angeles Times* sportswriter Paul Zimmerman effectively describes the city that visitors saw as they arrived for the games in "Olympics Put LA on the Map," page 2 of *Los Angeles, the Olympic City, 1932–1984,* a document edited and published in 1984 by the photographer Delmar Watson (I found it at the LA84 Foundation Library). Doris Pieroth, drawing from Zimmerman, also describes the city in *Their Day in the Sun,* pp. 84–85. My list of hotel room rates draws from "Hotel Reservations: List of Select, Centrally-Located Hotels, and Prices," a document issued by the Hotel Reservation Committee of the Tenth Olympiad, which I found at the LA84 Foundation Library.

My account of the vibrant atmosphere in Los Angeles as the games began draws from "Thousands crowding into LA for Opening of Olympics Games Tomorrow," *New York Times,* July 29, 1932; "Curtis Today Opens the Olympic Games in Colorful Scene," *New York Times,* July 29, 1932; "Games Visitors Throng Hotels," *Los Angeles Times,* July 27, 1932; "Visitors Thronging City," *Los Angeles Times,* July 28, 1932; "Influx to City Gains Impetus," *Los Angeles Times,* July 29, 1932.

My description of Hollywood luminaries' involvement with the athletes draws from "Every Foreign Champion Must Meet Film Stars," *Los Angeles Times,* July 24, 1932; and Malcolm Metcalf's oral history in the Olympian Oral Histories archive, LA84 Foundation Library. My description of gate-crashers at the Olympic Village draws from "Fair Damsel Crashes Village Gate," *Los Angeles Times,* July 29, 1932; and *Canada at the Xth Olympiad 1932,* edited by W. A. Fry. My report of "calmer" conditions at the Chapman Park Hotel draws from Jean Shiley's and Jane Fauntz's oral histories, LA84 Foundation Library, and from *Canada at the Xth Olympiad 1932*, edited by W. A. Fry.

Hector Dyer and Jane Fauntz tell of their encounter with celebrities in their oral histories, part of the Olympian Oral Histories archive, LA84 Foundation Library. The parties hosted by Billy Garland, Louis B. Mayer, and Mary Pickford and Douglas Fairbanks are described in *Official Report, the Games of the Xth Olympiad, Los Angeles 1932*. The village's role as unexpected if temporary equalizer is reported in "Garland Lauds Games Village," *Los Angeles Times*, July 31, 1932; "Prince and Butcher Live Side by Side," *New York Times*, July 30, 1932; *Canada at the Xth Olympiad 1932*, edited by W. A. Fry.

My account of the attack by federal troops on the Bonus Army encampment draws from multiple sources. Among them are a number of *New York Times* articles: "Washington Orders B. E. F. To Evacuate," July 22, 1932; "Anacostia Camp No More: Troops Move Into Last Bonus Army Refuge as Flames Start," July 29, 1932; "Bombs and Sabres Win Capital Battle," July 29, 1932; "Chronology of Day's Swift B. E. F. Eviction," July 29, 1932; "Fires Compel Final Action," July 29, 1932; "Hoover Orders Eviction," July 29, 1932; "Camps Now Charred Ruins," July 30, 1932; "Grand Jury Inquiry Ordered by Hoover," July 30, 1932. I draw also from "Last Bonus Band Ousted; Hoover Praises Troops; Camps Burn; Reds Seized," *Los Angeles Times*, July 30, 1932.

Events at Will Rogers's luncheon are reported in "Will Rogers Refuses to Take Babe's Offer," *Los Angeles Times*, July 28, 1932; and *Canada at the Xth Olympiad 1932*, edited by W. A. Fry. Los Angeles' official welcome to IOC members in the new city hall tower is described in "City Welcomes Olympic Heads," *Los Angeles Times*, July 29, 1932; and *Official Report, the Games of the Xth Olympiad, Los Angeles 1932*. Vice President Curtis's encounter with hecklers in Las Vegas is reported in "Hecklers of Curtis Draw Quick Jailing," *Madera Tribune*, July 29, 1932. My description of Curtis's arrival and first day in Los Angeles draws from several *Los Angeles Times* stories, including "Vice President Due Today," July 29, 1932; "VP Given Welcome," July 30, 1932; "State Building Dedicated: VP Presents Flying Cross to Amelia Earhart," July 30, 1932.

My account of the LA Olympic Organizing Committee's ceremonial dinner in the ballroom of the Biltmore Hotel draws from "Olympic Ball Notable Affair," *Los Angeles Times*, July 30, 1932; *Official Report, the Games of the Xth Olympiad, Los Angeles 1932*; "Last Bonus Band Ousted; Hoover Praises Troops; Camps Burn; Reds Seized," *Los Angeles Times*, July 30, 1932. I found the program for this dinner, including the menu, in the Avery Brundage Collection, Box 85, LA84 Foundation Library.

**CHAPTER 19. THE GAMES**

The headlines Billy Garland saw on the morning the games were to begin appeared on the front page of the *Los Angeles Times* on July 30, 1932. My description of the city on that morning draws from two *New York Times* stories: "Curtis Formally Opens Olympic Games," July 31, 1932, and "Curtis Proclaims the Olympics Open," July 31, 1932. I draw also from *Official Report, the Games of the Xth Olympiad, Los Angeles 1932*. The tally of participating athletes at the 1932 games varies. The boosters and the later official reports claim 2,000 participating athletes, but in most other accounts the number ranges between 1,328 and 1,503.

My account of the opening ceremony draws from multiple sources. Among them: "Stirring March of Athletes Brings Out Goose Pimples," *Los Angeles Times,* July 31, 1932; "Throng of 105,000 Roars Welcome to Olympics," *Los Angeles Times,* July 31, 1932; *Official Report, the Games of the Xth Olympiad, Los Angeles 1932.* In her oral history for the LA84 Foundation Library, Jean Shiley tells the story of Norma Shearer falling over the fence. In his oral history, the runner Hector Dyer tells the story of Buster Crabbe and Georgia Coleman goofing around. In her oral history, Jane Fauntz talks about Helene Madison being an aloof loner with bright red fingernails and toenails. In their oral histories, Evelyne Hall and Jean Shiley recount kicking off the tight buckskin shoes.

Billy Garland's introductory speech at the opening ceremony is reproduced in *Report of the American Olympic Committee: Games of the Xth Olympiad, Los Angeles, California, July 30–August 14, 1932,* edited by Frederick W. Rubien. Vice President Curtis's speech is described in "Curtis Proclaims the Olympics Open," *New York Times,* July 31, 1932; *Report of the American Olympic Committee;* and *Official Report, the Games of the Xth Olympiad, Los Angeles 1932.* In his oral history, Hector Dyer tells the story of the athletes playfully covering their heads.

My account of the elite social events on Saturday and Sunday after the opening ceremony, including the reception at Louis B. Mayer's home, derives from "Curtis Leaves, Telling Thrill: Tribute Paid to Garland," *Los Angeles Times,* August 1, 1932. I draw my description of Mayer's beach house from several sources, including "Louis B. Mayer's Former House—the Birthplace of the Academy Awards," by Lindsay (no last name listed), iamnotastalker.com, February 26, 2013; and "The Legendary Ghosts of 625 Beach Road," by Alicia Mayer, hollywoodessays.com, September 9, 2012. (Louis B. Mayer was Alicia's great uncle.) Vice President Curtis learned of Jim Thorpe's situation by reading "Jim Thorpe Denied One Little Ticket; Weeps as Huge Parade Passes," *Los Angeles Times,* July 31, 1932. Curtis's parting tribute to Billy Garland is reported in "Curtis Leaves, Telling Thrill: Tribute Paid to Garland," *Los Angeles Times,* August 1, 1932.

Ellen Galford discusses Babe Didrikson's choice of three events in *The X Olympiad,* p. 8. My account of Babe's javelin throw draws from several sources. Among them: "Five Marks Broken in Olympics: Babe Didrikson Cracks World Javelin Record," *Los Angeles Times,* August 1, 1932; "'Gee, My Hand Slipped,' Wails Babe in Smashing Record by Eleven Feet," *Los Angeles Times,* August 1, 1932; and "Record-Breakers Fall by Wayside," *New York Times,* August 1, 1932. I draw also from *Report of the American Olympic Committee: Games of the Xth Olympiad, Los Angeles, California, July 30–August 14, 1932,* edited by Frederick W. Rubien and *Official Report, the Games of the Xth Olympiad, Los Angeles 1932.* Doris Pieroth describes this event in *Their Day in the Sun,* p. 101, as does Ellen Galford in *The X Olympiad,* pp. 8–9. Both Pieroth and Galford correctly note that Babe in fact did not break the world record, held by Nan Gindele; I confirmed this by a review of the *International Association of*

*Athletics Federations Statistic Handbook* and Gindele's biography on Sports-reference.com.

My account of the eighty-meter hurdles race between Evelyne Hall and Babe Didrikson derives from a number of reports published in the *Los Angeles Times* and *New York Times* on August 5, 1932, including articles in the *LA Times* by Braven Dyer, Grantland Rice, and Jean Bosquet, and a dispatch in the *New York Times* by Arthur Daley. Babe's comment at the end, "Sure, I slowed up a little," appeared in "Sister A-Jitter As Babe Wins," by Muriel Babcock, *Los Angeles Times*, August 5. I draw also from "Olympic Games in Los Angeles: In the Midst of a Depression, L.A. Put On a Record-Breaking, Money-Making Extravaganza," a retrospective by Paul Zimmerman in the *Los Angeles Times*, July 23, 1984. I draw as well from Evelyne Hall's oral history at the LA84 Foundation Library; *Report of the American Olympic Committee: Games of the Xth Olympiad, Los Angeles, California, July 30–August 14, 1932*, edited by Frederick W. Rubien; and *Official Report, the Games of the Xth Olympiad, Los Angeles 1932*. Doris Pieroth writes about this event in *Their Day in the Sun*, pp. 108–10.

My account of the high jump competition between Jean Shiley and Babe Didrikson derives from reports published in the *Los Angeles Times* on August 8, 1932, including "Track Records Toppled in Sensational Time: Girl Wins High Jump Title From Babe Didrikson" by Braven Dyer, and "All Hail—She Beat Mighty Babe!" by Muriel Babcock. I draw also from "Olympic Games in Los Angeles: In the Midst of a Depression, L.A. Put On a Record-Breaking, Money-Making Extravaganza," a retrospective by Paul Zimmerman in the *Los Angeles Times*, July 23, 1984. I draw as well from Jean Shiley's oral history at the LA84 Foundation Library; *Report of the American Olympic Committee: Games of the Xth Olympiad, Los Angeles, California, July 30–August 14, 1932*, edited by Frederick W. Rubien; and *Official Report, the Games of the Xth Olympiad, Los Angeles 1932*. Doris Pieroth writes about this event in *Their Day in the Sun*, pp. 112–13; the story of teammates begging Jean to beat Babe comes from an interview Pieroth conducted with Shiley. Ellen Galford also writes about the high jump event in *The X Olympiad*, pp. 16–17.

Babe's fateful round of golf with the sportswriters has been recounted many times. Paul Zimmerman tells the story in "Olympic Games in Los Angeles: In the Midst of a Depression, L.A. Put On a Record-Breaking, Money-Making Extravaganza," as does Ellen Galford in *The X Olympiad*, p. 17. Jane Fauntz reports Babe's score for that day in her oral history, LA84 Foundation Library. Fred Steers's comment about the seventeen American track and field women appeared in *Report of the American Olympic Committee: Games of the Xth Olympiad, Los Angeles, California, July 30–August 14, 1932*, edited by Frederick W. Rubien; and *Official Report, the Games of the Xth Olympiad, Los Angeles 1932*, p. 121.

Helene Madison's predictions, struggles, and early concerns are reported in "All Records 'To Go Boom': Helene Madison Predicts Sensations," *Los Angeles Times*, July 23, 1932. The press report doubting Helene could beat Willie came after the fact, in "Miss Madison Captures Olympic Swim Title, *New York Times*, August 9, 1932. My account of Helene's hundred-meter freestyle race derives from reports published in the *Los Angeles Times* and *New York Times* on August 8 and 9, 1932. I draw also from *Report of the American Olympic Committee: Games of the Xth Olympiad, Los Angeles, California, July 30–August 14, 1932,* edited by Frederick W. Rubien; and *Official Report, the Games of the Xth Olympiad, Los Angeles 1932.* Doris Pieroth writes about this event in *Their Day in the Sun,* pp. 118–19.

My account of Eleanor Holm's hundred-meter backstroke race derives from reports published in the *Los Angeles Times* and *New York Times* on August 10 and 12, 1932. I draw also from *Report of the American Olympic Committee: Games of the Xth Olympiad, Los Angeles, California, July 30–August 14, 1932,* edited by Frederick W. Rubien, and *Official Report, the Games of the Xth Olympiad, Los Angeles 1932.* Doris Pieroth writes about this event in *Their Day in the Sun,* pp. 119–20. My account of the springboard divers' competition derives from reports published in the *Los Angeles Times* on August 11, 1932, and Jane Fauntz's oral history at the LA84 Foundation Library. Doris Pieroth writes about this event in *Their Day in the Sun,* pp. 120–21. My account of the platform divers' competition derives from reports published in the *Los Angeles Times* and *New York Times* on August 13, 1932. Doris Pieroth writes about this event in *Their Day in the Sun,* pp. 122–23.

The new system of presenting medals is described in *Official Report, the Games of the Xth Olympiad, Los Angeles 1932.* Ellen Galford writes about it in *The X Olympiad,* pp. 53–54. My account of the women's 4 x 100-meter freestyle relay race derives from reports published in the *Los Angeles Times* and *New York Times* on August 13, 1932. Doris Pieroth writes about this event in *Their Day in the Sun,* pp. 123–24. My account of the women's four-hundred-meter freestyle race derives from reports published in the *Los Angeles Times* and *New York Times* on August 14, 1932. Doris Pieroth writes about this event in *Their Day in the Sun,* pp. 126–27.

Jane Fauntz tells of seeing Helene Madison dancing with Clark Gable at the Cocoanut Grove in her oral history, LA84 Foundation Library; this is also reported in *Canada at the Xth Olympiad 1932,* edited by W. A. Fry. The slavering over the women athletes appears in Jean Bosquet, "Stars and Stripes Wave After Victories Won," *Los Angeles Times,* August 3, 1932; and Muriel Babcock, "Olympic Champions Hear Siren Song of Screen," *Los Angeles Times,* August 7, 1932.

My account of the hundred-meter and two-hundred-meter races between Eddie Tolan and Ralph Metcalfe derives from reports published in the *Los Angeles Times* and *New York Times* on August 2, 1932, and August 4, 1932, including articles in the *LA Times* by Braven Dyer, Paul Lowery, and Muriel Babcock and a dispatch in the *New York Times* by Arthur Daley. I draw also from Paul Zimmerman's retrospective looks at the 1932 games in *Los Angeles, the Olympic City, 1932–1984* and "Olympic Games in Los Angeles: In the Midst of a Depression, L.A. Put On a Record-Breaking, Money-Making Extravaganza." I draw as well from *Report of the American Olympic Committee: Games of the Xth Olympiad, Los Angeles, California, July 30–August 14, 1932,* edited by Frederick W. Rubien, and *Official Report, the Games of the Xth Olympiad, Los Angeles 1932.* Ralph Metcalfe's complaint about rooming with Eddie Tolan appears in the oral history of the runner Hector Dyer at the

LA84 Foundation Library. Ellen Galford writes about Tolan, Metcalfe, and their competition in *The X Olympiad*, pp. 51–53 and 60–65.

My description of the Japanese men swimmers derives from reports published in the *Los Angeles Times* and *New York Times* on August 10, 1932. I draw also from Paul Zimmerman's retrospective look at the 1932 games in *Los Angeles, the Olympic City, 1932–1984*. I draw as well from *Report of the American Olympic Committee: Games of the Xth Olympiad, Los Angeles, California, July 30–August 14, 1932*, edited by Frederick W. Rubien, and *Official Report, the Games of the Xth Olympiad, Los Angeles 1932*. Allan Guttmann reports on the "disturbing rumors" that oxygen was administered to Japanese swimmers in *The Olympics: A History of the Modern Games*, p. 52. Jane Fauntz talks about these rumors in her oral history, LA84 Foundation Library. Harry Carr writes that "the contestants were pumped full of oxygen," in *Los Angeles: City of Dreams*, p. 188.

My report on Buster Crabbe's four-hundred-meter freestyle race derives from articles published in the *Los Angeles Times* and *New York Times* on August 11, 1932, including Bob Ray's article in the *LA Times*, "Crabbe Annexes Swim Thriller By Inches." I draw as well from *Report of the American Olympic Committee: Games of the Xth Olympiad, Los Angeles, California, July 30–August 14, 1932*, edited by Frederick W. Rubien, and *Official Report, the Games of the Xth Olympiad, Los Angeles 1932*. Ellen Galford writes about this race in *The X Olympiad*, p. 87.

My account of the four-hundred-meter race between Bill Carr and Ben Eastman derives from reports published in the *Los Angeles Times* and *New York Times* on August 6, 1932, including Braven Dyer's article in the *LA Times*, "Carr Beats Eastman, Sets Mark; Wee Willie Breaks All Marks for 400 Meters." I draw as well from *Report of the American Olympic Committee: Games of the Xth Olympiad, Los Angeles, California, July 30–August 14, 1932*, edited by Frederick W. Rubien, and *Official Report, the Games of the Xth Olympiad, Los Angeles 1932*. Ellen Galford writes about this race in *The X Olympiad*, pp. 65–67.

My account of the high-jump competition between Bill Miller and Shuhei Nishida derives from reports published in the *Los Angeles Times* and *New York Times* on August 4, 1932. I also draw from *Report of the American Olympic Committee: Games of the Xth Olympiad, Los Angeles, California, July 30–August 14, 1932*, edited by Frederick W. Rubien, and *Official Report, the Games of the Xth Olympiad, Los Angeles 1932*. Ellen Galford writes about this event in *The X Olympiad*, pp. 82–83.

My account of the twenty-six-mile marathon derives from reports published in the *Los Angeles Times* and *New York Times* on August 8, 1932. I also draw from Paul Zimmerman's "Olympic Games in Los Angeles: In the Midst of a Depression, L.A. Put On a Record-Breaking, Money-Making Extravaganza." I draw as well from *Report of the American Olympic Committee: Games of the Xth Olympiad, Los Angeles, California, July 30–August 14, 1932*, edited by Frederick W. Rubien, and *Official Report, The Games of the Xth Olympiad, Los Angeles 1932*. Ellen Galford writes about Zabala and this event in *The X Olympiad*, pp. 39–41.

My account of the fifteen-hundred-meter race derives from reports published in the *Los Angeles Times* and *New York Times* on August 5, 1932, including articles in the *LA Times* by Braven Dyer, Grantland Rice, and Jean Bosquet, and a dispatch in the *New York Times* by Arthur Daley. I also draw from *Report of the American Olympic Committee: Games of the Xth Olympiad, Los Angeles, California, July 30–August 14, 1932,* edited by Frederick W. Rubien. The anecdote about Beccali's treatment by teammates at the village after the race is related in *Canada at the Xth Olympiad 1932,* edited by W. A. Fry. Ellen Galford writes about Beccali and the fifteen-hundred-meter race in *The X Olympiad,* pp. 74–76.

My account of Robert Tisdall and the four-hundred-meter hurdles race derives from reports published in the *Los Angeles Times* and *New York Times* on August 2, 1932. I also draw from *Report of the American Olympic Committee: Games of the Xth Olympiad, Los Angeles, California, July 30–August 14, 1932,* edited by Frederick W. Rubien, and from *Official Report, the Games of the Xth Olympiad, Los Angeles 1932.* Ellen Galford writes about Tisdall in *The X Olympiad,* pp. 68–71, as does David Guiney in *The Friendly Olympics,* pp. 55–58. Galford recounts Tisdall's visit to Pickfair after the race, as does Franklin D. Kjorvestad in an undated, unpublished pamphlet titled "The 1932 Los Angeles Xth Olympiad: Its Development and Impact on the Community," which I found in the LA84 Foundation Library archives.

My account of the Brazil water polo team's fracas draws from articles published in the *Los Angeles Times* and *New York Times* on August 9, 1932. My report of the five-thousand-meter race derives from articles published in the *Los Angeles Times* and *New York Times* on August 6, 1932. I also draw from Paul Zimmerman's retrospective looks at the 1932 games in *Los Angeles, the Olympic City, 1932–1984,* and "Olympic Games in Los Angeles: In the Midst of a Depression, L.A. Put On a Record-Breaking, Money-Making Extravaganza." I draw as well from *Report of the American Olympic Committee: Games of the Xth Olympiad, Los Angeles, California, July 30–August 14, 1932,* edited by Frederick W. Rubien. Ellen Galford writes about this event in *The X Olympiad,* pp. 78–81.

Evelyne Hall talks about the meeting at the Biltmore, to review race results, in her oral history, LA84 Foundation Library. Avery Brundage wrote to *New York Herald Tribune* columnist W. O. McGeehan on November 29, 1932; I found this letter in the Avery Brundage Collection, Box 85, at the LA84 Foundation Library. The Amateur Athletic Union's vote to recognize Ralph Metcalfe and Evelyne Hall as coholders of the American records set in their races is reported in "Metcalfe, Mrs. Hall Share in 2 Marks: Adjudged Co-holders of US Records," *New York Times,* November 22, 1932.

My account of Takeichi Nishi and the equestrian individual jumping competition derives from newspaper reports published in the *Los Angeles Times* and *New York Times* on August 15, 1932. Ellen Galford writes about Nishi in *The X Olympiad,* p. 43. I draw the concluding figures on attendance, ticket sales, and world records from multiple sources, relying chiefly on *Official Report, the Games of the Xth Olympiad, Los Angeles 1932.*

My report on the closing ceremony derives from "95,000 Attend Closing of the Olympics; U.S. Finishes Far Ahead on Point Basis," *New York Times,*

August 15, 1932; *Official Report, the Games of the Xth Olympiad, Los Angeles 1932;* and *Report of the American Olympic Committee: Games of the Xth Olympiad, Los Angeles, California, July 30–August 14, 1932,* edited by Frederick W. Rubien. My description of the missing athletes, and their eviction from the village, draws from "Athletes Must Pay Or Vacate Quarters," *New York Times,* August 10, 1932; and "Olympic Village A Deserted City," *New York Times,* August 15, 1932. The public adulation for the games appeared in Grantland Rice, "Japan Triumphs Before 100,000: Olympic Games End As Thousands Sing 'Aloha,'" *Los Angeles Times,* August 15, 1932; "Will Rogers Remarks," *Los Angeles Times,* August 15, 1932; Allison Danzig, "95,000 Attend Closing of the Olympics; U.S. Finishes Far Ahead on Point Basis," *New York Times,* August 15, 1932.

President Hoover's congratulatory letter of August 19 to Billy is reproduced in Gwendolyn Babcock's *The Ancestry of John Jewett Garland.* Billy Garland's closing comments about the games appear in "Garland Credits Entire Nation for Success of Olympics, Hailed as Finest Ever Held," *New York Times,* August 16, 1932. Al Stump reports on Billy's remarks in "1932, the 'Hopeless' Dream of William May Garland" and "The Olympics That Almost Wasn't."

#### CHAPTER 20. A FOOTING IN THE WORLD

Warren Christopher, secretary of state in the Clinton administration, listened to radio broadcasts of the 1932 games as a seven-year-old boy in Scranton, North Dakota. "A beacon of light" is how he described the experience to me when we talked about my book project and the 1932 Olympics; the memory clearly fanned his passions. Billy called the village "the brilliant jewel" in a letter he wrote to Coubertin on October 12, 1932; Robert Barney quotes from it in "Resistance, Persistence, Providence." My description of the village's dismantling draws from "Olympic Village a Deserted City," *New York Times,* August 15, 1932; and *Official Report, the Games of the Xth Olympiad, Los Angeles 1932.* Will Rogers's comment about the coming political "hooey" appeared in "Will Rogers Remarks," *Los Angeles Times,* August 15, 1932. Ellen Galford recounts George Roth's experience in *The X Olympiad,* p. 54, as do David Wallechinsky and Jaime Loucky in *The Book of Olympic Lists,* p. 17.

My account of Eddie Tolan's life after the 1932 games derives from a number of *Los Angeles Times* articles, including "All Michigan Honors Tolan: Colored Star's Achievements in Games to Be Recognized," August 31, 1932; "Tolan Sick on Victory Wine: Feted Little Colored Hero's Dreams of Becoming a Great Physician Shattered as He Toils at County Clerk's Job," *Los Angeles Times,* January 24, 1933; "Eddie Tolan Ruled 'Pro' by A.A.U.," *Los Angeles Times,* June 24, 1933. I draw also from "Tolan, Olympic Star, Appears in Vaudeville to Help Family, Finance Study Medicine," *New York Times,* November 29, 1932. Ellen Galford writes about Tolan's postgames experiences in *The X Olympiad,* pp. 64–65.

My report on Jean Shiley's life after the 1932 games draws from Jean Shiley's oral history, LA84 Foundation Library. Doris Pieroth also writes about Shiley's postgame experience in *Their Day in the Sun,* p. 132. My description of Helene Madison's life after the games draws from "Madison, Helene (1913–

1970)" by Alan Stein, a History.Link.org essay; "Helene Madison, Record Swimmer," an obituary of Helene that ran in the *New York Times* on November 27, 1970; and "Helene Madison Biography and Olympic Results," an obituary at Sports-reference.com. Doris Pieroth writes about Madison's later years in *Their Day in the Sun*, p. 139.

My account of 1932 Olympic athletes successfully finding their footing in the world draws from "Eleanor Holm Whalen, 30's Swimming Champion, Dies," *New York Times*, February 2, 2004; "Buster Crabbe, Swimmer and Actor, Dies at 75, *New York Times*, April 24, 1983; Evelyne Hall oral history, LA84 Foundation Library; "Rep. Ralph H. Metcalfe Dies," *Washington Post*, October 11, 1978; "Ralph Metcalfe: Olympian with Jesse Owens Went on to Chicago Politics," *Chicago Tribune*, March 24, 2016. Doris Pieroth writes about Eleanor Holm's later years in *Their Day in the Sun*, p. 140. Jean Shiley talks about how the games "changed my whole life forever," in the Jean Shiley oral history, LA84 Foundation Library.

My description of how the 1932 games proved a turning point in the Olympic movement derives from *Official Report, the Games of the Xth Olympiad, Los Angeles 1932;* and *Report of the American Olympic Committee: Games of the Xth Olympiad, Los Angeles, California, July 30–August 14, 1932,* edited by Frederick W. Rubien. My report on the 1932 games' significant impact on the development of Southern California draws from a range of sources, including Franklin D. Kjorvestad, "The 1932 Los Angeles Xth Olympiad: Its Development and Impact on the Community," LA84 Foundation Library; and "Games Guests Extend Marts: Chamber Reports 500 Sign Register: City Makes New Connections in Parts of World; Industry, Farms and Culture Studied by Visitors," *Los Angeles Times*, August 15, 1932. The *Los Angeles Times* celebrated the fame the games brought the city in "The Tenth Olympiad—And After," *Los Angeles Times*, August 14, 1932.

The discrimination experienced by the Japanese Olympics team, as well as the support they received from spectators and officials at the Coliseum, is reported in "Japan's Athletes Tell Impressions," *New York Times*, October 9, 1932. Mark Dyreson, drawing from this source, writes about the Japanese athletes' experience in "Marketing National Identity: The Olympic Games of 1932 and American Culture," p. 37.

### EPILOGUE

Gwendolyn Babcock offers her comparisons of the Garland and Chandler families, and her memories of Casa Ladera, in *The Ancestry of John Jewett Garland*, pp. 2–3, and pp. 54–56. Her parents' betrothal is reported in "Miss Helen Chandler to Wed John Garland," *Los Angeles Times*, December 24, 1933.

My account of Chief Davis's call for hard-labor "rock pile" penal camps for vagrants and the sealing of state borders draws from a number of *Los Angeles Times* articles, including "Light on Transient Problem," November 12, 1935; "Vagabonds Will Labor in Quarry: Chief Davis Directs Move as Part of Drive Against Influx of Indigents," February 9, 1936; "Davis Seeks State Aid in Drive on Indigents," February 16, 1936; and "Davis Urges Patrol Aid: Wants Stricter

Vagrant Curb," February 20, 1936. Kevin Starr offers a comprehensive report about this phase of Los Angeles history in *Endangered Dreams,* pp. 197–227. Billy Garland's concern over Upton Sinclair's candidacy for governor of California is reported in "Realty Seen Endangered; Garland Sounds Warning," *Los Angeles Times,* September 23, 1934.

My description of the battle over the 1932 games surplus derives from correspondence I found in the Avery Brundage Collection (Boxes 85, 56). Among the documents: a letter from Brundage to Billy, dated September 26, 1932, in which Brundage first broaches the idea of the AOC getting the surplus, and a second from him, on December 9, 1932, further pressing his claim; a telegram from Zack Farmer to Brundage, on February 21, 1933, asking why a lawyer representing the AOC had "injected himself" into the matter of the surplus; and a letter from Brundage to Farmer, dated March 1, 1933, explaining why the AOC was intervening. In a letter to Brundage dated May 7, 1935, Billy expressed the thought that the AOC brief was "full of downright lies and disgusting claims." I draw also from the records of a related legal proceeding, "In the Matter of the Funds Realized From the Olympic Games Held in California in 1932," which I obtained at the LA84 Foundation Library. I draw as well from "Games Profits Battle Begins: Rush of Claimants Unlovely Sequel to Olympiad: 'Friendly Suit' Fast Losing Character as Such," *Los Angeles Times,* September 29, 1933.

My account of the Berlin games dispute derives generally from a range of reports in the *Los Angeles Times* and *New York Times,* listed below, and correspondence I found in the Avery Brundage Collection, Box 56. I draw also from "The Nazi Olympics," chap. 6 of Allen Guttmann's biography of Brundage, *The Games Must Go On,* pp. 62–81.

The March 1933 attack on six Americans in Berlin by men wearing Nazi uniforms is reported in "3 More Americans Attacked in Berlin as Raiding Goes On: Anti-Semites Compel Shops to Close," *New York Times,* March 10, 1933. My report on both the IOC meeting in Vienna, and Billy's comments after that meeting, draws from "No Ban on Jews at Berlin: Assurance Given By German Olympic Committee," *Los Angeles Times,* July 14, 1932; and "Garland Home With Awards," *Los Angeles Times,* July 21, 1933. Allen Guttmann writes about the Vienna meeting in *The Games Must Go On,* p. 66.

Charles Ornstein, who served as chair of the AOC Housing Committee for the 1932 games, wrote his "it would be unthinkable to hold the Games in Berlin" letter to Brundage on April 13, 1934. I found this letter in the Avery Brundage Collection, Box 234. Allen Guttmann writes about the AOC boycott resolution in *The Games Must Go On,* p. 67. My summary of the IOC session in Athens and Billy Garland's opposition to a boycott draws from "Garland Says Games Spirit Not Violated," *Los Angeles Times,* June 22, 1934. Allen Guttmann writes about the Athens IOC session in *The Games Must Go On,* p. 68. The American Jewish Congress's disagreement with Billy's views is reported in "Jewish Body Disagrees with Garland Views," *Los Angeles Times,* June 22, 1934.

My account of Avery Brundage's report in favor of accepting the German invitation draws from "Vote on Olympics Set For Tonight," *New York Times,* September 26, 1934; and "U.S. Will Compete in 1936 Olympics: Germany's Bid is Accepted Without Dissenting Vote After Brundage Report," *New York Times,*

September 27, 1934. Allen Guttmann writes about Brundage's report in *The Games Must Go On*, p. 70. My description of resistance to Brundage's position, and a mounting boycott campaign, draws from a number of *New York Times* articles, including "Demands Open Hearing: Jewish Athletes Still Are Proscribed, Cellar Says," September 27, 1934; "Brundage Favors Berlin Olympics: U.S. Sports Official Says He Knows of No Reason to Boycott Germany," July 27, 1935; "Catholic Boycott on Olympics Urged: Brundage is Disputed," July 31, 1935; and "Brundage Combats Foes of Olympics," August 2, 1935. Helene Madison's support of the boycott is recounted in her obituary, "Helene Madison, Record Swimmer," *New York Times*, November 27, 1970. Allen Guttmann writes about the boycott campaign in *The Games Must Go On*, pp. 70–71.

Billy Garland wrote his supportive letter to Brundage on August 7, 1935. Billy wrote his letter to Lewald on October 15, 1935, and sent a copy to Brundage. Billy wrote his letter to Count de Baillet-Latour on October 16, 1935, and sent a copy to Brundage. I found all these letters in the Avery Brundage Collection, LA84 Foundation Library, Box 56. Ernest Lee Jahncke's letters to Lewald and Count de Baillet-Latour, openly disputing Billy's views, are reported in "Jahncke Asks Ban On Olympic Games," *New York Times*, November 27, 1935. Allen Guttmann writes about Jahncke's challenge in *The Games Must Go On*, pp. 74–75.

My summary of Billy's pushback response to Jahncke draws from "Garland Condemns Fight on Olympics," *New York Times*, November 30, 1935; "Fight on Olympics Gets New Support: Zack Farmer, Director of 1932 Games, Joins Opposition to Our Participation," *New York Times*, November 28, 1935; "Garland Urges Entry of Yankees in Games: Senior American Member of International Board Condemns Proposed Boycott of Olympiad," *Los Angeles Times*, November 30, 1935. Billy expressed his "intense disappointment" with Jahncke in a letter to Brundage on December 27, 1935, which I found in the Avery Brundage Collection, Box 56.

My account of the AAU's eventual decision to reject the boycott draws from a number of *New York Times* articles, including "Even Split in A.A.U. On Olympic Issue: Board Puts an Anti-Berlin Resolution Up for Vote Today 'Without Recommendation,'" December 7, 1935; "A.A.U. Blocks Vote on Olympics Ban; New Fight Today," December 8, 1935; "A.A.U. Backs Team in Berlin Olympic; Rejects Boycott," December 9, 1935. The IOC 35th Session Minutes, Berlin, July 30, 1935, records Jahncke's expulsion and Brundage's election, events Allen Guttmann writes about in *The Games Must Go On*, p. 81. Billy expressed his ambition to have Brundage elected to the IOC, as Jahncke's replacement, in a letter to Brundage on December 27, 1935, which I found in the Avery Brundage Collection, Box 56.

Billy's 1937 tour of the Orient, and enthusiasm for Japan's hosting of the 1940 Olympics, is reported in "Garland Back From Orient: He Reports Japanese Will Make Success of Olympic Games," *Los Angeles Times*, June 10, 1937. Billy's 1938 tour of the Orient, and continued belief in the 1940 Tokyo Games, is reported in "Col. Garland Returns Home: Angeleno Describes Tokio's Extensive Plans for Olympic Games," *Los Angeles Times*, May 10, 1938. Tokyo's withdrawal and Billy's question, "Does Los Angeles want the

Olympic Games in 1940?," appears in "Garland Asks if City Wants 1940 Olympics," *Los Angeles Times,* July 17, 1938.

Gwendolyn Babcock writes about coming down with polio, and a hard-of-hearing Billy visiting her in Children's Hospital, in *The Ancestry of John Jewett Garland,* pp. 4 and 26. Harry Chandler's passing is reported in "Harry Chandler Called By Death," *Los Angeles Times,* September 24, 1944. Estimates of Chandler's estate vary. Robert Gottlieb and Irene Wolt, in *Thinking Big,* put it at half a billion dollars, as does David Halberstam in *The Powers That Be.* Gottlieb and Wolt report that Chandler on his deathbed "is said" to have ordered destruction of his and General Otis's papers (p. 126).

The Tribute to Victory celebration is reported in "Coliseum Throng Views Tableau of War Scenes," *Los Angeles Times,* October 28, 1945. The recognition of Billy on his eighty-second birthday appeared in "Col. Garland Observes 82nd Birthday Tomorrow," *Los Angeles Times,* March 30, 1948. Billy's letter to an IOC colleague, resigning and reporting he could not attend the 1948 games in London, is in the Garland Collection, LA84 Foundation Library.

My account of Billy Garland's passing draws from a number of *Los Angeles Times* articles: "Civic Leader W. M. Garland Dies at 82," September 27, 1948; "Garland Funeral Rites Scheduled for Friday: City Council Adjourns in Memory of Man Who Led Scores of Community Projects," September 28, 1948; "William May Garland, A Great Influence," September 28, 1948; and "Sportscripts" by Paul Zimmerman, *Los Angeles Times,* September 28, 1948. My report of Billy's funeral service draws from "Notables Attend Funeral of William May Garland," *Los Angeles Times,* October 2, 1948; and "Realty World Mourns Passing of Col. Garland," *Los Angeles Times,* October 3, 1948.

A photograph of Billy's bronze bas-relief plaque in the Coliseum's Memorial Court of Honor appears in Gwendolyn Babcock's *The Ancestry of John Jewett Garland.*

# BIBLIOGRAPHY

**BIBLIOGRAPHICAL NOTE**

Because my book follows a range of storylines, I have divided my bibliography into a number of categories, which reflect how I organized my research materials. I list first all that I found at the remarkable LA84 Foundation Library on West Adams in Los Angeles, which for me constituted its own "category." (Created with a share of the 1984 Olympic Games surplus, LA84, among many other activities, maintains the world's premier Olympic and sports library collection.)

I list separately various scholarly essays on the LA 1932 Olympics published over the years in academic sports journals, though most of these can be obtained via the LA 84 Foundation website. In other categories, I list articles on the Olympic Games, and articles on Los Angeles, intended for a general readership; graduate-level dissertations about the 1932 games and Los Angeles; books on the Olympics Games; books on Southern California history; books on the United States in the 1920s; and multiple sources for my segments on the 1924 plague outbreak and the Greystone murder-suicide in Los Angeles.

Many of my key primary sources derive from the LA84 Foundation Library. They include:

William May Garland Collection, correspondence, 1921–37.
William May Garland's "Story of the Origin of the Xth Olympiad Held in Los Angeles, California in 1932," a thirty-four-page typescript letter to his wife, Blanche.
Avery Brundage Collection, a vast library of its own, on microfilm, that includes, among other useful documents, Brundage's correspondence with Billy Garland regarding the LA 1932 Olympic Games.
Olympian Oral Histories, transcripts of interviews of various athletes of the 1932 games conducted by George Hodak.

Wolf Lyberg. *The IOC Sessions: 1894–1955*. Vol. 1. N.p.: W. Lyberg, 1989.

Los Angeles Olympic Organizing Committee (LAOOC). *Olympic*. May 1930, September 1930, April 1931, October 1931, May 1932.

American Olympic Committee. *Olympic News*. January 1930, February 1930, March 1930, April 1930, June 1930, July 1930, August 1930, October–November 1930, March–April 1931, May–June 1931, September–October 1931, January–February 1932, August 1934.

*Official Bulletin of the International Olympic Committee,* meeting of the IOC, Berlin, May 22–24, 1930; Olympic Congress of Berlin, May 25–30, 1930.

*Report of the American Olympic Committee, Seventh Olympic Games, Antwerp, Belgium, 1920*. N.p.: American Olympic Committee, 1920.

*Official Program, Xth Olympiad*. July 30 through August 14, 1932.

Other primary sources include:

Correspondence and 1932 games memorabilia in the Bill Henry Collection at Occidental College.

A bound manuscript at the Huntington Library titled "Plague in Los Angeles, 1924–25," produced by the California State Board of Health.

"Minutes of the Board of Directors, Los Angeles Chamber of Commerce, October–November 1924" and "Stenographer's Reports, Board of Directors Meeting, Los Angeles Chamber of Commerce, October–November 1924," which I obtained from USC Libraries Special Collections in the Doheny Memorial Library.

My primary sources also include many hundreds of newspaper articles published in the *New York Times* and in the *Los Angeles Times* and a range of other Southern California publications. I accessed these scanned historical newspaper accounts online via ProQuest Historical Newspapers, available to me through the UC Irvine Library. I also drew from the California Digital Newspaper Collection: Repository of Digitized California Newspapers from 1846 to the present.

These newspaper databases allowed me to closely follow all manner of events unfolding in Southern California over a wide span of time in LA's early years. Particularly revealing was my extended search, year by year, from 1890 (Garland's arrival in LA) to 1948 (his death), for all stories about William May Garland: This is how I learned how prominent he was, not just in the bidding for and staging of the Olympic Games, but also in many other matters concerning the emergence and growth of Los Angeles. I was fortunate indeed that Billy didn't lurk in LA's "shadow government" but rather willingly seized the public stage.

The newspaper articles also allowed me to constantly burrow further into, and corroborate, events I read about in secondary sources concerning the games and LA history. Many of the specific articles I drew from are listed in my source notes. Others more generally inform my narrative.

I found no books focused on Billy Garland's role in Southern California's development, including his quest for and staging of the games. Mine is the first book to view the city's history through this lens. Yet I was aided by a number of scholarly essays in academic sports journals that do look at Garland's quest as part of their examination of the 1932 games. Among those, the most useful and comprehensive was Robert Barney's "Resistance, Persistence, Providence: The 1932 Los Angeles Olympic Games in Perspective," published in *Research Quarterly for Exercise and Sport,* June 1, 1996. For my book, I returned to most of Barney's primary sources, and added others, but Barney provided me a quite helpful roadmap. So did Steven A. Riess in "Power without Authority: Los Angeles' Elites and the Construction of the Coliseum," published in *Journal of Sport History* 8, no. 1 (Spring 1981).

I was aided also by two books that focus on the athletes and athletic events of the 1932 games: Doris H. Pieroth's *Their Day in the Sun: Women of the 1932 Olympics* (Seattle: University of Washington Press, 1996), and Ellen Galford's *The X Olympiad* (Los Angeles: World Sport Research and Publications, 1997), which is an official history, a joint editorial project between the International Olympic Committee and the United States Olympic Committee. For my book, I again returned to the primary sources, and added others, but Pieroth and Galford provided me two additional helpful roadmaps.

I was aided as well, greatly, by Gwendolyn Garland Babcock's finely researched, self-published history of her family, *The Ancestry of John Jewett Garland.*

I must offer a word of appreciation for Hadley Meares, who writes historical accounts about Los Angeles for LA Curbed and KCET.org. Wherever my research took me, I seemed to find an interesting piece by Meares: four of them are listed in my bibliography.

I offer another word of appreciation for Laura Redford, whose 2014 PhD dissertation, "The Promise and Principles of Real Estate Development in an American Metropolis: Los Angeles 1903–1923," insightfully identifies the key role of the Los Angeles Realty Board in the city's development.

Finally, I bow to the justly celebrated major books of Los Angeles history, all listed below. The pantheon of LA historians (among them Kevin Starr, Carey McWilliams, Mike Davis and William Deverell) inform my narrative throughout.

## FROM THE LA84 FOUNDATION LIBRARY ARCHIVES

American Olympic Committee. *Olympic News,* January 1930, February 1930, March 1930, April 1930, June 1930, July 1930, August 1930, October–November 1930, March–April 1931, May–June 1931, September–October 1931, January–February 1932, August 1934.

Avery Brundage Collection (on microfilm).

Cahoon, John. "Los Angeles 1932." *TERRA* (Natural History Museum of Los Angeles County) 22, no. 5 (May–June 1984).

Coubertin, Pierre de. *Olympic Memoirs.* Lausanne: International Olympic Committee, 1979.

———. *Olympism: Selected Writings,* edited by Norbert Muller. Lausanne: International Olympic Committee, 2000.

Fry, W.A., ed. *Canada at the Xth Olympiad 1932.* Dunnville, Ontario: n.p., 1932.

Garland, William May. "Mixing Games and Business Profitably." *Southern California Business* 3, no. 11 (December 1924).

———. "Real Estate, the Basis of All Wealth." In *Realty Blue Book of California*. N.p., 1924.

———. "Story of the Origin of the Xth Olympiad Held in Los Angeles, California in 1932." Thirty-four-page typescript letter to his wife, Blanche.

*IOC General Session Minutes.* "Session de 1923, Rome." In French.

Kjorvestad, Franklin D. "The 1932 Los Angeles Xth Olympiad: Its Development and Impact on the Community." Unpublished pamphlet, n.d.

Los Angeles Olympic Organizing Committee. *Olympic.* May 1930, September 1930, April 1931, October 1931, May 1932.

Lyberg, Wolf. *The IOC Sessions: 1894–1955,* vol. 1. N.p.: W. Lyberg, 1989.

*Official Bulletin of the International Olympic Committee.* Meeting of the IOC, Berlin, May 22–24, 1930; Olympic Congress of Berlin, May 25–30, 1930.

*Official Program, Xth Olympiad.* July 30 through August 14, 1932.

*Official Report, the Games of the Xth Olympiad, Los Angeles 1932.* Los Angeles: Xth Olympiade Committee [Los Angeles Olympic Organizing Committee], 1933.

Olympian Oral Histories. Interviews of Olympics athletes conducted by George Hodak.

Reiner, Burt. "U.S.A.—1932." *TERRA* (Natural History Museum of Los Angeles County) 22, no. 5 (May–June 1984).

*Report of the American Olympic Committee, Seventh Olympic Games, Antwerp, Belgium, 1920.* N.p.: American Olympic Committee, 1920.

Rubien, Frederick W., ed. *Report of the American Olympic Committee: Games of the Xth Olympiad, Los Angeles, California, July 30–August 14, 1932.* New York: American Olympic Committee, 1933.

William May Garland Collection. Correspondence, 1921–37.

Wilson, Rusty. "Douglas Fairbanks and the Birth of Hollywood's Love Affair with the Olympics." In *Cultural Imperialism in Action, Critiques in the Global Olympic Trust: Eighth International Symposium for Olympic Research,* edited by Nigel B. Crowther, Robert K. Barney, Michael K. Heine, Cesar R. Torres, and Wanda Ellen Wakefield. London, Ontario: University of Western Ontario, 2006.

### HISTORICAL NEWSPAPERS [SCANNED]

California Digital Newspaper Collection: Repository of Digitized California Newspapers from 1846 to present.

ProQuest Historical Newspapers: *Los Angeles Times.*

ProQuest Historical Newspapers: *New York Times.*

### SCHOLARLY ESSAYS ON THE LA 1932 OLYMPIC GAMES

Barney, Robert. "Resistance, Persistence, Providence: The 1932 Los Angeles Olympic Games in Perspective." *Research Quarterly for Exercise and Sport* (June 1, 1996).

———. "William Garland and California's Quest to Host the Olympics." In *The World of Games: Political, Social and Educational Aspects* (Berlin: n.p., 1996), 144–52.

Dinces, Sean. "Padres on Mount Olympus: Los Angeles and the Production of the 1932 Olympic Mega-Event." *Journal of Sport History* 32, no. 2 (Summer 2005).

Dyreson, Mark. "Marketing National Identity: The Olympic Games of 1932 and American Culture." *Olympika: The International Journal of Olympic Studies* 4 (1995): 23–48.

Dyreson, Mark, and Matthew Llewellyn. "Los Angeles Is the Olympic City: Legacies of the 1932 and 1984 Olympic Games." *International Journal of the History of Sport* 25, no. 14 (December 2008): 1991–2018.

Lucas, John A. "Almost the Last American Disciple of Pure Olympic Games Amateurism: John J. Garland's Tenure on the International Olympic Committee, 1948–1968." *Olympika XV* (2006): 113–25.

———. "Prelude to the Games of the Tenth Olympiad in Los Angeles, 1932." *Southern California Quarterly* 64, no. 4 (Winter 1982): 313–18.

Riess, Steven A. "Power without Authority: Los Angeles' Elites and the Construction of the Coliseum." *Journal of Sport History* 8, no. 1 (Spring 1981).

Somerby, Grace A. "When Los Angeles Was Host to the Olympic Games of 1932." *Historical Society of Southern California Quarterly* 34, no. 2 (June 1952): 125–32.

Welky, David B. "Viking Girls, Mermaids, and Little Brown Men: U.S. Journalism and the 1932 Olympics." *Journal of Sport History* 24, no. 1 (Spring 1997).

White, Jeremy. "The Los Angeles Way of Doing Things: The Olympic Village and the Practice of Boosterism in 1932." *Olympika: The International Journal of Olympic Studies* 11 (2002): 79–116.

## GENERAL INTEREST ARTICLES ON THE OLYMPIC GAMES

Belcher, Jerry. "LA's '32 Olympics—Bright Days amid Dark Times." *Los Angeles Times,* May 21, 1978.

*Literary Digest.* "Olympic Games as a Depression-Buster." 113 (June 18, 1932).

Metro Digital Resources Librarian. "80 Years Ago This Week: Los Angeles Welcomes (and Transports) the World to the 1932 Summer Olympics." July 25, 2012. metroprimaryresources.info.

Murray, Carolyn S. "Olympics an Ongoing Legacy." *Los Angeles Times,* July 25, 1982.

Shirley, Bill. "Rookie Wins '32 Games for LA." *Los Angeles Times,* December 10, 1983.

Stump, Al. "1932, the 'Hopeless' Dream of William May Garland." *Olympic Review* 274 (August 1990).

———. "The Olympics That Almost Wasn't." *American Heritage* 33, no. 5 (August–September 1982).

Tunis, John R. "The Olympic Games." *Harper's Magazine,* June 1, 1928.

Zimmerman, Paul. "Olympic Games in Los Angeles: In the Midst of a Depression, L.A. Put On a Record-Breaking, Money-Making Extravaganza," *Los Angeles Times,* July 23, 1984.


## GENERAL INTEREST ARTICLES ON LOS ANGELES

Bartlett, James. "The Strangest Club in Los Angeles, the L.A. Breakfast Club." KCET.org, March 16, 2017.

Guinn, J.M. "The Great Real Estate Boom of 1887." *Historical Society of Southern California* 1, no. 5 (1890).

Meares, Hadley. "Chester Place: The Grandeur of L.A.'s First Gated Community." KCET.org, August 8, 2013.

———. "Death at Hotel Barclay: Behind the Beautiful Façade, Gruesome Slayings and Bloody Accidents." Curbed LA (la.curbed.com), October 20, 2017.

———. "The People's Playground: How the Memorial Coliseum Put Los Angeles on the Map." Curbed LA (la.curbed.com), July 21, 2016.

Miller, Danny. "West Adams and the Movies." *West Adams Matters,* newsletter of the West Adams Heritage Association, December 2005.

Rasmussen, Cecilia. "L.A. Then and Now: Colossal Undertaking Left an Enduring Landmark." *Los Angeles Times,* May 18, 2003.

Sitton, Tom. "Did the Ruling Class Rule at City Hall in 1920s Los Angeles?" In *Metropolis in the Making: Los Angeles in the 1920s,* edited by Tom Sitton and William Deverell. Berkeley: University of California Press, 2001.

Treffers, Steven. "How a Visionary Scoundrel Created Woodland Hills in the 1920s." Curbed LA (la.curbed.com), April 16, 2014.


## DISSERTATIONS AND THESES

Moore, Roger D. "The 1932 Los Angeles Olympics: A Model for a Broken System." Master's thesis, Graduate College of the Oklahoma State University, May 2015.

Paul, Jonathan Robert. "Melting Resources: A Historical Analysis of the 1932 Olympic Winter and Summer Games." Master's thesis, University of Windsor, Faculty of Graduate Studies and Research, 2004.

Redford, Laura. "The Promise and Principles of Real Estate Development in an American Metropolis: Los Angeles 1903–1923." PhD diss. University of California, Los Angeles, 2014.


## BOOKS ON THE OLYMPIC GAMES

Findling, John E., and Kimberly D. Pelle, eds. *Encyclopedia of the Modern Olympic Movement.* Westport, CT: Greenwood Press, 2004.

Galford, Ellen. *The X Olympiad.* Vol. 10 of *The Olympic Century: The Official History of the Modern Olympic Movement.* Los Angeles: International Olympics Committee, United States Olympic Committee, 1st Century Project, and World Sport Research and Publications, 1997.

Goldblatt, David. *The Games: A Global History of the Olympics*. New York: W. W. Norton, 2016.

Guiney, David. *The Friendly Olympics*. Dublin: PR Books Ireland, 1982.

Guttmann, Allen. *The Games Must Go On: Avery Brundage and the Olympic Movement*. New York: Columbia University Press, 1984.

———. *The Olympics: A History of the Modern Games*. Urbana: University of Illinois Press, 1992.

Henry, Bill, and Patricia Henry Yeomans. *An Approved History of the Olympic Games*. Sherman Oaks, CA: Alfred Publishing, 1984.

Johnson, William Oscar, and Nancy P. Williamson. *"Whatta Gal": The Babe Didrikson Story*. Boston: Little, Brown, 1977.

Pieroth, Doris H. *Their Day in the Sun: Women of the 1932 Olympics*. Seattle: University of Washington Press, 1996.

Wallechinsky, David. *The Complete Book of the Olympics*. New York: Penguin Books, 1984.

Wallechinsky, David, and Jaime Loucky. *The Book of Olympic Lists*. London: Aurum Press, 2012.

Yeomans, Patricia Henry, ed. *Behind the Headlines with Bill Henry, 1903–1970*. Los Angeles: Ward Ritchie Press, 1972.

Zimmerman, Paul. *Los Angeles, the Olympic City, 1932–1984*. Hollywood, CA: Delmar Watson, 1984.


## BOOKS ON SOUTHERN CALIFORNIA HISTORY

Babcock, Gwendolyn Garland. *The Ancestry of John Jewett Garland*. San Marino, CA: n.p., 1992.

Boyarsky, Bill. *Inventing L.A.: The Chandlers and Their Times*. Santa Monica, CA: Angel City Press, 2009.

Buntin, John. *L.A. Noir: The Struggle for the Soul of America's Most Seductive City*. New York: Broadway Books, 2009.

Carr, Harry. *Los Angeles: City of Dreams*. New York: D. Appleton-Century, 1935.

Davis, Margaret Leslie. *Dark Side of Fortune*. Berkeley: University of California Press, 1998.

Davis, Mike. *City of Quartz: Excavating the Future in Los Angeles*. London: Verso, 1990.

Deverell, William. *Whitewashed Adobe: The Rise of Los Angeles and the Remaking of Its Mexican Past*. Berkeley: University of California Press, 2004.

Federal Writers Project. *Los Angeles in the 1930s: The WPA Guide to the City of Angels*. Berkeley: University of California Press, 2011.

Flacco, Anthony, with Jerry Clark. *The Road out of Hell: Sanford Clark and the True Story of the Wineville Murders*. New York: Diversion Books, 2013.

Fogelson, Robert M. *The Fragmented Metropolis: Los Angeles, 1850–1930*. Berkeley: University of California Press, 1967.

Gottlieb, Robert, and Irene Wolt. *Thinking Big: The Story of the Los Angeles Times, Its Publishers and Their Influence on Southern California*. New York: G. P. Putnam's Sons, 1977.

Halberstam, David. *The Powers That Be*. New York: Alfred A. Knopf, 1979.

Mann, William J. *Tinseltown: Murder, Morphine, and Madness at the Dawn of Hollywood*. New York: HarperCollins, 2014.

McDougal, Dennis. *Privileged Son: Otis Chandler and the Rise and Fall of the L.A. Times Dynasty*. Cambridge, MA: Perseus, 2001.

McWilliams, Carey. *Southern California: An Island on the Land*. Salt Lake City: Peregrine Smith Books, 1946.

Sitton, Tom, and William Deverell, eds. *Metropolis in the Making: Los Angeles in the 1920s*. Berkeley: University of California Press, 2001.

Sloper, Don. *Los Angeles's Chester Place*. San Francisco: Arcadia, 2006.

Starr, Kevin. *Endangered Dreams: The Great Depression in California*. New York: Oxford University Press, 1996.

———. *Inventing the Dream: California through the Progressive Era*. New York: Oxford University Press, 1985.

———. *Material Dreams: Southern California through the 1920s*. New York: Oxford University Press, 1990.

Starr, Kevin, David Ulin, and Jim Heinmann. *Los Angeles: Portrait of a City*. Los Angeles: Taschen, 2009.

Tygiel, Jules. *The Great Los Angeles Swindle: Oil, Stocks and Scandal during the Roaring Twenties*. New York: Oxford University Press, 1994.

Weaver, John. *Los Angeles: The Enormous Village, 1781–1981*. Santa Barbara, CA: Capra Press, 1980.

Zimmerman, Tom. *Paradise Promoted: The Booster Campaign That Created Los Angeles, 1870–1930*. Santa Monica, CA: Angel City Press, 2008.


## BOOKS ON THE UNITED STATES IN THE 1920S

Allen, Frederick Lewis. *Only Yesterday: An Informal History of the 1920s*. New York: Harper Perennial Modern Classics, 1931.

Dumenil, Lynn. *Modern Temper: American Culture and Society in the 1920s*. New York: Hill and Wang, 1995.

Grossman, Mark. *Encyclopedia of the Interwar Years, from 1919 to 1939*. New York: Facts on File, 2000.

Kyvig, David E. *Daily Life in the United States, 1920–1940: How Americans Lived through the Roaring Twenties and the Great Depression*. Chicago: Ivan R. Dee, 2002.


## PLAGUE OUTBREAK, LOS ANGELES, 1924

Bogen, Emil. "The Pneumonic Plague in Los Angeles." *California and Western Medicine* (February 1925).

California State Board of Health. "Plague in Los Angeles, 1924–25." Bound manuscript in the Huntington Library, San Marino, California.

———. *Weekly Bulletin,* November 8 and 15, 1924.

Deverell, William. "Ethnic Quarantine." Chap. 5 of *Whitewashed Adobe: The Rise of Los Angeles and the Remaking of Its Mexican Past,* 172–206. Berkeley: University of California Press, 2004.

Feldinger, Frank. *A Slight Epidemic: The Government Cover-Up of Black Plague in Los Angeles*. Los Angeles: Silver Lake, 2008.

Los Angeles Chamber of Commerce. "Minutes of the Board of Directors Meetings." October 30 and November 6, 13, and 26, 1924. Los Angeles: Doheny Memorial Library, USC Libraries Special Collections, University of Southern California.

————. Stenographer's Reports, Board of Directors Meetings, October 30, November 6, 13, and 26, 1924. USC Libraries Special Collections, University of Southern California, Doheny Memorial Library.

Martin, Helen. "The Plague Epidemic." Chap. 15 of *The History of the Los Angeles County Hospital (1878–1968) and the Los Angeles County–University of Southern California Medical Center (1968–1978)*. Los Angeles: University of Southern California Press, 1979.

Viseltear, Arthur. "The Pneumonic Plague Epidemic of 1924 in Los Angeles." *Yale Journal of Biology and Medicine* 47, no. 1 (March 1974): 40–54.

## GREYSTONE MURDER-SUICIDE

Davis, Margaret Leslie. "Night of Terror." Chap. 13 of *Dark Side of Fortune*, 229–45. Berkeley: University of California Press, 1998.

Meares, Hadley. "We Shall Never Know: Murder, Money and the Enduring Mystery of Greystone Mansion." KCET.org, July 25, 2014.

Moss, Robert F. "Cracking the Cassidy Case." Criticism and Scholarship: The Raymond Chandler website. Palmettonewmedia.com.

Welton, Benjamin. "Vintage Noir: The Tragedy at Greystone." Crimemagazine.com, May 16, 2013.

White, Leslie T. "The Doheny Murder Mystery." Chap. 18 of *Me Detective*, 106–14. New York: Harcourt, Brace, 1936.

# INDEX

Page references in italics refer to illustrations.

Founded in 1893,
UNIVERSITY OF CALIFORNIA PRESS
publishes bold, progressive books and journals
on topics in the arts, humanities, social sciences,
and natural sciences—with a focus on social
justice issues—that inspire thought and action
among readers worldwide.

The UC PRESS FOUNDATION
raises funds to uphold the press's vital role
as an independent, nonprofit publisher, and
receives philanthropic support from a wide
range of individuals and institutions—and from
committed readers like you. To learn more, visit
ucpress.edu/supportus.